MYTHS AND MEMORIES
OF THE
EASTER RISING

BOOKS OF RELATED INTEREST FROM
IRISH ACADEMIC PRESS

The GPO and the Easter Rising
Keith Jeffery

The Northern IRA in the Early Years of Partition 1920–1922
Robert Lynch

Patrick Pearse: The Triumph of Failure
Ruth Dudley Edwards

Florence and Josephine O'Donoghue's War of Independence A Destiny That Shapes Our Ends
Editor: John Borgonovo

Republican Internment and the Prison Ship Argenta 1922
Denise Kleinrichert

Our Own Devices National Symbols and Political Conflict in Twentieth-Century Ireland
Ewan Morris

The Last Days of Dublin Castle
The Diaries of Mark Sturgis
Editor: Michael Hopkinson

MYTHS
AND
MEMORIES
OF THE
EASTER RISING

*Cultural and Political
Nationalism in Ireland*

JONATHAN GITHENS-MAZER
Nottingham Trent University

IRISH ACADEMIC PRESS
DUBLIN • PORTLAND, OR

First published in 2006 by
IRISH ACADEMIC PRESS
44, Northumberland Road, Dublin 4, Ireland

and in the United States of America by
IRISH ACADEMIC PRESS
c/o ISBS, Suite 300, 920 NE 58th Avenue
Portland, Oregon 97213-3644

WEBSITE: www.iap.ie

British Library Cataloguing in Publication Data
An entry can be found on request

ISBN 0-7165-2823-1 (cloth)
ISBN 0-7165-2824-X (paper)

Library of Congress Cataloging-in-Publication Data
An entry can be found on request

Typeset in 11/13pt Sabon by FiSH Books, Enfield, Middx.
Printed by MPG Books Ltd., Bodmin, Cornwall

Contents

Acknowledgements

My experience as a PhD student at the LSE, in so far as I found myself surrounded by an ever present core of junior and established scholars who express a keen interest in the study of ethnicity and nationalism, has been vital to the writing of this book. This is a function of one organisation – the Association for the Study of Ethnicity and Nationalism (ASEN) – and one dedicated and generous individual – Professor Anthony D. Smith. The PhD thesis and book would not have been possible without Professor Smith's sage and patient advice, both at the LSE and in his home, and I am eternally indebted to him and his family for his help, constant encouragement and intellectual guidance. This book would also not have been possible without the further support of my kind and generous colleagues in the Division of Politics and Sociology at Nottingham Trent University.

While at the LSE, I have also been lucky enough to be a student and friend of another scholar of ethnicity and nationalism, and an expert in Irish nationalism as well – Dr John Hutchinson. Dr Hutchinson has consistently given me excellent advice, and helped to rein in my occasional 'romantic' tendencies, and for all his help I am also very grateful.

While carrying out the research for this book, I have been truly lucky to have found such generous and supportive librarians in the Manuscripts Reading Room of the National Library of Ireland and at the Public Records Office at Kew. One individual in particular, David Sheehy, stands out for his commitment to historical documentation and research, for his intellectual clout, and for his academic generosity. The Diocesan Archivist at the Archbishop's Palace in Dublin pointed me in invaluable directions with this material – and helped stimulate my ideas over lunches while researching in the Archives.

An academic life is consistently punctuated by ups and downs, but there have been three individuals who have provided constant love and support I am so grateful for all the help and support of my mother, Dr Marianne Githens, who has not only provided 'motherly love' but also acted as an intellectual sounding board for my ideas, and provided a variety of support while writing this thesis. My wife, Gayle, has also gone through this entire process with me – seeing the highs and the lows, and the book would have been quite impossible without her love, her help and especially her patience.

Lastly, this book would not have been possible without the love and help of my father, Dr Stanley Z. Mazer, who sadly passed away before the completion of my PhD. While I know that he loved me and was proud of me, I think he would have been especially pleased to see its completion as a book. For this reason, I dedicate this book to him.

List of Tables and Figures

Tables

Figures

Foreword

Recent debates in the theory of nations and nationalism have focused on the social, political and cultural factors in the origins and characterisation of nations and the role of nationalism in their creation. Recently, the dominance of the modernist paradigm which holds that nations, as well as nationalism, are the products exclusively of modernity, has been challenged both by 'neo-perennialists' who claim that we can locate nations in pre-modern epochs, and by 'ethno-symbolists' who trace the origins of modern nations and nationalism back to pre-modern ethnic communities. Ethno-symbolists make a further claim: the character of nations is largely determined by the repertoire of myths, symbols and memories that derive from earlier ethnic cultures in the same geopolitical area or of the same presumed descent group.

It is to this latter debate that Jonathan Githens-Mazer's study has made a major contribution. Taking the pivotal Easter Rising of 1916 and its dramatic aftermath as his focus, he skilfully constructs a 'before-and-after' model of its effects as the 'cultural trigger point' of a crucial shift in the political allegiances and actions of the majority Catholic population in Ireland. Within this robust framework, Githens-Mazer's analysis highlights the many factors and developments that occurred in the vital years of the Great War, especially the role of British policy in Ireland, the effects of conscription and the decline of Redmond's moderate constitutional nationalism. But the burden of his explanation for the character of the radicalisation of Irish nationalism and the growing appeal of Sinn Féin, falls on the ways in which the repertoire of pre-existing myths, symbols and memories of a long suffering Irish nation, going back to the Great Famine and the Penal Laws, and internalised by a large number of

Irish men and women, was able to provide a framework for ordering and reinterpreting the unfolding events of 1916. Moreover, as he so clearly demonstrates, this framework was not simply descriptive; the messages which it conveyed prescribed certain kinds of action and injected a sense of urgency, thereby mobilising many Irish men and women who till then had been content to pursue a moderate Home Rule programme.

In this invaluable study, Jonathan Githens-Mazer has given us a rich and innovative account of a critical moment in the creation of an Irish national state. He has provided both an original interpretation of the role of the Easter Rising, and an imaginative application of an ethno-symbolic approach to the study of a crucial historical development. Above all, he has shown us how Ireland's cultural heritage informed the thoughts and actions of Irish Catholics in the early twentieth century, and how it was able to furnish a guide to political action at a decisive juncture in Irish history. His book will have great significance both for our understanding of the role of cultural factors in the development of nationalism, and for the ways in which an ethno-symbolic approach can illuminate the study of historical change.

Anthony D.Smith
Professor Emeritus of Nationalism and Ethnicity
University of London (LSE)

January 2006

Introduction

Having seen the power of culture and politics in my own life and on the ground in Northern Ireland, I was led by personal and intellectual curiosity about these issues to the London School of Economics in the autumn of 1998 to study with Professor Anthony D. Smith. Smith's work on ethno-symbolic approaches to nationalism were based, in large part, on the idea that myths, memories and symbols were important in the maintenance and development of some 'older' nations, and/or a necessary element for the construction of 'new' nations. This theoretical orientation meshed well with my initial work in the field. It was readily apparent that while some scholars had examined the links between culture and political action, these were often times written from an un-nuanced 'primordialist' standpoint. Others had dismissed any power in such links, rather emphasising the instrumental use of culture by dominant elites to achieve their personal political ambitions. Other scholars overlooked these links entirely, or took them for granted in pursuit of various institutional or structural explanations of group political behaviour.

As this project began to take shape and come into focus, the lacuna in an explanation for the popular appeal of radical nationalism, specifically in the wake of the Irish Easter Rising of 1916, became apparent. A group of previously unpopular and, in many cases, little-known radicals had walked into the General Post Office in Dublin and simply declared the existence of an Irish Republic. The ensuing insurrection was short lived and a total military failure. The leaders of the Rising were arrested and shot or interned. In the wake of their executions and the draconian implementation of martial law in Ireland, the ideas of this minority of radical nationalists caught on at the grassroots level throughout Ireland.[1]

Scholars such as Lyons, Lee, Foster, Garvin, Fitzpatrick, O'Day, Boyce, Augusteijn, Hart and Hennessey have, in various ways, accounted for the 'revolution' in Irish nationalism through changing political, economic or structural factors in Irish society. Such factors included an emerging Catholic middle class, changes in rural social structures, changes in a variety of economic factors, the effects of Catholic emancipation, and so on. There exists, however, a gap in the literature on the role of the popularly held myths, memories and symbols of the Irish nation in the radicalising effects of the Easter Rising. Only one account, written in 1967, explicitly attempts to unpack the effects of the Rising in terms of the power of the content of cultural nationalism to stimulate a popular reaction. Thompson's *The Imagination of an Insurrection* argues that the action of Pearse and the other leaders of the Rising had tapped into a rich vein of potent nationalist symbolism. Other works, such as those of Dudley Edwards and Moran, deal with Pearse and 'The Triumph of Failure' or 'The Politics of Redemption'. These works analyse the role that cultural nationalism plays in Pearse's own actions, thereby concentrating on the role of culture, but from an elite perspective. Hutchinson's *Dynamics of Cultural Nationalism* also demonstrated the important role of cultural nationalism in the broad project of Irish nationalism, over the course of the eighteenth, nineteenth and twentieth centuries, in the periods of Gaelic revival. None of these works, however, elaborate on how the events of the Rising and its aftermath account for the popular and mass transformation of sympathy in Irish nationalism, from moderate to radical.

This book therefore represents an attempt to fill this gap. How could the transformation in popular support from moderate constitutional to radical and violent nationalism be explained in the wake of Easter Week? Is there some sort of 'process' or phenomenon that explains how this 'radicalisation' occurred?

My contention is that the Easter Rising and the events that occurred in its aftermath constituted a *cultural trigger point* that accounted for this new popular sympathy for radical nationalism in the wake of the Rising. This concept of the cultural trigger point is based on aspects of social movement theory, in so far as it defines a moment or set of events that bring together a self-aware group to react with a sense of agency and urgency to a perceived injustice. This concept is also based on an ethno-symbolic approach to nationalism, in so far as the group, i.e. the Irish nation, and what it perceives as 'unjust' is underpinned by a repertoire of national myths, memories and symbols. Even what is deemed by the group as a reasonable response to this injustice is, in part, determined by this repertoire. The Easter Rising and its aftermath constituted just such a cultural trigger point for the Irish nation. In this way, the myths, memories and symbols that spoke to the Irish national perception of the Anglo-Irish and Protestant-Catholic relationships were unleashed, and informed interpretations of and reactions to the Rising, providing a basis by which a grassroots radical nationalist movement emerged in the political vacuum of legitimate parties and leaders in the wake of the Rising.

This hypothesis can only be confirmed by demonstrating that Irish national myths, memories and symbols did have a significant and definitive impact on the political behaviour of individuals in the Irish nation in the aftermath of the Easter Rising. It must therefore demonstrate:

1) the lack of popular support for radical nationalism before the Rising despite the presence of the relevant repertoire of Irish national myths, memories and symbols
2) the transformation from support for moderate constitutional nationalism to a variety of violent radical nationalism that occurred as a direct result of the Rising and its associated events, and
3) the ensuing emergence of a grass-roots movement of support for radical nationalism resulting from a reliance by individuals on the Irish national repertoire of myths, memories and symbols to make sense of these events.

In order to accomplish this, the book charts contemporary popular responses to the Rising and compares pre- and post-Rising attitudes towards radical nationalism, Home Rule, and the outbreak of the First World War, as well as the content of religious and cultural nationalisms.

The methods utilised to support this hypothesis are limited by being applied to a historical case study. As these events occurred over 90 years ago, this ruled out the possibility of conducting interviews with those who participated in these events. Instead, I have consulted a variety of archival sources. Letters and diaries, such as those in the collection of the National Library of Ireland (NLI) have provided many contemporary accounts of these events and the attitudes towards them. The intelligence reports of the Crimes Special Branch (CSB) section of the Dublin Metropolitan Police

(DMP), which are available in the National Archives of Ireland (NAI), are not complete, but provide some helpful insight in to the activities of radical and moderate nationalists. The intelligence reports of the County Inspectors of the Royal Irish Constabulary (RIC), which can be found at the Public Records Office (PRO) Kew are much more complete and extensive, and provide evidence for actions and ideas amongst a broad range of members of the Irish nation during this period. Archbishop Walsh's Papers, generously provided by the Dublin Diocesan Archives, proved a veritable goldmine for contemporary accounts and analysis of events in Ireland and especially in Dublin from 1914–1918. In particular, the combination of Monsignor Michael Curran's statement to the Bureau of Military History (MS. 27728), available in the NLI, with the Archbishop's papers provided real elucidation of many events which would have otherwise remained shrouded in the mists of forgotten history. Many historical works about this time, including those of Kee, Hennessey, and Fitzpatrick, have also provided invaluable insight into debates over the exclusion of Ulster and the partition of Ireland, the events of the Rising and its aftermath, and the downfall of John Redmond and the Irish Party.

Despite its reliance on historical works and archival sources, this book has not attempted to provide a general history of the Rising nor of the critical period of the Great War or of constitutional or indeed of radical nationalism. My focus is exclusively on the relationship between radical nationalism and the myths, memories and symbols of the Irish nation, as these had been handed down and elaborated over the last few generations or possibly earlier. Various other scholars have carried out these other tasks ably, charting the various intricacies that accompanied this turn of events. Furthermore, this book has not attempted to explain the transformation of Ireland in terms of economic or class factors over the course of the 'long nineteenth' century, and it does not, therefore, expound on a resource mobilisation account of how and why radical nationalism emerged in the wake of the Rising. Space and time have placed limitations on my ability to demonstrate the effects of various structural transformations in Irish society which might have accounted for the eventual shift in popular sympathy from moderate to radical nationalism in reaction to the Rising. Such transformations include the broader international context in which questions of Irish national self-determination were become politically salient and legitimate, something covered in great detail by Dr Bill Kissane. Limitations in time and space have also prevented me from being able to chart the role played by a variety of geographic factors, in this transformation, in terms of a particular county or region's attachment to a set of myths, memories and symbols as a potentially interesting line of enquiry. Rather, I have concentrated on the role played by popularly held and resonant national myths, memories and symbols in determining the political behaviour of individuals in the Irish nation as a result of the Easter Rising and its aftermath.

The first chapter proposes the theoretical underpinnings of the phenomenon of the cultural trigger point, and establishes its strengths and limitations as an explanatory phenomenon. Chapter 2 considers popular attitudes towards radical nationalism before the Rising. Chapter 3 examines attitudes towards the outbreak of the First World War, and the recruiting efforts of the British Army. Chapter 4 sets out the content of Irish cultural and religious nationalism before the Rising, exploring several important and pervasive cultural themes in the repertoire of Irish myths, memories and symbols in the run-up to the Rising.

The following chapters detail the situation in the Irish nation after the Easter Rising. Chapter 5 lays out the events of the Rising, and popular reactions to these events as they unfolded. Chapter 6 provides evidence of how the Rising constituted a cultural trigger point. Chapter 7 demonstrates the decline of moderate nationalist political institutions in the wake of the Rising, and Chapter 8 establishes the rise in popularity of a reorganised Sinn Féin, culminating in the party's sweep to power in the General Election of 1918.

NOTE

1   It should be noted that this book has concentrated entirely on the perspective of the Irish nation. By no means, however, is this a reflection on a particular claim of greater legitimacy for this group over any other, especially the Unionist community or British government. While for the sake of brevity this book has concentrated on the Irish national perspective, a natural companion piece to this book would be an analysis of the cultural trigger point, and repertoire of myths, memories and symbols which made the Unionist struggle against Home Rule and for the exclusion of Ulster seem rational, reasonable and just to Unionists throughout Ireland, and especially in Ulster. Such a study might include conceptions of religious identity, loyalty, and so on, which underpinned Unionist participation in and sacrifice for the United Kingdom, especially in light of the events of the time, such as the Battle of the Somme.

1

Ethno-Symbolism, Memory and Social Movements

Though a great deal has been written on each of the fields of nationalism and social movements independently, there exists a difficulty in explaining how the nation creates an impetus for individuals to get involved with a collective movement, and therefore how the nation becomes a causal determinant of an individual's behaviour. How does being Irish affect individual and collective political behaviour – and in the wake of the Easter Rising, how did it colour how individuals interpreted the actions of Anglo-Protestants and British authorities? Is there an observable mechanism that lies behind a process of how or why an Irishman participated in a movement of sustained collective action based on the nation in the wake of the Rising? How does the nation, through processes of personal attachment, identification, interpretation, and so on, inspire individuals to participate in collective political actions based on their membership in the Irish nation?

This book proposes to show how the Irish nation's repertoire of myths, memories and symbols constituted a significant causal factor in determining an individual's participation in a radical nationalist movement. It will do this by establishing a mechanism which accounts for the processes of filtration or contextualisation of contemporary events through the prism created by the nation's repertoire of myths, memories and symbols. In the case of Irish nationalism, this repertoire serves as a prism through which to break down contemporary events, so that an individual member of the Irish nation interprets contemporary events in light of the images, symbols, myths and memories that are salient to an Irish national past – a process which may lead this individual to believe that the symbolic resonance of a contemporary event reflects a set of 'inherent truths', established by and extant in popular and resonant national myths, memories and symbols – the stories grandparents, parents and teachers tell children to help them 'make sense of the world'. In the Irish case, examples of this are events which affect land or the food supply being viewed in the context of the Famine, and events and actions which are related to religion being seen down through the perspective of Catholicism and the traumas associated with the disestablishment of the Catholic Church. This means that there are situations in which myths, memories and symbols of the Irish nation's past serve as a significant causal factor in determining an individual's senses of agency, urgency and injustice – ultimately resulting in collective political action (nationalism). In this way, this chapter, and this book overall, seek to account for the impact of the collective (nation) on the individual's perception of contemporary events, and how the Irish nation comes to be a causal factor in determining what are subsequently perceived as appropriate and accepted responses to the events of the Easter Rising.

In order to accomplish this, this chapter will begin by examining the phenomenon of nations and nationalism, making special reference to ethno-symbolism. It will then move on to examine Social Movement Theory and to relate this body of literature to ethno-symbolic approaches to nationalism. At this point, the chapter will introduce how myths, memories and symbols of the nation are disseminated and maintained through the phenomenon of collective memory, creating a defined and delimited, as well as popular and resonant, though dynamic and often contradictory, repertoire of myths, memories and symbols for the nation. Ultimately, the chapter suggests that senses of injustice and perceptions of agency, which are necessary for a social movement to occur, emanate from the Irish nation's repertoire of myths, memories and symbols. This process accounts for a shift from latent to active nationalist political behaviour, leading to popular support for radical nationalism in the wake of the Rising – thus explaining how culture, national myths, memories and symbols can be a causal factor in the transformation and radicalisation of collective political action in the name of the nation.

The Collective and Causality

While it is intuitively apparent that being Irish impacts the individual, this impact is difficult to prove, analyse and assess in a rigorous, quantifiable and scientific manner. How does one measure the Irish nation – and Irish nationalism – especially when looking at historical examples of these phenomena? When considering methodological strategies to employ in examining contemporary cases of nationalism, what varieties of evidence actually prove causality, and how much of this evidence, if it exists, is needed to prove causality or how little is needed to disprove it, pose real problems. When dealing with historical case studies of nationalism, it is impossible to carry out surveys, interviews, and so on in order to ascertain the emotional attachment to, and political, social and emotional effects of, the nation on the individual. In such cases the evidence available is clearly limited and specific. Of course the same issues are to be found at the coalface of the social sciences, with questions continually arising as to the role of the individual and/or society, in terms of cause and effect as opposed to a variety of other very real and significant social, economic, political, moral, and/or biological or environmental factors. While society is the collection of interactions amongst individuals, can a 'collection of interactions', let alone the character of these interactions, ever serve to determine the action of the individual?[1]

Measurement of the impact of *culture* on an individual's political behaviour is difficult but can be observed and the existence and use of the repertoire of myths, memories and symbols of the nation has rational and tangible benefits for those who accept and engage in meaningful interactions based on them. The repertoire of national myths, memories and symbols is most potent when they are popularly resonant. A myth, memory or symbol is resonant when it strikes a common chord in the nation, denoting a common or universal significance for members of the nation. Resonance occurs when personal experience, whether real, vicarious or imagined, corresponds to these myths, memories or symbols in the repertoire of the community, in this case the nation. Beyond providing tangible benefits for the individual locked into the everyday interconnections of their society, can myths, memories and symbols of the nation be understood to come to form a basis for an individual to assess the relative costs and benefits of participating in a potentially dangerous and/or personally detrimental action such as a nationalist movement?

Definitions: Nation, Nation-State, Nationalism

The nation will be defined after Smith, though slightly modified, as 'a group of human beings, possessing common and distinctive elements of culture ... citizenship rights for all members, a sentiment of solidarity arising out of common experiences, and occupying a common territory'.[2] The nation encompasses a common culture, history, territory and destiny and a political self-awareness that distinguishes it from other forms of collective political or sociological organisation. Being a nation entails an awareness of rights, privileges and responsibilities as a condition of membership. Nationalism will be defined as the movement for the attainment of a state on behalf of an existing or 'potential' nation.[3] Nationalism is a variety of collective movement by the nation, its elites and masses, to gain congruence between the institutions of the state and the identity of the nation. There are a variety of forms of nationalist movements, cultural and political, instrumental and romantic, differing in form and content, aims and means. Despite this variation, the important unifying factor of all nationalisms is that they are all movements and/or ideological positions which argue that the nation should be congruent with the state or that the nation should possess the requisite political power and/or legitimacy which those in the nationalist movement believe to be the nation's due political, social, cultural and economic recognition. The nation-state is defined after Giddens and Tilly as the territorially bordered container of legitimate violence, with the powers to tax, raise armies, and so on. The nation-state, nationalism and the nation are related phenomena as they tie the state to the nation through the use of 'a myth of origin, conferring cultural autonomy upon the community which is held to be the bearer of these ideals'.[4]

Theories of nations and nationalism are generally split into three main streams, though there are many scholars' works that bridge the divide between these streams, or cannot be easily categorised within them. These three streams are those of modernism, perennialism and primordialism. Within the debate on theories of nationalism, a main point of contention which distinguishes these streams concerns the role of elites in the (re)discovery and/or (re)appropriation of national myths and symbols. Are elites instrumentally choosing national myths, memories and symbols to promote personal political power and economic gain, or are elites instead 'Weberian switchmen', who provide ideology and imagery recognised and therefore 'chosen' by the demanding masses?[5] In some approaches the masses are portrayed as a *tabula rasa*, on to which the wills, desires and ambitions of the elites can be imprinted.[6] In this perspective, the masses are easily coaxed and prodded, instrumentally manipulated to act through a series of conscious and orchestrated efforts on the part of a driven group of elites. Modernist orthodoxy dictates that the relationship between the state and the nation is an instrumental one, brokered by these elites and/or state institutions, whether intentional or accidental.[7] The institutions of the state, resulting from various processes of modernity, a need for armies, factories, taxes and unified linguistic populations, centre–periphery conflicts and blocked upward mobility are all proposed, in varying and combined degrees, as being the rationale behind the state's drive to create a coherent and unifying political identity. In this model, the nation and nationalism serve to amalgamate disparate populations to the infrastructure of the state.[8] In this theory, nationalism creates a reason why people should fight and die for each other or pay taxes, and it ultimately creates a mechanism by which to 'imagine' the nation. While there was no state 'to make' the Irish nation prior to the Rising and the Anglo-Irish Treaty, this theory can be adapted to the Irish case, to argue, for example, that Irish nationalism was a movement of a emerging Catholic middle class who felt that their economic, social and political progress was blocked by the Anglo-Irish elite and British authorities and the British state – controlled by the English – or British nation, to gain benefits for its members. Such theories, dependent on conceptions of a middle-class sense of 'blocked upward mobility', go on to argue that a group of Irish nationalist intelligentsia, culled from this blocked middle class, is subsequently responsible for the (re)emergence or (re)creation of nationalist myths, memories and symbols in their quest to unblock their social, economic and political progress. Alternatively, it can be argued that the Irish nation was solely the instrumental creation of elites living in Ireland who sought political power which was otherwise not afforded them – and in this way they did nothing more than stir up populist and reactionary anti-British/Protestant sentiment in a transparent effort to gain political power.

Modernist theories of nations and nationalism are often compared and contrasted with primordialist accounts of nations and nationalism. Primordialism suggests that the nation is either part of a persistent pattern of human cultural, social and political organisation, or that the nation is based on various socio-biological conceptions of genetic fitness and/or 'otherness'. This primordialist approach suggests that the persistence of cultural or political patterns or conceptions of genetic fitness account for the political and/or social/cultural organisation of the nation. Primordialism deems the pre-modern/modern divide irrelevant, in so far as it fails to account for the emergence of political and social organisations in the nation, or the conceptions of the genetic fitness that underpin the nation and nationalisms.[9] Primordialism, as applied to the Irish nation, would have it either that there is something biologically given about being Irish, that it is somehow in the blood, which distinguishes them from the Anglo-Protestant other, or that the cultural elements which distinguish the Irish nation are from 'time immemorial' – ultimately suggesting that the Irish nation is a given and continuous entity.

In the Irish case, neither of these approaches satisfactorily explains the Irish nation and Irish nationalism. Modernism does not seem immediately applicable in Ireland, as while the elites may have been collecting, cultivating and disseminating the Irish national repertoire of myths, memories and symbols, they could find them only in the countryside and amongst the masses of the Irish nation. Dublin-based members of the Gaelic League considered rural Ireland to be the location of their romantic nationalist ideal, and the Catholic Church saw the romantic conservative ideals of a Catholic Ireland in the countryside. In Ireland and beyond, instrumentalist accounts often fail to note adequately this phenomenon of popular resonance. As is clear in the Irish case, the processes of (re)discovery or (re)appropriation of an ethnic past are limited in the scope and content of their message by the confines of ethno-history, and the popular conceptions of history, myth and symbols.[10] Primordialism also does not seem to account for any of the subtleties of the Irish nation and Irish nationalism, not least the constant ability of a pre-modern Irish entity to merge with and accommodate what were at first considered to be alien communities and cultures – the Normans, the Old English and then the New English. Intellectually and scientifically answering the question of 'why is there an Irish nation?' with 'because it's genetic or in the blood' does not seem to provide a coherent answer for political behaviour. Yet there are elements of cultural continuity and distinction and instrumental dissemination and maintenance of the Irish nation – so how can scholars of Irish nationalism account for the emergence of a nationalist political elite drawing on certain popular myths, memories and symbols to mobilise an Irish nation to gain political power and legitimacy?

Ethno-Symbolism

There is a third approach between modernist and primordialist accounts of the nation. Perennialist theories of nationalism propose that the broad phenomenon of the nation has occurred and/or recurred throughout history, but that it is not part of the human condition as such, not part of 'nature,' but rather part of recorded history. *Some* nations reach back to these myths and memories of the collective from a pre-modern era in order to (re)construct, (re)invigorate, or transform this community into the modern phenomenon of the nation. In this way, *some* nations can be seen to bridge the pre-modern/modern divide. Other nations, competing with these 'pre-modern' nations seek to demonstrate their claims of political, social or cultural legitimacy and authenticity through a process that requires extensive processes of (re)discovery, (re)appropriation, (re)affirmation, and (re)imagination in order to complete their transformation into a nation. From a perennialist standpoint, the Irish nation contemporary with the Easter Rising can be understood as fulfilling the social, political and economic needs of its members at the time, but its existence is not 'constructed' by elites or an intelligentsia *ex-nihilo*, simply frustrated with their blocked upward nobility, nor is it reflective of 'Irish blood'.

The ethno-symbolist approach to nationalism fits broadly within perennialist understandings of the nation. Ethno-symbolists broadly recognise that the nation is a modern phenomenon, but argue that *some* nation's cultural and/or political antecedents pre-date the modern era. In fact, in the field of nationalism, ethno-symbolic approaches rendered it less contentious to argue that some nations have, at the very least, various forms of proto-national, and therefore proto-modern, institutional and/or cultural antecedents.[11] More controversially, ethno-symbolists suggest that some nations may actually be based on pre-modern cultural, political and ethnic groups which are (re)constituted in a modern period as nations. The repertoire of this shared ethnic past stems from the ethnic group or *ethnie*. An *ethnie* is defined by Smith as 'a named human population with shared ancestry, myths, histories and culture, having an association with a specific territory and a sense of solidarity'.[12] In this argument, the core of ethnicity – the 'myth-symbol complex' and the *mythomoteur* – diffuses the myths, memories and symbols of the group contemporarily through the ethnic group and across generations, preserving and maintaining the form of the group, and the content of its identity over the *longue-durée* – i.e. those myths, symbols, values and memories that make the *ethnie* distinct and separate.[13] The nation emerges from this *ethnie* in response to the pressures and needs of a modern world, to changes in trade, administration, the rise of secularism and mass culture and education.

National myths, memories and symbols must have meaning and potency or they fail to unite or excite, politically or culturally, the nation.[14] Myths, in the context of ethnic groups and nations, serve to 'establish and determine' a nation's foundation and system of values, creating a set of beliefs put forward as a narrative about the group itself.[15] The value of national myths, memories and symbols comes from their being 'founded on living traditions of the people (or segments thereof) which serve both to unite and to differentiate them from their neighbours'.[16] They can be persistent, and ethno-symbolists argue that in some cases they are observable phenomena within the *longue-durée*, but this does not denote an historical or factual continuity in the content of the myths, memories and symbols of the nation. St Patrick had a religious significance in Ireland prior to the disestablishment of the Church, and this importance persisted for Catholics and the members of the Church of Ireland throughout the nineteenth and twentieth centuries, so that in Armagh, duelling cathedrals face each other across the town. The symbolic importance of St Patrick is a matter of context – from original 'Christian' to 'Catholic', from Celtic intellectual to Welsh slave, to the very embodiment of Victorian values. Myths, memories and symbols are not only defined by context, but also dynamic and constantly being recast or reinvoked to maintain contemporary pertinence and meaning. The national repertoire of myths, memories and symbols are therefore recast and invoked by the nation – either as a project of the nationalist elites, or through grassroots movements – in order to address the needs of the collectivity of the nation. A nation encompasses certain 'types' of myths to affirm its foundation, and ensure the transference and maintenance of the repertoire of myths, memories and symbols of the nation.[17] As a simultaneous function of this process, the 'myth–symbol complex' serves to unite disparate individuals to the collective phenomenon of the nation through the shared meanings and values attached to the myths, symbols and memories of the nation.

An *ethnie* that did not participate in the initial move towards nationhood may find itself burdened by a subservient or lesser status in alternative forms of political organisation – empire, state, federal union, and so on. Non-recognition of the nation's cultural, social, political and economic claims for legitimacy, authenticity and autonomy is a common condition for these 'subservient' nations in relation to other more established or politically powerful nations. For many other 'non-historical' or 'less deeply rooted' *ethnies*, there was often an active process of seeking out the myths, memories and symbols which lent credibility and legitimacy to their claims of nationhood in order that they might state their claim for equal or greater legitimacy to their 'historical' or 'deeply rooted' cousins. Regardless of the origins of the nation, collective senses of injustice occur when an 'opponent' is perceived as holding back the development of their *ethnie* into nation, or their nation into state. In such cases, the intelligentsia of an *ethnie* or nation often seeks to turn to a virile political form of nationalism in order to strongly stake out the autonomy of their community in the contemporary inter-state and international order, thereby providing legitimacy and authenticity to the various cultural and political claims of their nation.[18] In this top-down elite led approach, the elites/intelligentsia must accomplish this within the rubric of the delimited and defined repertoire of the nation's myths, memories and symbols – a repertoire defined and delimited in part by these same elites/intelligentsia, but also bounded by the limits of what is 'resonant' in the nation's collective memory.

Popular resonance accounts for the balance between the will of the elites and the needs of the masses of the nation, and it underpins the myths, memories and symbols of the nation as bases for a collective identity and the 'authenticity' and 'legitimacy' of the community.[19] After the Rising, popular resonance becomes politically evident in phenomena such as the rejection of Griffith's dual monarchy platform for the Sinn Féin party, and it is evident later in the eventual limiting of Count Plunkett's electoral pull and power in the aftermath the Rising. By carefully defining and studying the popular resonation of national myths, memories and symbols, it is evident that the factors which define the Irish nation as a collectivity are causal factors in the shaping and informing of an Irish individual's views on and interpretations of a contemporary event, and help to determine reaction to this event. In this way an individual's assessment of a contemporary event, and the process of determining the appropriate course of response to this event, is greater than an individual analysis of personal cost and benefit. Both masses and elites are particularly fertile ground for those myths, memories and symbols which appear to speak to their individual situations as members of the struggling nation. In particular, periods of social, economic, political and/or cultural crises may lead to members to introspectively relate their membership in the nation to this crisis – simultaneously requiring and reifying appropriate myths, memories and symbols of the nation. It is this particular point where modernist and ethno-symbolic approaches to nationalism intersect – not on the origins of myths, memories and symbols, but their ultimate necessity for members of the nation at such moments.

Popular resonance of a nation's repertoire of myths, memories and symbols is dependent on this repertoire having a collective meaning for individual member of the nation. The literature on collective memory, especially the work of Halbwachs, looks at how social groups remember, forget or re-appropriate the past – clearly a core component for the proposed cultural trigger point.[20] This becomes salient when assessing Ireland during and after the Easter Rising – why was a certain repertoire of myths, memories and symbols more resonant and popular than another? Collective memory can be defined as 'those memories of a shared past that are retained by members of a group, class or nation … [it] refers to shared memories of societal-level events especially extreme, intense events that have led to important institutional changes'[21] Collective memories are based on oral stories, rumours, gestures or cultural styles, in addition to literature and institutionalised practices.[22] Collective memory links an individual's memory of collectively significant events from the past to the official, delimited and defined set of narratives of this event, as defined by the nation. Collective memory, in so far as it relates to the collective construction of meaning for past events, will therefore be proposed as a causal factor in the interpretation of contemporary events. In this way the mythic, memorial and symbolic repertoire of the Irish nation, including successes, failures, disasters and golden ages, can be understood to tangibly and demonstrably affect an individual's contemporary contextualisation of the Rising in light of the memories of experiences such as the Famine. This means that an individual makes contemporarily sense of an event within the rubric of the past in the 'national memory'.

Through individual remembering, collective memory serves to create a backdrop for and perpetuate the individual's own identity in the context of the community. It helps locate the individual in the broader nation. However, memory, at both the collective and individual levels, is dynamic – as the needs of a society change in relation to contemporary events, situations and so on, so too do individual memories. This change in individual memory occurs as the individual reassesses and re-places herself in the new and variable historical, political and social contexts. Whatever changes take place in the memory, they do so in the context of limitations placed by society through its repertoire of collective memory on an individual, and in response to changing personal circumstances and situations. In this process of reassessment and re-placing 'our imagination remains under the influence of the social milieu'.[23] In this way, according to Halbwachs,

> Society from time to time obligates people not just to reproduce in thought previous events of their lives, but also to touch them up, to shorten them, or to complete them so that, however convinced we are that our memories are exact, we give them a prestige that reality did not possess.[24]

The question emerges, however, to what extent can one talk about an individual remembering in the face of the monolith of 'society' demanding the retouching and reassessment of these memories. This is to say, does everyone in the nation remember an event in exactly the same manner? Halbwachs does not deny that there is individual memory, and that there is variation in this individual memory, it is simply that

> individual memory is nevertheless a part ... of group memory since each impression and each fact, even if it apparently concerns a particular person exclusively leaves a lasting memory only to the extent that one has thought it over –to the extent that it is connected with the thoughts that come to us form the social milieu ... In this way the framework of collective memory confines and binds our most intimate remembrances with each other ...[25]

Halbwachs therefore proposes a binding relationship between the collectivity and the individual. The collective memory of the nation is dynamic and subject to degrees of differentiation and variation due not only to individual perspective and context, but to the needs of the collectivity, ultimately accounting for variations and deviations in collective memory over time. The collective memory serves to form the basis for a collective identity and impacts on the individual's process of interpretation of contemporary events.

Through collective memory, society 'represents the past to itself' in order that it might modify its current conventions to suit present needs – just as the repertoire of national myths, memories and symbols has to be dynamic in order to maintain its salience and resonance.[26] In this way, collective memory serves not only to 'nourish our thought' but pronounces judgements on individuals and events, reflecting the thoughts of the society as a whole.[27] Within this process, the collective past is construed in light of the present. Thus, for the purposes of this book, and to paraphrase Halbwachs, there is no national thought that is not an idea of an atomised individual and that is not at the same time composed of a series of recollections, of images or events or persons located in space and time and delimited and bounded in form and content by the nation.[28] The purpose of collective memory is therefore to ensure that knowledge – the content of culture as practised in the transference of memory and ritual – is transmitted across time and built upon by successive generations of the nation. It ensures that a nation's experiential gains – through success and suffering – can be consolidated and rendered into a single coherent narrative so as to anchor the moral compass of the collective, even if this anchor is subject to changes over the *longue-durée*.

The nation, again to paraphrase Halbwachs, can live only if there is a sufficient unity of outlooks among the individuals and groups comprising it – therefore accounting for the phenomenon of the popular resonance of Irish national myths, memories and symbols. Social movements flourish where individuals believe that their fellow members in the community are experiencing similar cognitive processes and changes.[29] In this way, the existence of a collective memory of the nation demonstrates that certain symbols, memories and myths communicate a singularly understood meaning and message despite their myriad atomised interpretations. When the needs of the nation change, or the perceived needs of the nation diverge, the collective memory adjusts or the nation splits. In response, those in sympathy with or participating in the social movement must redefine their own beliefs to make them congruent with organised collective political action. To this extent, according to Halbwachs, 'as soon as each person ... and historical fact has permeated this memory, it is transposed into a teaching ... or symbol and takes on a meaning ... it becomes an element of the society's system of ideas'.[30] For a society to exist, not only must it possess unity in outlook, but these memories and ideas must be constantly repeated and re-enacted, so that they retain their meaning – accounting for a moral anchoring ensuring the salience of the content of collective memory for the individual and the persistence of the collective memory in the *longue-durée*, in form if not in content.[31] Collective memory can therefore be said to offer a 'normative view of the past that guides present-day behaviours ... it allows one to defend the positive image of the ... collectivity, using social identity ... retrospectively'.[32]

Of course a symbol that exists in the national repertoire is not thought of, interpreted or understood by one single brain, or in one single context alone. There is a danger of reifying the nation, and national myths, memories and symbols, in such a manner as to treat them as a 'unitary empirical datum'.[33] The nation is not a living being – it is the sum of its individual parts. In this way, myths and memories of significant and/or traumatic events may have different connotations for a member of a nation living in Dublin, as opposed to someone who lives in Mayo, as each area may be affected differently and experience this event in light of different internal and external contexts. Broadly speaking, however, and in the *longue-durée*, both parties, despite their geographical separation, would recognise the invocation or use of the myth/symbol in a national context, and in the case of a traumatic event, often commonly understand attached conceptions of suffering, guilt and injustice to the use of such a symbol.[34] In this way, myths and memories of the Great Hunger in Ireland in 1848 may have different connotations for a member of the Irish nation living in Dublin as opposed to Skibbereen, as each area was affected differently and experienced this event in light of different internal and external contexts. Common myths, memories and symbols create a 'consistency' through communication and action (ritual) even when they may be conflicting.[35] The myths, symbols and memories of the nation are individually experienced, yet communally shared.

While collective memory does not mean a singular 'national' memory of past events there is a further complication – as not all events from the past are passed on in the collective memory. It is retrospectively, through a process of (re)casting and (re)assessment, that the long-term impact of an event determines the contents of collective memory.[36] The events that form the repertoire of the collective memory need not only be glorious and successful, referring to the golden age of a nation. Myths of disasters, tragedies and thorough and utter defeats often form the foundations of national myths, memories and symbols.[37] Such commemorations can be based on 'distinctly emotional sources' within the collective memory of the nation, and these emotional sources emanate from experiences such as repeated periods of suffering, prolonged anxiety about one's fate and the fate of one's family, loss of family, imprisonment under threat of life, and torture.[38] The effects of these repressive experiences are permanent, creating unsolved problems and incorrigible expectancies, permanently undermining a belief in a 'just' or 'safe' world and potentially aiding in the cultivation of a collectively shared perception of injustice.[39] Towards this end, public commemoration of events remembered in the collective memory can be thought of as forms of 'social sharing of emotions' in which 'emotions are shared mutually or collectively'.[40] In this process of sharing, the bonds of the community are strengthened and reinforced, contributing to seeing and experiencing national myths, memories or symbols over a broad spectrum and further under-pinning the mutually shared phenomenon of national identity.[41] Through this collective sharing of national traumas in the past, individuals are much more likely to see the factors of not only agency, but especially urgency and injustice as being resonant with and highly relevant to their own experience and influencing their political behaviour.

The basic assumption of this work is that the ethno-symbolist perspective best explains the Irish nation. The Irish nation is based on a pre-modern *ethnie* which provided the Irish nation with a repertoire of myths, memories and symbols, which were dispersed through various *mythomoteurs*, not least of all education, popular culture and institutions such as the Catholic Church, all of which ensured the transmission and maintenance of the repertoire of myths, memories and symbols over the *longue-durée*. As Ireland's position in relation to England, Britain and then the United Kingdom became more complex, and the question of its equal status in versus subservience to the English Crown and British Parliament came to the fore through events such as the disestablishment of the Catholic Church, the establishment of the Plantations in Ulster, the Penal Era and later the Act of Union, the Irish nation emerged in response to pressures of the modern world. The emergence of the Irish nation from the mists of a pre-modern era into a modern nation are well documented in many alternative works, including events such as the Gaelic Revivals, and these illustrate the constraint of collective memory on the emergence of the modern nation.[42]

As for the role of what was clearly the important factor of a rising Catholic middle class in Ireland during the nineteenth century, in this framework, Irish nationalist elites and/or intelligentsia were not only involved in furthering individual power and authority, but were also intimately concerned with the gaining of official political, social, cultural and economic recognition for the claims of their community. Within this perspective on nationalism, nationalist elites/ intelligentsia in Ireland and beyond are understood to be actively engaged in a process of reinforcing collective identity, persuading those that are sympathetic to the injustices being perpetrated on the *ethnie*/nation, and convincing those around them that a nationalist movement is the form of agency that will permanently and completely remedy these injustices. To this extent, the disaster of the Famine provided a modern window and framework for Irish nationalist elites/intelligentsia to reinforce how the Irish nation was a remedy for the perceived injustice and devastation of the Famine. As the elites/intelligentsia's claims of power and privilege depend on their 'action' for the nation, they must continue to put forward their ideas and maintain and cultivate the repertoire of national myths, memories and symbols, even when the injustices to which they are reacting may seem petty and/or irrelevant. This role for nationalist elites/intelligentsia has clear parallels with the suggested role of elites in social movements, in so far as elites must continually engage in the cultivation of their movements in order to attract potential participants. It is therefore the argument here that the radicalisation of Irish nationalism in the wake of the Rising is in part mobilised by radical nationalist elites/intelligentsia who helped to transform the interpretations of these events into one which triggered all three factors that motivate a social movement – identity, injustice and agency.

Defining Nationalism as a Social Movement?

A social movement can be defined as a collective struggle by a group of individuals who come together with a common purpose and solidarity to challenge groups of elites, opposing collectives and authorities.[43] To achieve its objective, a social movement mounts disruptive actions against elites, authorities, other collectives and institutional codes in the name of common claims against these opponents. The basis for the collective action is rooted in feelings of solidarity or collective identity, and sustained action on the part of this collective constitutes the basis for a social movement.[44] While participation in a social movement inherently signifies sympathy for its arguments and intentions, many individuals may sympathise with a social movement's aims, ambitions and actions without actively participating. Some reasons for being in sympathy with a movement, but failing to participate in it, may be fear of repression for participation or alternatively the 'free rider' dilemma.[45] This dilemma can be understood as occurring when an individual decides not to participate in a movement because the 'free-rider', the non-participating individual, believes that they will receive all of the benefit of collective action, with out extending any personal effort.

Social movement theory, as a body of academic literature, has been utilised to investigate and explain popular political action in a number of settings. Often, it has been used to account for participation in grassroots political activism, in non-nation contexts – such as anti-nuclear proliferation movements, environmental movements, local cultural movements, and in movements against elites and institutions by communities who feel themselves to be deprived or discriminated against, but again who may not define themselves or their issues vis-à-vis the nation and/or ethnicity (such as groups based on class, occupation, race and/or geography.) Participation in a social movement is generally accepted as being broadly motivated by three key factors. The first of these factors is a sense of injustice – a sense of 'moral indignation' concerning what participants in a movement feel to be collective grievances – which often takes the form of 'outrage' about the way in which the authorities are treating a problem that affects the collective.[46] Second, a sense of collective identity must be present for the emergence of a social movement, where the motivating sense of injustice is shared by the collective and is therefore equally informed by shared beliefs and a sense of what actually constitutes the injustice itself.[47] The third factor that must be present for the emergence of a social movement is a factor of agency, a belief that the individual can, in so far as they participate in sustained collective action, alter conditions and politics through the mechanisms, institutions and actions of the social movement.[48] The emergence of shared perceptions of injustice, the reinforcement of the collective identity, and the sense of agency occur at different levels of the collective, at different rates and in differing contexts. These conditions emerge in response to various contextual factors and may be cultivated by those in the movement trying to persuade potential sympathisers of their take on these three factors (in this case nationalist elites and/or intellectuals.) Debates over whether such sentiments which motivate social movements are organic and popular or instrumentally concocted and imposed from above correspond to the modernist/perennialist debate in theories of ethnicity and nationalism.

Socialisation may, in part, help to account for certain shared 'common' aspects of these factors, but so too do the institutions of these movements and the efforts of participants to organise and persuade others of their cause. Throughout this book, examples of newspapers writing about events and issues with certain biases and perspectives, as well as various examples of handbills and posters, provide some evidence for this process of socialisation. Participation in the sustained collective action of a social movement can also 'dramatically' change an individual's perspective on the merits of participation. This is evident again and again in the way in which individuals participating in the GAA and/or Gaelic League go on to have very strong views about or participate in radical nationalism. One may be socialised or persuaded into sympathy for a social movement, but the experience of a specific action or event, especially an experience of repression carried out by the challenged 'opponents' of the social movement, may cause an individual to cross the threshold from sympathy to participation.[49] Of course in this case the experience of the Rising, and especially the aftermath of the Rising, is viewed as one of the experiences of repression. There are some occasions, too, where events and occurrences that form part of the basis of the nation's collective memory are forbidden to be re-enacted or actively remembered, in the guise of the collective memory of silent events, or are actively repressed by the community's 'opponents'. Repression of collective memory can occur through the nation's own sets of institutions and structures, or by the application of repression by external and opposing forces wishing to suppress these specific memories.[50] Such 'silent events' can be potent in the formation of collective memory, and can increase their likelihood to 'display aggression and initiate fights with friends and acquaintances'.[51] If the expression of this collective memory takes the form of protest activity (especially peaceful protest) and this activity is repressed by the movement's opponents, then it is highly likely that more protest and political violence will result.[52]

Acts of repression by a movement's opponents not only serve to locate, reify and focus a conception of the collective grievance, but also help to define the available and appropriate actions to rectify this grievance.[53] This becomes even more apparent when one considers the 'Black and Tan War'. Repression of social movements may be accomplished through various sets of institutions, in this case, after the Rising, repression of radical nationalism was most obviously carried out through the institutions of British authority – the Royal Irish Constabulary (RIC), the Dublin Metropolitan Police (DMP), especially its Special Branch, and the British military. The similarity in the outlook amongst the participants in a social movement is not only a result of a common identity but also part of the collective response to these institutions which the social movement is trying to change, not least as set by the common outcry concerning and interpretations of events such as those at Bachelor's Walk (1914) and Bloody Sunday (1920).[54] Therefore a social movement's encounters with opposing and especially repressive institutions are crucial. In particular this may effect what myths, memories and symbols may subsequently appear pertinent, potent and salient to the elites/intelligentsia and participants alike in light of the strategies and tactics employed by the movement and in its repression.[55] Social movements develop their own 'cultures' in response to the organisations, groups, authorities, codes and institutions with which they are engaged in their nationalist struggle, and they are therefore reflexively defined by this struggle.[56] This is important in terms of the emergence of a nationalist movement, in so far as the participants in the nationalist movement find themselves in conflict with other groups, authorities and/or institutions, and the need emerges 'to separate allies from foes and … to turn general predispositions into specific decision structures on ideological debate', which helps to account for the polarisation of a conflict, and the emergence of a unified agenda or 'voice' within a social movement.[57] This may in no small part help to account for how moderate constitutional nationalism dissipated in the years following the Rising.

It therefore follows that the movement of a nation to gain what is perceived by its members as its legitimate status *vis-à-vis* the nation's opponents, mobilised through a popularly resonant repertoire of national myths, memories and symbols and triggering perceptions of identity, injustice and agency, constitutes a social movement. This link opens many new directions for the field of the study of nationalism as a whole, let alone in Ireland. Nationalism is a challenge by a collectivity, the nation, with a common purpose, to gain control of the state, and as a movement is typified by engaging in sustained confrontation with opposing elites, institutions, and authorities. How does it engage in this struggle? Like social movements, nationalist movements mount disruptive actions against opposing elites, authorities, and the legal and cultural codes of various significant opposing institutions over the course of years, decades and/or centuries. This had been occurring in Ireland in a modern capacity at least since O'Connell, and throughout the nineteenth and early twentieth centuries. However, the method and tactics of how this disruption should be carried out was hotly debated and often varied, not least as epitomised in the debates between physical force and constitutional nationalists. In all nations, let alone the Irish nation in the run-up to the Rising and in its aftermath, the type and degree of collective action that are perceived as justified and/or necessary are often hotly disputed within the nation, especially during times of crisis and trauma.

Ultimately the link between nationalism and social movements relies on the role that myths, memories and symbols play in the conception of the identity of the collective and the way in which this informs individual members of the collective causes of injustice, agency and identity. This means that myths, memories and symbols define conceptions of national history, and 'secure' an individual's attachment to the nation.[58] Collective memory plays a crucial part in defining the context in which individuals who comprise the nation pursue their movement. In Ireland, this meant that individuals who supported radical nationalism in the aftermath of the Rising did so in light of the myths, memories and symbols of the Irish nation. The executions of the leaders of the Rising, the internment of participants and others, the repressive character of British rule and the inability to find a way forward on the exclusion of Ulster in a Home Rule solution all triggered this support because of the high degree of resonance between these contemporary events and traumas and disasters in the Irish national past. In particular, collective memory, through popular resonance, helps to establish what events or actions are considered to be unjust, and what events or actions create the urgency necessary for the emergence of a nationalist movement. This repertoire underpins what all members of the nation are able to collectively recognise and identify as injustices and grievances perpetrated against the individual as a member of the nation.[59] This has the practical effect of embedding personal experiences of traumatic history in the national narrative, and means that personal experiences are interpreted in light of this narrative. The murder of Francis Sheehy-Skeffington during Easter Week is then an event which, beyond a tragedy, is at first interpreted in light of the broader narrative of the Anglo-Irish relationship and then retold, reaffirming this same narrative. The occurrence of a cultural trigger point depends on the interpretation of this event through the 'cultural stock of movement symbols and speech' which mobilise individuals within the social movement.[60] This is to say that the transformation which occurred in the wake of the Rising depended on the framing and packaging of relevant myths, memories and symbols, promoting a relevant ideological package emphasising the primacy of the nation, and creating a model by which radical collective action on behalf of the Irish nation became understood as well as carried out.[61] While national myths, memories and symbols are chosen by elites, they must also be resonant and relevant not only within the context of the collective memory, but also perceived to be directly salient to the situation.

The Cultural Trigger Point

In the Irish case, immediately after the Rising, it is not novel to assert that an Irish nation already existed, or that there was a social movement to gain political power for the nation – in the form of constitutional nationalism. The novel aspect of this case is the way in which sympathy for and participation in this social movement was transformed in a way that would have been unimaginable in 1905 or even 1912 – from support for moderate constitutional to popular radical and violent nationalism in the wake of the Rising. There had been a nationalist movement in place throughout the nineteenth century, although the content varied in response to the context. It was therefore variously characterised by its engagement with issues such as repeal, land reform and Feinianism. In the movement of Irish nationalism, various contenders attempted to mobilise the nation by making exclusive claims to political control.[62] The task at hand is to understand why the form of Irish Nationalism that had the most appeal in the wake of the Rising was radical – why, in Tilly's words, there was 'a rapid increase in the number of people accepting those [radical] claims and/or rapid expansion of [its] coalition'.[63] Here this process of transformation is located in the cultural trigger point, a moment/event or series of events that trigger a radicalisation in identity, a sense of injustice and perceptions of agency, therefore accounting for a shift from moderate to radical politics and political behaviour in the popular sympathy for and participation in an Irish nationalist movement.

The cultural trigger point, and the process by which this radicalisation is triggered in the Irish nation, is located in its popularly resonant repertoire of myths, memories and symbols, perceptions of injustice and a sense of agency. The executions of Pearse, Connolly and others and acts of repression on the part of the British authorities triggered a response that interpreted these events to a ready-made package of myths, memories and symbols that subsequently radicalised perceptions of identity, injustice and agency in the wake of the Rising. These elements of the Irish nation's past became focal points, because they translated fears amongst individual members of the Irish nation into meaningful events that explained contemporary events, through suffering that was not only ingrained in national memory, but was also tangible through living memory.

The main hypothesis of this book is that the events of the Easter Rising, especially the actions and extent of repression in the British response to the Rising, led to a radicalisation of the Irish nationalist movement because of the way in which individuals in the Irish nation interpreted the repressive actions on the part of the British authorities, institutions and opposing groups. In the wake of the Rising moderate constitutional nationalists failed to react in a way that was interpreted by members of the Irish nation as being adequate and/or appropriate and hence did not resonate widely in the circumstances. There was an anxiety that while an injustice had occurred, little had been or could be done by moderate constitutional nationalism to rectify the perceived injustices of the executions of its leaders and internment of its participants. The sense of injustice was so great that it was deemed the culmination of a fundamental threat to the very basis of the Irish collective identity. In this period of crisis and confusion, individual interpretation of these events became directly informed by their engagement with the collective memory – and the Irish collective memory was particularly marked by memories of repression, at the individual and collective levels, often in sectarian experiences and memories of proselytism at the hands of the Anglo-Protestant 'other'.

The added external social pressures of the First World War, fears of conscription amongst the members of the Irish nation, and an apparent Irish ambivalence towards the British war effort, as well as the unfinished but dramatic and violent sectarianism of the Home Rule question, had already served to heighten the fears of the Irish nation, or more accurately its sensitivity to any event amongst its component individual members. The events of the Rising, when interpreted through the Irish national collective memory, and in the context of these tensions, triggered a shift towards radical perceptions of injustice at the hands of Anglo-Protestant-controlled and -dominated elites, authorities and institutions. This radicalising shift was informed by the collective identity of members of the Irish nation, who in the wake of these events latched on to the existing and reorganised set of radical nationalist institutions in the guise of Sinn Féin, the IRA, and so on. The organisations that lie behind radical collective political action had been in place since Griffiths had created the Sinn Féin League in 1905, although his efforts were initially ignored as they lacked agency and popular support. It took the events of the Rising to trigger members of the Irish nation to personally acknowledge, sympathise with, and/or participate in the radical nationalist institutions, support the radical nationalist leaders and carry out actions under its specific, unifying rubric. The specific Irish taxonomy of myths, memories and symbols was accessible and mobilised by a radical nationalist movement because it demonstrated already existing perceptions of:

1) the binary opposition of radical Irish nationalism, in its core senses of identity, injustice and agency, to the Anglo-Protestant opponents of the Irish nationalist movement, and
2) the relative strength of the popular resonance of the Irish national collective memory because of the Famine, and the manner in which all previous and subsequent 'national' events are broken down through this defining experience.

In short, the case of the Easter Rising is marked by a sense of injustice arising out of the executions and other policies carried out by the British in the aftermath of these events. This sense of injustice was stoked at regular intervals after the Rising, by policies of repression such interment, censorship and physical oppression, accounting for a sustained movement of collective political action in the form of radical Irish nationalism. Repression on the part of the Anglo-Protestant opponents of Irish nationalism had the ultimate effect of ensuring that Irish nationalism was galvanised in its pursuit of national freedom outside of the British Imperial framework, and seemingly confirmed the more extreme content of the national collective memory. It is therefore the moment of the Rising, inclusive of the repression in its aftermath, which can be said to cause a radicalisation in individual sympathies with, if not participation in, Irish nationalism.

NOTES

1 For several interesting analyses of these questions and the general state of the field see especially Johnston, H. and Klandermans, B. (eds), *Social Movements and Culture*, (London: UCL Press, 1995). This question is of course part of many broader debates within the social sciences, such as Weber, Durkheim, via Parsons and Geertz.

2 Smith, A. D., *Nationalism and Modernism* (London: Routledge, 1998), p. 188.

3 Ibid.

4 Giddens quoted in ibid., p. 72.

5 See Weber as quoted in Swidler, in Johnston and Klandermans (eds), 1995, pp. 25–6.

6 See the accounts for this process in Breuilly, J., *Nationalism and the State* (Manchester: Manchester University Press, 1993) and Hobsbawm, E. J., *Nations and Nationalism Since 1780: Program, Myth, Reality* (Cambridge: Cambridge University Press, 1992).

7 This 'orthodox modernism' represents an amalgamation of modernist approaches, and admittedly does not do justice to the depth of complexity and nuance within the various modernist approaches to nations and nationalism. However, for the sake of brevity, this presentation of 'orthodox modernism' represents an attempt at the distillation of this vast body of excellent theory. The modernist orthodoxy, as described above, does not exist as such. It is an amalgamation of theories as put forward by Hobsbawm, 1992, Breuilly, 1993, Gellner, E., *Nations and Nationalism* (Oxford: Blackwell, 1983), Mann, M., 'A Political Theory of Nationalism and its Excesses', in Periwal, S. (ed.), *Notions of Nationalism* (Budapest: Central European University Press, 1995); Nairn, T. *The Break-up of Britain: Crisis and Neo-Nationalism* (London: NLB, 1977), and others.

8 For an extensive analysis of 'orthodox modernism' see especially Smith, 1998.

9 Shils, E., 'Nation, nationality, nationalism and civil society', *Nations and Nationalism*, Vol. I No. 1, 1995 pp. 93–118; Van Den Berghe, 1995; Grosby, 1995; and Geertz, 1963.

10 See especially Hutchinson's discussion of archaeology in Ireland for a discussion of attempts in the Irish case to construct new and/or ethno-nationally encompassing identities, and the way that such processes are often included and reinterpreted in such a way as to maintain a 're-interpreted' and readjusted conception of the national status-quo (Hutchinson, J., 'Archaeology and the Irish Rediscovery of the Celtic Past', *Nations and Nationalism*, Vol. 7, No. 4, October 2001, pp. 505–19).

11 Smith, 1998; Hobsbawm, 1992.

12 Smith, 1998, p. 191.

13 Smith, A. D., *The Ethnic Origins of Nations* (London: Blackwell, 1986).

14 Smith, 1998, p. 198.

15 Schöpflin, G., 'The Functions of Myth and Taxonomy of Myths' in Hosking, G. and Schöpflin, G. (eds), *Myths and Nationhood* (London: Hurst, 1997, p. 17).

16 Smith, 1998, p. 46.

17 See especially Smith, 1986 and Schöpflin, 1997.

18 Smith, 1986.

19 Hutchinson, 2001.

20 Paez, D., Basabe, N. and Gonzalez, J-L., 'Social Processes and Collective Memory: A Cross-Cultural Approach to Remembering Political Events' in Pennebaker, J., Paez, D. and Rimé, B. (eds), *The Collective Memory of Political Events* (New Jersey: Erlbaum Associates, 1997), p. 150.

21 From Halbwachs in Paez, Basabe and Gonzalez, 1997, p. 150.

22 Paez, Basabe and Gonzalez, 1997, p. 150.

23 Halbwachs, M., *On Collective Memory* (Chicago: University of Chicago Press, 1992), p. 49.

24 Ibid., p. 51.

25 Ibid., p. 53.

26 Ibid., p. 173.

27 Ibid., p. 175.

28 Ibid.

29 White, R., 'From Peaceful Process to Guerrilla War: Micromobilisation of the Provisional Irish Republican Army' *American Journal of Sociology*, Vol. 64, No. 6, May 1989, p. 1294.

30 Halbwachs, 1992, p. 188.

31 Shils, in Pennebaker and Banasik, 1997, p. 7.

32 Igartua, J. and Paez, D., 'Art and Remembering Traumatic Events: The Case of the Spanish Civil War' in Pennebaker, J., Paez, D. and Rimé, B. (eds), *The Collective Memory of Political Events* (New Jersey: Erlbaum Associates, 1997), p. 81.

33 Klandermans, B., *The Social Psychology of Protest* (Oxford: Blackwell, 1997), p. 3.

34 Drumm, Fr. M., 'Irish Catholics: A People Formed by Ritual' in Cassidy, E. (ed.), *Faith and Culture in the Irish Context* (Dublin: Veritas, 1996) discusses this process in light of the Irish Famine.

35 Schöpflin, 1997, p. 21.

36 Pennebaker and Banasik, 1997.

37 Smith, 1986; Smith, 1998.

38 Frijda, N. 'Commemorating' in Events' in Pennebaker, J., Paez, D. and Rimé, B. (eds), *The Collective Memory of Political Events* (New Jersey: Erlbaum Associates, 1997), p. 106

39 See the extensive discussion of Holocaust survivors in Frijda, 1997.

40 Frijda, 1997, p. 123.

41 Ibid., p. 123.

42 See especially, Hutchinson, J., *The Dynamics of Cultural Nationalism: The Gaelic Revival and the Creation of the Irish Nation State* (London: Allen and Unwin, 1987).

43 Tarrow, in Klandermans, 1997, p. 2.

44 Klandermans, 1997, p. 2.

45 For an extensive review of the debate on the 'free rider' dilemma see Klandermans, 1997. Though not discussed here, there is often a counterbalancing force to the fear of repression by an opponent for participation in movement, which is the reward from the participant's own collective (nation) associated with participation, and the potential collective penalty – ostracisation or worse.

46 Klandermans, 1997, pp. 17–19.

47 Ibid.

48 Ibid.

49 See Klandermans' discussion of these factors, Klandermans, 1997.

50 Pennebaker and Banasik, 1997, p. 10. For example, in the run-up to the Irish Easter Rising of 1916, the British state had tried to suppress the practice of Roman Catholicism from the disestablishment, and the theological and cultural content of this religion was repressed by various state institutions until the repeal acts of the nineteenth century. Furthermore, the official narrative of the Famine, when combined with survivor's guilt encouraged by the Cullenisation of the Catholic Church (Drumm, 1996) served to create a silent collective memory which manifested itself in other forms of commemoration and remembrance.

51 Pennebaker and Banasik, 1997, p. 11.
52 White, 1989, p. 1281.
53 Ibid., p. 1294.
54 Swidler, A., 'Cultural Power and Social Movements' in Johnston, H. and Klandermans, B. (eds), *Social Movements and Culture* (London: UCL Press, 1995), p. 37.
55 Ibid., p. 38.
56 Ibid., p.38.
57 Ibid., pp. 35–9.
58 Smith, 1998, p. 180.
59 White, 1989, p. 1294.
60 Johnston and Klandermans, 1995, p. 14.
61 Smith, 1998, p. 46.
62 Tilly, C., *From Mobilisation to Revolution* (New York: Random House, 1978), pp. 216–19.
63 Ibid., pp. 217–19.

2

Reactions to the Outbreak of War

Introduction

The First World War brought about a massive set of transformations in Ireland, politically, economically and culturally, and it had a massive effect on everyone in Ireland, nationalist and unionist, radical or moderate, all classes and in all geographical locations. Initially, it was believed that the war would be over by Christmas, and therefore these dramatic effects were surprising and unforeseen. Contemporary experiences of war, for example in South Africa, had not prepared Britain or Ireland, government or population, for this war's devastation. Ultimately, however, even for moderate nationalists, recruiting and conscription came to be issues analysed and broken down through the prism of the myth, memories and symbols that lay at the heart of the Irish nation.

The effects of the First World War in Ireland can be categorised into five broad themes: 1) recruiting into the army, 2) conscription and its application to Ireland, 3) the initial enthusiasm for the war, 4) the emergence of sectarian division, and 5) the eventual emergence of a sense of regularity and weariness as to the pursuance and suffering associated with the war. This chapter will attempt to demonstrate the presence of these themes, and examine their effects on the Irish nation before the Rising. This will come to provide a basis for comparison to demonstrate the transformation in attitudes towards these issues after the Rising.

Irishmen in the British Army

The actual outbreak of the war came as a great shock. While there were some general reports of the troubles in 'Servia' and regular reports about the overthrow of the king in Albania, there was no contemporary evidence of in-depth analysis of these events in newspapers which saw these events as leading directly or imminently to a possible war between the great powers of the time.[1] There was, however, contemporary evidence of militarisation. In Ireland, there had been a clear 'militarisation' of politics, with the arming of paramilitary groups. In Britain there had been a build-up of forces, in reaction to imperial competition and events on the continent since the start of the twentieth century. The build up of the British Army was important enough to be noted in British intelligence reports, prior to the outbreak of the war in August 1914. These make constant references to recruiting efforts and the endeavours of Sinn Féin and radical nationalists to undermine them. This indicated that even before the outbreak of the war, the issue of recruiting and enlistment was a contentious one in Ireland.

After the outbreak of the war, the reporting of events on the continent as well as Nationalist politics shaped attitudes amongst the Irish nation. Reporting of war news was severely curtailed in a policy of secrecy, which often served to exacerbate pre-existing anxieties.[2] It had the effect of adding oxygen to the flame of rumour. Rumours abounded as to the location of Irish regiments, and as to what exactly they were up to. All such rumours were tempered with the belief that 'the Irish regiments are always the first into and the last out of any of Britain's wars'.[3] This anxiety put further pressure on individuals to decide how to accommodate loyalty to the nation and the Empire in light of the outbreak of the war.

Attitudes towards the outbreak of the war were mixed. On the one hand, there were many reports of the dissipation of sectarian tension, with many stories of the National Volunteers providing 'emotional' send-offs for Protestant/Unionist recruits as well as their own colleagues. The intelligence reports from the period make explicit references to the transformations brought about by the outbreak of the war; it 'worked a revolution in the state of party feeling ... which was shown by the turning out together of the Ulster and National Volunteers with bands to escort troops during the mobilisation of the Army'.[4] This particular report is not unique, as there are consistent references to the 'strong patriotic and anti-German feeling, irrespective of creed and politics in giving a hearty send off to reservists and recruits'.[5] This enthusiasm was tempered by a sense of trepidation, as there was a recognition of a sense of 'grimness' in Ireland, which demonstrated 'none of the confidence and self-assurance now as ... at the time of the Boer War'.[6]

Overall, pro-war and pro-British propaganda abounded, and there was a great deal of support, excitement and enthusiasm which accompanied the outbreak of the war. There was a sense that this was something different from the Boer War or the 'little Wars such as occur twice or thrice a year in India'.[8] Along with the realisation, that this War was to be an undertaking of unknown proportions, there was some accompanying anxiety, 'The Great War may "fizzle out" – it may be Armageddon. No one knows.'[8] The association of the image of Armageddon with the outbreak of the war is a common one. The *Daily Freeman* reported that with the outbreak of the war 'We are confronted by an Armageddon as the climax to all our boasted modern progress ...'[9] With the constant merging of the cultural, religious and political a recurrent element of Irish nationalism it is hardly surprising that a religious concept, such as Armageddon, should be used to help contextualise the events of the war.

Support for Britain and the British army was strong even amongst those who had been ready to confront Westminster and the British establishment over the apparent failure to gain Home Rule without the exclusion of Ulster a month or two previously. According to the intelligence reports of the period there was a strong patriotic and an anti-German sentiment.[10] Accounts of spontaneous demonstrations of support for British soldiers, the singing of 'God Save the King' by Nationalist Volunteers, and vast crowds generally enthusiastic in their support of England, had been an 'unheard of thing hitherto among our nationalists'.[11] When reservists were called up and reported for duty, it was described as being accompanied by 'scenes of great enthusiasm', where the National Volunteers accompanied the troops to railway stations and recruiting centres, and in the North, there was even astonishment that the Ulster Volunteers 'fraternised' with reservists and the National Volunteers to give the men a 'good send off'.[12] In the House of Commons, Sir Edward Grey stated at the outset of the war that things had for once and all dramatically changed in Ireland, and that 'The general feeling throughout Ireland ... does not make the Irish question a consideration which we feel we have now to take into account ...'[13]

Other reports make specific mention of sectarian and political tension increasing on a daily basis prior to the outbreak of the war, but after the start of the war, 'matters quieted down considerably and the political tension was relieved'.[14] Another report from Co.

Tyrone details the way the outbreak of war 'worked a revolution in the state of party feeling'; demonstrated in the 'turning out together of the Ulster and National Volunteers with bands to escort troops during the mobilisation of the Army'.[15] In Tyrone, the report continues that 'amongst all people in the country the feeling against Germany was very strong ... party politics being eschewed for the time being'.[16] The *Irish Catholic* believed the outbreak of the war had put an end to radical politics in Ireland and that 'if there are any persons crazy and criminal enough to imagine that they could in any degree benefit Ireland by creating a disturbance within our shores ... when the Empire is fighting for its existence we can only say that small show of sympathy will be extended to them if they are compelled to pay the penalty of their folly'.[17] Interestingly, the dissipation in sectarian tensions may not have been as spontaneous as it appears to be – Orange marches and contentious demonstrations were banned during the war, in order that they might not affect recruiting levels in Ireland.

Although sectarian and political tensions seemed to dissipate in the face of the new crisis, all sources point to an anxiety still being expressed over the fate of Home Rule.[18] The County Inspector's reports make mention of the fact that while 'party feeling died down to a considerable extent, a good deal of anxiety was evinced on both sides as to the fate of Home Rule'.[19] Archbishop Walsh expressed similar anxieties to his secretary, Msgr Curran; he felt Redmond's entire pro-recruiting strategy to be indicative of the 'Irish Parties' subservience to the Liberals', as opposed to a strategy predicated on gaining the full implementation of Home Rule for Ireland.[20]

Recruitment

The issue of recruitment demonstrates some of the inherent splits between British political institutions and Irish young men. Support for, or opposition to, British army recruiting in Ireland was not a matter that simply emerged in response to Kitchener's drives at the beginning of the First World War. Indeed, from the 1790s onwards, recruitment into the British army was a political and nationalist issue.[21] The Boer War had seen the issue of recruitment come to the fore in Ireland. During this period, it had been generally the policy of the Irish Party to discourage recruitment, although it often raised the issue of the welfare of Irish soldiers in the army.[22] Of course, the

Boer War had special significance to physical force nationalists in Ireland, as it was seen as broadly demonstrative of how 'minority' nations throughout the Empire could mobilise an effective military insurrection against the impaired military juggernaut. John MacBride, later a major figure in the Irish Volunteers who was executed for his participation in the Easter Rising, had led a Brigade comprising mainly Irish-Americans against the British in South Africa.[23] The Boer War was also of particular importance, because it saw Irish participation in armed conflict, not only in the British army, but also in an Irish Brigade in support of the Boers fighting against the British. Indeed, some constitutional nationalists were, while not in explicit sympathy with their cause, broadly sympathetic to or proud of this Irish Brigade.[24]

By 1905, anti-recruiting sentiments had become a core plank of radical nationalism in Ireland. For the newly formed Sinn Féin League in 1907, anti-recruitment was a full-blown policy of radical nationalists in Ireland.[25] The power that the issue of recruiting had for Irish nationalists was not lost on the relevant British authorities. In the run-up to the war, activities that did not overtly support recruiting efforts were treated by British intelligence reports as being seditious and disloyal.[26] During the Home Rule crises, especially from 1912 onwards, reports regularly mention both Unionist and Protestant Church leaders making statements considered to be 'disloyal' to the Crown. However, inspector reports rarely, if ever, mentioned specifics of who, where or when such statements were being made. In contrast, during this same period the intelligence reports on nationalist anti-recruiting activities include specific details, such as the names and addresses of Nationalist agitators and Catholic clergy, and paid particular attention to the contents of sermons or statements amongst these groups which were considered not to explicitly support recruitment, or were explicitly anti-recruiting in character. Such reports and concerns were not without some merit. So much of the anti-recruiting and anti-army sentiments prior to the war, and even after its outbreak, came from cultural nationalist institutions such as the GAA and the Gaelic League.[27] In February 1914, well before the outbreak of the war, Archbishop Walsh of Dublin had refused to bless the colours of the City of Dublin Cadets, on the grounds that the prayers used at this event were 'unsuitable'.[28] That this refusal could occur at this (elite) 'official' level, illustrates the power, resonance and potentially polarising effects that the issue of recruitment possessed.

The intelligence reports regularly indicated the origin of British army recruits in terms both of religion and 'volunteer' orientation. These figures allowed the military and British government to assess the effects of their recruiting efforts, and to see whether or not they were successful amongst Catholics and Nationalists. Even if such data was kept for innocuous purposes it served to consistently reify the differences that existed between Nationalists and Unionists, Catholics and Protestants, Irish and English. The figures kept are indicated in Table 1.

Table 1: Recruits into the British Army, 1915

Irish (National) Volunteers	Ulster Volunteers	N/A	TOTAL
10,794	8,203	23,144	51,151

Source: Intelligence Reports, CO 903/8 PRO, Kew.

Figure 1: Recruits by Volunteer Affiliation in the British Army, 1915

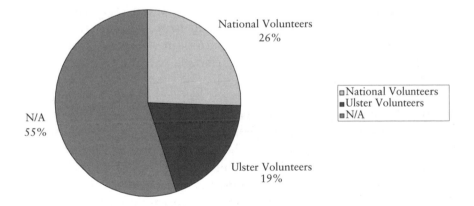

Source: Intelligence Reports, CO 903/8 PRO Kew

Table 2: Religious Denomination of British Army Recruits, 1915

Roman Catholics	Protestants	Total
31,412	19,729	51,141

Source: Intelligence Reports, CO 903/8 PRO, Kew.

Figure 2: Religious Affiliation amongst British Army Recruits, 1915

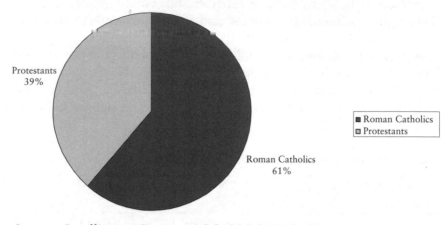

Protestants
39%

Roman Catholics
61%

■ Roman Catholics
▢ Protestants

Source: Intelligence Reports, CO 903.8 PRO, Kew

These tables and figures demonstrate the difficulty faced by the British Army in mobilising the Catholic population of Ireland. While they show the majority of recruits were Catholic, the ratio of roughly 40/60 Protestant to Catholic was not reflective of the religious makeup of Ireland. In fact, from the perspective of the British Army the question of recruitment demonstrated the problematic nature of Irish participation in the war effort. The army's attitudes appeared to be sectarian, so was the response to its calls for enlistment.

A great deal of Nationalist scepticism concerning recruitment emanated from Kitchener's perceived snub to the National Volunteers. The contentious events of the Home Rule Crisis (discussed in the following two chapters), including the 'Curragh Mutiny' the difference between how Unionists and Nationalists were treated when landing arms at Howth and Larne, culminating in the Bachelor's Walk incident did little to make the Nationalist community feel at ease with the British authorities. While the Ulster Volunteers were accepted *en masse* as an entire division in the British army, it took some time before the same *privilege* was extended to the National Volunteers, and even when the Gorgeous Wrecks, so called for the GR insignias on their uniform, were recognised, it was not in the same manner as the Ulster Division. This perceived snub when combined with the lack of any national badges and regalia for other Irish troops serving in the British army, the failure to establish an adequate Catholic Chaplaincy Corps, no censorial exemption for Episcopal correspondence with Rome, and the perceived failure to facilitate commissions for Nationalists, especially moderate Nationalists, did little to inspire confidence in Redmond's pro-British, pro-Imperial policies.[29] The lack of Catholic priests was a significant blunder on the part of the British army and War Office, and constituted what the *Irish Catholic* called 'a new display of War Office stupidity'.[30] Recruiting from moderate nationalists was also not helped by the simultaneous appeals made by Unionist leaders to members of the Ulster Volunteers and other Unionist groups on the grounds that those who would remain behind would 'be strong enough and bold and courageous enough to keep the old flag flying ... while you are away we are not going to abate ... our opposition to Home Rule ... you will come back just as determined as you will find us at home'.[31] For Nationalists, there was a great deal of sensitivity to the language being used by the Unionists counterparts. This sensitivity was typically heightened by comments such as those of General Richardson, an ex-Indian Army officer and commander of the Ulster Volunteers who urged Ulstermen to join the army because the British army had 'come to the help of Ulster in the day of trouble, and would do so again,' i.e. that the army had undertaken the Curragh Mutiny to protect the Ulster Unionists.[32] Nor had recruitment benefited from the British army's actions at Bachelor's Walk in the summer of 1914, an event that was heavily played upon in an Irish Volunteer handbill distributed on the anniversary of its taking place, in July 1915.[33]

The prevailing popular depiction of Irish soldiers in the British mainstream as drunken, lazy, irrational and stupid, fulfilled broader traditional sectarian stereotypes.[34] This stereotype could be found in the writings of Rudyard Kipling, who managed to distil all of the images and fears of the British imperial elite about the Irish masses, expressing fears that these 'drunken louts' could not be trusted – that they might 'prove to be susceptible to Nationalist subversion'.[35] This was despite the army's pragmatic recognition of their need for Irish manpower regardless of religion. This dependence, however, did nothing to reduce the expression of sectarian tensions.

Recruiting Propaganda in Ireland

In order to overcome Nationalist reluctance to enlist, the British army employed a vigorous recruiting campaign in Ireland. There were four broad kinds of propaganda which were used in Ireland by the British army and its agents to promote recruiting 1) exaggerated

German atrocities, such as stories of the raping of nuns and destruction of Catholic churches in Belgium, 2) the 'spectre' of German occupation, often relayed in Ireland as the threat of Lutheran domination, 3) real German atrocities, such as the sinking of the *Lusitania*, and 4) the fears of a 1798/Wolfe Tone-style rebellion.[36] This last variety of pro-recruiting propaganda specifically referred to the atrocities committed by the 'Hessian' mercenaries, and raised the potential for the same kinds of things to occur again, despite the fact that these Hessians had been deployed by the Anglo-Protestant forces in Ireland, therefore making it a problematic theme for propaganda for obvious reasons.[37]

This propaganda attempted to tap into pre-existing ideas about Irish national morality and bravery, and these were regularly apparent in cultural outlets for popular expression. In early June 1914, newspapers such as the *Irish Catholic* proclaimed with pride that the Irish youth had not succumbed to the 'anti-patriotic poisons of anti-militarism' and that 'the children of a soldier race are as ready as they ever were of yore to risk all in defence of the constitutional liberties and rights of the motherland'.[38] Of course, while this referred to the establishment of the Irish National Volunteers, it served broadly to underpin the later themes of propaganda employed in the British recruitment drive. Such statements were double edged – on the one hand they referred to the 'bravery' and patriotism of the Irish National Volunteers, on the other hand it was this same language that was deployed by British propaganda about Ireland being the 'defender of small nations', which was deployed to attract recruits from Redmondite Volunteers.

From as early as 7 August, newspapers reported 'heroic deaths' of French priests, shot for ringing church bells to warn of an impending German invasion.[39] This report appeared the day after the first recruiting advertisement appeared in the pages of *The Daily Freeman's Journal*.[40] Stories about corpses of naked, mutilated and violated girls hanging in trees were common. By 15 August, some two weeks after the onset of the conflict, reports were already appearing describing German 'treachery' in Belgium with the discovery of German spies disguised as nuns.[41] This sacred imagery was potent, combining the treachery of espionage with the perversion of the Catholic religion. Overall, German atrocities were almost always described in the pages of Irish papers in terms of their denigration of the Catholic Church.

These stories, officially reported in the press, sparked a variety of rumours amongst nationalists in the Irish nation. One diary mentions the rumour spreading through Dublin about a young girl, who had been brought over from Belgium with her hands and ears cut off, to prevent her from struggling against her 'Hun' abductors, and there were many other stories of rape and murder circulating.[42] Other headlines in the *Daily Freeman*, the organ of the Irish Party, point out the 'Horrors of War – German and Austrian Atrocities'.[43] Such atrocities included 'Old People Murdered', the rape and mutilation of Belgian women and children, the especially 'heinous' atrocity of the raping and mutilation of the nuns, the firing on the Red Cross and White Flags, and, most powerfully a priest being shot and then interred without a coffin.[44]

The relevant authorities thought that these stories about atrocities in foreign lands were not enough to get young Catholic and nationalist men to enter the British army. To reinforce the cultural and political sympathy of Irish nationalists, beyond the constant stories of 'Hun atrocities' against nuns and Catholic churches, the fight for land reform was also used a recruiting tool. In October 1914, the *Irish Catholic* ran a story stating the way that the German Kaiser was looking for possessions in distant lands 'in order that he may find homes therein for the surplus Lutheran-Socialist population of his fatherland'.[45] By some strange twist, were the Germans to gain possession of Ireland, the *Irish Catholic* asserted that:

> It would be a comparatively simple thing to so alter the provisions of the tenant purchasers acts as to make the positions of the tenant purchasers hopeless, and then to evict them and transplant Lutherans ...[46]

Such propaganda or analysis served to touch upon all the fears that had historically dogged the Catholic nation, that they would be replaced by Protestants on their land again, this time not just Protestants, however, but socialists as well. Indeed, for some three decades prior to the outbreak of the war, land and land reform dominated Irich nationalism.[47] The idea that they would be removed from their land refers to the way in which the Catholics were removed from the land during the sixteenth and seventeenth centuries by the plantations in Ulster and the English disestablishment of the Catholic Church. The idea that the Kaiser intended to send over settlers – socialist and/or Lutheran settlers – to Ireland in order to provide them with land at the cost of driving out Irish Catholics was of course ridiculous. Yet, at this time, an author thought such a story not only worth recording but one consumable by an Irish reading public. Nor were these kinds of references unique. Bishop Browne of Cloyne was quoted in the *Daily Freeman* in April 1916 saying that Irishmen were fighting in the British army to ensure that Ireland would not be 'made like unfortunate Belgium or Poland, the battle ground of the mighty legions of Europe'.[48] Irishmen were therefore expected to fight off the 'heathens' – and the fates of the two Catholic nations of Belgium and Poland, were mentioned to spur them on.

Within these headlines and descriptions, the intent of the recruiting propaganda was to appeal to Irish nationalism to exploit the linkage between religion and the myths, memories, and symbols of the Irish nation. To this end, German militarism was ultimately described as the 'negation of Christianity' by one priest, while another poster depicted the spirit of St Patrick hovering over a burning Belgian Catholic Church, with a strapline urging an Irish ploughman to enlist.[49] The title of this poster was 'Isle of Saints and Scholars'.[50] In fact, the religious quality of the Irish soldiers was used to account for the great bravery in the Irish soldiery; as, for example 'there is a blend of piety and militarism which makes [an Irishman] an effective soldier'.[51] This moral cleanliness was even equated to corporal cleanliness, with one advertisement for soap in an Irish paper claiming British army soldiers were 'the cleanest fighters in the world'.[52] Of course such depictions stood in direct contrast to Kipling's portrayal of the Irish soldiery, and the use of religious symbols jarred with the reality of the initial lack of sensitivity on the part of the army for Catholic recruits.

There were also some appeals to Irish nationalists that represented a more overt attempt to mobilise nationalist support for the war in light of political, rather than cultural, sensibilities. Regular references mention the 'nobility' of Redmond's pledging of the National Volunteers to the defence of Ireland, as it freed up the British army to go to Belgium and France so that they might more effectively defend the rights of small nations.[53] In this way, the argument was presented that Irishmen should support British efforts to liberate Belgium, because if they wanted freedom as a small nation, so too should they fight for the freedom of the small Catholic nation of Belgium. The war was described at times as a 'War of Liberation,' with a victory for the Allies being a victory 'for causes of the same nature as Ireland's own'.[54] In this way it was thought that working-class men, left behind in Ireland and up to no good, should join the army and go to the front 'to get plenty of fighting' because ultimately 'Duty obliges us to join England … [who] had not always justice on her side, but in the present case she and Ireland are mutually interested in keeping the Germans at Bay.'[55] In this view there was no alternative other than to participate fully and happily in the conflict on the Continent, as 'No nation that is free or hopes to be free or to maintain its freedom can escape the fortunes of this conflict'.[56] There was some sense of irony that here was a 'small nation' struggling for its own freedom, answering the call of an Imperial power, its larger and often oppressive neighbour. However, any concerns were broadly mitigated by Redmond's strategy of Ireland proving its worthiness of Home Rule by support-ing the Imperial war effort.

There was some contemporary recognition that these stories were, even though officially circulated, often second, third or fourth hand, and this is admitted and noted in newspapers and diaries. Such stories were more than likely examples of of propaganda, and despite the pro-war frenzy amongst members of the Irish nation, there is some evidence that these stories were recognised as such. The heady mixture of religion, sexual violence and treachery was a constant point of reference for the pro-recruiting forces in Ireland and, whether or not propaganda, touched on sensitive issues in the repertoire of Irish national myths, memories and symbols. This meant that even though the exaggeration was recognised, it still stimulated a response typified by one journal entry which read – 'I admit that many of these stories were probably the exaggerations of fear – but enough, too much remains solidly established. The corpses are there, they cry to God and to men, too, for vengeance against the terrorists.'[57]

Redmond's Strategy

Redmond's commitment to this strategy went beyond simple encouragement, stating that he would feel 'personally dishonoured if I did not say to my fellow countrymen … that it is their duty … to take their place in the firing line in this contest'.[58] In this way, Redmond not only committed the National Volunteers to the Imperial War effort generally, but also urged them to serve 'wherever the firing line extends in defence of right and freedom and religion in this war'.[59] As part of this effort, the Central Council for the Organisation of Recruiting in Ireland (CCORI) had been founded by constitutional nationalists to show how Ireland could carry out recruiting methods 'by their own methods in their own way'.[60] In this way, they aided in recruiting drives, replete with pamphlets, posters, etc., with a distinctly Irish 'flavour'. These efforts of course went hand in hand with Redmond's conception of recruitment in Ireland – as a function of the nation establishing its trustworthiness and merit to receive Home Rule. Recruiting themes of CCORI-based drives therefore included ideas of reconciliation, recognition and Christian Brotherhood, which was reflected in the culmination of the granting of Home Rule.[61]

Redmond's political gamble, that an Irish commitment to the war would ensure their receipt of Home Rule, meant for him that, whereas in the past Ireland had been 'estranged' from Britain, now there were 'altered views of the democracy of this country towards the Irish question, and I believe that ... Ireland will turn with the utmost anxiety and sympathy to this country in every trial and every danger that may overtake it'.[62] As part of this project, the National Volunteers were 'the great rampart of defence against any attempt to defeat or delay Home Rule' and were therefore physically and metaphorically Redmond's lever by which to show Ireland's worthiness for Home Rule.[63] In light of the 'new standing' and equal footing of Ireland given the passage and immediate suspension of the Home Rule Act after the outbreak of the war, Ireland was just as 'morally compelled' as England to respond to the plight of small nations in peril, such as Belgium.

Contemporary attitudes towards these recruiting drives must be understood within the context of the Home Rule question. The pages of the *Freeman's Journal* often include small political laments, such as 'How differently we should have all confronted this situation ... if we had been given the chance to confront this prospect as a free nation of brothers in arms.'[64] Redmond's own statement in the House of Commons served to further reinforce these ideas. The statement refers to the historical estrangement of Irish nationalists from England and Britain, but that in the current crisis 'Ireland will turn with the utmost anxiety and sympathy to this country, in every trial and every danger that may overtake it.'[65]

Wavering Enthusiasm

As the war progressed support became mixed. Rumours, stories and concerns about personal tragedies, such as the death of loved ones, all belied a gradual resumption of a wartime status quo. Journal entries at the time become more irregular, not because of the stress and pressure of war, but rather because the events became part of a new 'status quo'. In part this was a function of the 'secrecy' of the conduct of the war.[66] The wartime status quo was punctuated from time to time with personal tragedy, such as that of Moylan, who describes the death of his cousin at the front. Such events led observers to question what and who the war was for and about.[67] Indeed Moylan returns to the same images of wailing horns, remembering the day that 11,000 had left in August 1914, but by Christmas 1915 the excitement had passed. Moylan states: 'War had lost all its glamour.'[68] This sense of general malaise was in part due to the disappointment that the war had not ended by the Christmas of 1914, and was now punctuated by moments of high anxiety on the home front about possible Zeppelin attacks.[69]

Perhaps because it was a major point of political contention for all types of Irish nationalism, the response to the recruiting drives dropped off after a period of official enthusiasm, and those that had been 'left behind' were much more reticent to enlist. Therefore after the dissipation of the original enthusiasm for the war, the push for Irish recruitment into the army grew more pointed. One observer blamed the dissipation of support for recruitment on the fact that Ireland was 'so remote from battle that recruiters could not make lads believe in it at all'[70] though as late as April 1916 there were still regular references to the fact 'Catholics should fight for liberation and liberty' – and that such a fight was a 'great' one and a unifying one.[71] Yet, even amongst the National Volunteers there was a notable 'decline in enthusiasm' from when the movement had first started.[72] Redmond was still pushing the fact that despite the problematic history between Ireland and England, 'the passing of Home Rule was a vital fact that had materially altered the situation'.[73] Redmond was doing everything he could to maintain 'an atmosphere favourable to recruiting' in Ireland and as part of this effort courted the press and relied on the leadership of the Irish Party to disseminate the message as the initial grassroots enthusiasm began to disappear.[74]

On the ground, in provinces, counties, regions, cities and towns, attitudes towards recruitment were heavily influenced by politics and parishes. In fact, overall recruitment in Ireland was a failure, although no more so that in Britain and throughout the Empire.[75] Attitudes towards recruiting became increasingly unsympathetic, though this was highly dependent on where one lived. For example, over 52 per cent of the recruits into the British army in County

Wexford, Redmond's home county, would come from the ranks of the National Volunteers, between the outbreak of the war and March 1915, and this represented a clear sympathy with Redmond's pleas to enlist.[76] However, even in the pages of sympathetic papers such as the *Daily Freeman*, the departure of new recruits was described as being very 'affecting', and included images of wives and friends crying, as well as noting the devastation that the departure left in the leadership structure of the National Volunteers.[77] While not explicitly anti-recruiting in its nature, this type of article shows that even recruiting was having a significant and sometimes depressing impact on the Irish nation.

The Response of the Catholic Church

Initially, the Roman Catholic Church throughout Ireland generally supported recruiting efforts and the British army.[78] This was not least in reaction to the stories of the 'German atrocities'. By 1915, however, the Roman Catholic clergy, even beyond the outspoken Archbishop of Dublin, were generally thought to be 'lukewarm' on recruiting and the war.[79] Part of this transformation was due to the apparent lack of concern or urgency about the role of Catholic clergymen in the British army – an issue that not only concerned the institutions of the Church, but also was regularly apparent in the pages of newspapers. This concern was typified by not only a desire for equality of status in the army as a whole, but also as part of the perception that Irish and Catholic soldiers would be without pastoral care in the absence of Catholic priest, and preferably an *Irish* Catholic priest.[80]

The Archbishop of Dublin, William J. Walsh, who from the outset did not support the Irish Party, was vehemently opposed to recruiting and particularly the propaganda that accompanied it.[81] Walsh refused to allow Red Cross or military recruiting drives, solicitations or posters either inside or outside of the churches in his archdioceses.[82] He was sceptical of British intentions, regarded these drives as new labels for British militarism, and openly and explicitly refused to engage with anything he perceived to be propagandistic, believing that collection money for Belgian refugees and churches were sent to England, but the only thing gained in return were 'great numbers of refugees'.[83] While Walsh and the Church did, at first, support relief drives for the Belgian refugees, later references are peppered with references to England shirking its own duty to these individuals. Such statements include notions that if Belgian clergymen were religious then they would remain in Belgium, in order to provide ministry to the suffering. Indeed, the persistent and lengthy, endless even, efforts on the part of English Bishops, British government, and British military to gain Walsh's support and sympathy for the war cause, especially by utilising the Belgian situation, only seemed to harden Walsh's opposition to these drives and his antipathy for the war effort.[84] In this context, Walsh had made it clear that rather than continuing collections for the British upkeep of refugees, he was now ordering collections 'for the unfortunate Belgians who are suffering so heavily at the present in their own devastated country'.[85] Indeed, Walsh regularly clashed with other members of the Catholic hierarchy, resisting the calls of colleagues such as Bishop Browne of Cloyne to publish the amounts raised by the Belgian relief fund to show those who 'are opposed to us in religion or political sentiment ... the generous contribution of our poor people'.[86] Of course such sentiments went well with Redmond's strategy to prove Irish loyalty to England and Ulster.

There was definitely an element of sectarianism associated with Walsh's rejection of these drives, in that the British military elite, and the British ruling classes, English Protestant elites, who were behind these drives, were detached from the business of his Catholic Church. Walsh was particularly infuriated with what he perceived to be British arrogance at the use of his own, and other clergyman's, sermons to promote recruiting efforts. In the spring of 1915, Walsh received a poster already drafted and printed intimating his belief that the sinking of the Lusitania was 'That Horrible Massacre' and encouraging young men to join an Irish Regiment in response. Walsh threatened to sue for the 'great liberty taken' in quoting 'some words spoken last Sunday'.[87] Walsh's disapproval went beyond his own efforts at dampening the recruiting efforts, and there are several accounts of parish priests being before the Vicars-General for making speeches on recruiting.[88]

Conscription

Beyond the recruiting drives and attempts to use nationalist imagery to help boost enlistment, conscription loomed large as a symbolic and pragmatic concern for members of the Irish nation. Before it could be implemented, there would have to be a complete failure to heed the calls to enlist, and this would represent the ultimate failure of Redmond's strategy to prove Ireland's worthiness for Home Rule. It would also emphasise Ireland's precarious political position – in so far as while Ireland had apparently gained Home Rule, Britain continued to override fundamental Irish sovereignty. Therefore Irish fears of conscription dogged Redmond from as early as October 1914.[89] This fear was significant enough for Count Plunkett to lead the calls for the formation of the 'All Ireland Public Meeting Against Conscription' at the end of 1915.[90] On the one hand, Redmond and the Irish Party opposed conscription because it was undemocratic, and on the other hand they recognised the harm that such a policy would inflict on the constitutional nationalist movement in Ireland.[91] They therefore tried to sail a middle path, demonstrating their loyalty to empire, and trustworthiness to induce Home Rule through encouragement for Kitchener's recruiting drives, while at the same time opposing a policy of conscription in Ireland, to the great annoyance of their Unionist counterparts. Opposition to conscription was not unique to Ireland, as conscription had barely been passed in Canada, and resulted in great hostility in Quebec. Australia's conscription referendum failed, twice, and conscription was never even proposed in South Africa.[92]

Rumours about conscription were rife in personal and journalistic accounts of this period. These fears culminated with the debates on the possible extension of the Derby Act to Ireland, in April/May 1916. There was anxiety and opposition to the application of conscription to Ireland, tinged with an acceptance of its inevitability. One diary states 'Personally I think conscription is bound to come … I am ready to do my share if I am called … If we are all to do our bit well and good. But until then, I remain where I am.'[93] This reaction was typical, a sense of inevitability combined with latent hostility towards the prospect of serving in the British army. The radical pamphlet, *The Spark*, quoting from a sermon by Father O'Reilly in Tang, Westmeath, proposed that when the 'man-stealers, the conscriptionists make their appearance just send a deputation of snipers, composed of your ten best shots to meet them'.[94] He assured people that this welcoming committee would 'put the lid on the conscriptionist coffin in a very brief space of time'.[95] This same article makes reference to Britain's claim to be the 'Champion of Small Nationalities' in light of their desire to now call upon the men of Ireland to people their army.[96] Various examples of radical nationalist paraphernalia, such as handbills, regularly make reference to a 'right of resistance to any scheme of compulsory military service under any authority except a free national government'.[97]

Of course not all anti-conscription measures were so radical, one example being Count Plunkett's All Ireland Public Meeting Against Conscription being one example. When writing to Archbishop Walsh, Plunkett requested that Walsh join with this group because 'it is incumbent upon them to give public expression to the undoubtedly universal detestation of any such measure in Ireland'.[98] When conscription was being debated in January 1916, three months prior to the Rising, it was clear that it had become a new issue to fight the old sectarian battles, as 'the Unionists are pressing conscription in the hope that nationalists will refuse it to the detriment of the fate of home rule, which is already in a pretty bad way'.[99] By March 1916, attitudes had not changed dramatically, but conscription was viewed within the confines of a zero-sum Nationalist/Unionist view of politics, and broken down through the prism of sectarianism. When conscription was not applied, the Irish Party took credit, while Unionists were described as rolling 'the whites of their eyes and thanked the Lord that they were not as other men, that they would wish for nothing better than that they should be compelled to serve willy-nilly'.[100] Ultimately recruitment and conscription was not an issue of loyalty or even strategy to Irish nationalists, but yet another indication and symbol of sectarian allegiance – denoting where one stood on the Volunteer or the Home Rule questions.

* * *

Catholic and Nationalist anxiety about the role of Ireland in the Imperial project was manifested in the politicisation of issues such as recruitment and conscription even prior to the Rising. Despite some popular misgivings evident in the lack of response to the recruiting drives, Redmond's support for the war effort made strategic sense to the bulk of moderate nationalists. If the war was a short one, than the commitment of the National Volunteers to service in the British army seemed a small price to pay in order to secure Home Rule by Christmas 1914.

However, the uncomfortable nature of the Irish relationship in respect to the war effort showed that while initial reactions were jubilant and 'strongly patriotic', the emergence of a wartime normality meant a fear of conscription and a desire to stay well away from the muddy trenches of Europe. Ultimately, fear of conscription was at least as strong as outrage over rumours of German atrocities and a desire to defend small Catholic nations, and they led to questions over the Anglo-Irish political relationship apparent in questions over the extension of the Derby Act to Ireland. Of course, the irony that recruitment propaganda provided, in terms of Britain's role as 'Defender of Small Nations', was not lost on nationalists of all hues. Nor were the past actions of the British army, at the Curragh and Bachelor's Walk.

Ultimately, what this chapter bears out is a highly charged Irish nation which displayed excitement, support and scepticism for the war simultaneously and independently. Perhaps this charged nature is the most significant aspect of all. For while sectarian and political tensions over the question of Home Rule may have appeared to fade in the heady days of August 1914, these same sectarian tensions apparently continued to fester under the surface of Irish society – directly affecting the interpretation and analysis of members of the Irish nation of the war, conscription and recruiting. This meant that initial interpretation of the events of the Rising and its aftermath would be carried out in the context of the myths and memories of the Anglo-Irish relationship, and that later radicalisation would occur more easily because of the accessibility of this set of political myths and memories.

NOTES

1   See various contemporary newspapers such as the *Daily Freeman, Evening Herald, Independent*, etc.
2   Taylor, A. J. P., *Politics in Wartime* (London: Hamish Hamilton, 1964).
3   'A Dubliner's Diary by Thomas King Moylan' 12 Aug 1914, MS. 9260 NLI.
4   County Inspector's Report, 1914, CO 903/19, PRO Kew.
5   County Inspector's Report, 1914, CO 903/19, PRO Kew.
6   'A Dubliner's Diary by Thomas King Moylan' 7 August, 1914, MS. 9260 NLI.
7   'A Dubliner's Diary by Thomas King Moylan' 5 Aug 1914, MS. 9260 NLI.
8   'A Dubliner's Diary by Thomas King Moylan' 5 Aug 1914, MS. 9260 NLI.
9   *Daily Freeman's Journal*, 3 August 1914.
10   County Inspector's Report, 1914, PRO CO 903/17 PRO Kew.
11   'A Dubliner's Diary by Thomas King Moylan' 6 Aug 1914, MS. 9260 NLI.
12   *Daily Freeman's Journal*, 3 August 1914.
13   Sir Edward Grey on Ireland and the European War, in Mitchell, A. and Ó Snodaigh, P. (eds), *Irish Political Documents* (Dublin: Irish Academic Press, 1989), p. 167.
14   County Inspector's Reports, 1914, PRO CO 903/17 PRO Kew.
15   Ibid.
16   Ibid.

17 *Irish Catholic*, 10 October 1914.
18 See especially County Inspector's Reports, 1914, PRO CO 903/17 PRO Kew for reports on this anxiety.
19 County Inspector's Reports, Belfast, 1914, CO 903/17, PRO Kew.
20 Statement of Monsignor Michael J. Curran to Bureau of Military History, MS 27728 NLI.
21 Denman, T. 'The Red Livery of Shame: the Campaign Against Army Recruitment in Ireland, 1899–1914' *Irish Historical Studies*, Vol. XXIX, No. 114, November 1994, p. 208
22 Ibid., 211.
23 Kee, R. *The Green Flag Volume 3: Ourselves Alone* (London: Quartet, 1982), p. 2.
24 Denman, 1994, p. 214.
25 Ibid., 225.
26 See the various reports from Dublin Metropolitan Police (DMP) Crimes Special Branch (CSB) Files in NLI and various Royal Irish Constabulary (RIC) Police Intelligence Reports in CO 903/7-24 at PRO Kew.
27 Denman, 1994, p. 228.
28 Letter from Walsh to Captain Cunningham, 14 February 1914, Archbishop Walsh Papers, 384/5.
29 McBride, L., *The Greening of Dublin Castle: The Transformation of Bureaucratic and Judicial Personnel in Ireland, 1892–1922* (Washington, DC: Catholic University Press, 1991), p. 181; Kee, R. *The Green Flag Volume 2: The Bold Feinian Men* (London: Quartet, 1983), p. 229.
30 *Irish Catholic*, 26 September 1914; also see Leonard, J., 'The Catholic Chaplaincy', in Fitzpatrick, D. (ed.), *Ireland and the First World War* (Dublin: Trinity History Workshop, 1986) and Fitzpatrick, D., *Politics and Irish Life: 1913–1921* (Cork: Cork University Press, 1998).
31 Speech cited in Kee, 1983, p. 229.
32 Kee, 1983, p. 229.
33 Irish Volunteer Handbill, 'The Present Crisis', in MS 31137, NLI.
34 See Denman, T. 'From Soldiers Three to the Irish Guards in the Great War: Rudyard Kipling and the Irish Soldier, 1887–1922', *The Irish Sword* Vol. XXII, No. 88, Winter 2000, pp. 159–73.
35 Ibid. p. 167.
36 Novick, B. 'Postal Censorship in Ireland, 1914–1916' *Irish Historical Studies*, Vol. XXXI, No. 123, May 1999, pp. 130–3.
37 Ibid.
38 *Irish Catholic*, 6 June 1914.
39 *Daily Freeman's Journal*, 7 August 1914.
40 First recruiting advertisement appeared in *The Daily Freeman's Journal*, 6 August 1914.
41 *Daily Freeman's Journal*, 15 August 1914.
42 'A Dubliner's Diary by Thomas King Moylan' 8 October 1914, MS. 9260 NLI.
43 *The Daily Freeman's Journal*, 26 August 1914.
44 See descriptions from *The Daily Freeman's Journal* throughout the war, though especially late August–November, 1914.
45 *Irish Catholic*, 3 Oct 1914.
46 Ibid.
47 Campbell, F., *Land and Revolution: Nationalist Politics in the West of Ireland, 1891–1921* (Oxford: Oxford University Press, 2005).
48 *Daily Freeman's Journal*, 11 April 1916.
49 Ellis, J. S., 'The Degenerate and the Martyr: Nationalist Propaganda and the Contestation of Irishness, 1914–1918' *Eire-Ireland* Fall/Winter 2001, p. 12.
50 Ibid.
51 MacDonagh, 1916 cited in Ellis, 2001, p. 13.

52   Advertisement cited in Codd, P., 'Recruiting and Responses to the War in Wexford', in Fitzpatrick, D. (ed.), *Ireland and the First World War* (Dublin: Trinity History Workshop, 1986), p. 22.

53   *Daily Freeman's Journal*, 11 August 1914.

54   *Daily Freeman's Journal*, 19 August 1914.

55   Newspapers, March and August, 1915 cited in Codd, 1986, p. 23.

56   *Daily Freeman's Journal*, 3 August 1914.

57   *Daily Freeman's Journal*, 25 August 1914.

58   Redmond in *Parliamentary Debates* cited in Boyce, D.G. and O'Day, A. (eds) *Ireland in Transition, 1867–1921* (London: Routledge, 2004), p. 94.

59   Redmond's Speech in Wicklow, 20 September 1914 cited in Boyce, 2004, p. 95; Lyons, F. S. L., *Ireland Since the Famine* (London: Fontana, 1985), pp. 329–30.

60   Ellis, 2001, p. 10.

61   Ellis, 2001, p. 11.

62   Redmond, Speech to Commons cited in Kee, 1983, p. 219.

63   Kee, 1983, pp. 218–20.

64   *Daily Freeman's Journal*, 3 August 1914.

65   Redmond's Statement in the House of Commons, 3 August 1914 in Mitchell and Ó Snodaigh, 1989, p. 167.

66   Taylor, 1964.

67   'A Dubliner's Diary by Thomas King Moylan', 31 May 1915, MS. 9260 NLI.

68   'A Dubliner's Diary by Thomas King Moylan' 22 December 1915 MS. 9260 NLI.

69   Letter from Walsh, 22 February 1916, Walsh Papers, 385/3.

70   Letter of Ismena (Rhodes), 21 May 1916, MS 15415, NLI.

71   *The Daily Freeman's Journal*, 8 April 1916.

72   County Inspector's Report, Belfast, 1915, CO 903/19 PRO Kew.

73   *Daily Freeman's Journal*, 10 April 1916.

74   Ellis, 2001, p. 10.

75   See Boyce and O'Day, 2001, McBride, 1999, Novick, 1999; Fitzpatrick 1998,

76   Codd, 1986, p. 21.

77   *Daily Freeman's Journal*, 14 August 1914.

78   Miller, D. 'The Roman Catholic Church in Ireland, 1865–1914' in O'Day, A. (ed.), *Reactions to Irish Nationalism, 1865–1914* (London: Hambledon Press, 1987), p. 196.

79   Ibid., p. 197.

80   For an in-depth discussion of the issues of the Catholic Chaplaincy in the British army, see Leonard, 1986.

81   For a description of Archbishop Walsh, and his place in the Catholic scene in Ireland at the end of the nineteenth century and beginning of the twentieth, see Miller, 1987.

82   Letter from Department of Recruiting to Archbishop Walsh, Walsh Papers, 385/6 and Statement of Monsignor Michael J. Curran to Bureau of Military History, MS 27728, NLI, and Walsh papers are replete with curt, almost rude responses to requests from Military authorities for his assistance in recruiting drives.; de Weil, J. A., *The Catholic Church in Ireland, 1914–1918* (Dublin: Irish Academic Press, 2003).

83   Letter from Walsh to Bishop Murphy in London, 4 November 1914, Walsh Papers, 384/5.

84   See also Walsh Papers, 384/5 14 February 1914, Letter from Walsh to Captain Cunningham on the Blessing of the Colours of the Dublin Cadets and 4 November 1914 Walsh's response to a letter from Bishop Murphy of London.

85   Letter from Walsh to Bishop Murphy in London, 4 November 1914, Walsh Papers, 384/5.

86   Walsh Papers, 1914, 384/4, Statement by R. Browne, Bishop of Cloyne, 31 December 1914.

87   For a full description of this exchange, see Statement of Monsignor Michael J. Curran

to Bureau of Military History, MS 27728, NLI, and Walsh's personal papers.

88   See Notes of Vicars Generals meetings in Walsh's Papers, and Statement of Monsignor Michael J. Curran to Bureau of Military History, MS 27728, NLI.

89   Finnan, J., 'Let Irishmen Come Together in the Trenches: John Redmond and Irish Party Policy in the Great War, 1914–1918', *The Irish Sword*, Vol. XXII, No. 88, Winter 2000, p. 185.

90   Letter from Plunkett to Walsh 10 December 1915, Walsh Papers: Special Papers/Political Papers.

91   Finnan, 2000, p. 185.

92   Finnan, 2000, p. 190.

93   'A Dubliner's Diary by Thomas King Moylan', 6 May 1915, MS. 9260 NLI.

94   *The Spark*, 14 November 1915, Vol. II No. 41.

95   *The Spark*, 14 November 1915, Vol. II No. 41.

96   *The Spark*, 14 November 1915, Vol. II No. 41.

97   Irish Volunteer Hand Bill, 'The Present Crisis', in MS 31137, NLI.

98   Special/Political Papers from Archbishop Walsh, letter from Plunkett to Walsh, 10 December 1915.

99   'A Dubliner's Diary by Thomas King Moylan', 5 Jan 1916, MS. 9260 NLI.

100 'A Dubliner's Diary by Thomas King Moylan', 1 Mar 1916, MS. 9260 NLI.

3

Radical Politics in Ireland
Prior to the Rising

They think that they have pacified Ireland. They think that they
purchased half of us and intimidated the other half. They think
that they have foreseen everything, think that they have
provided against everything; but the fools! the fools! the fools!
– they have left us our Feinian dead, and while Ireland holds
these graves, Ireland unfree shall never be at peace.

Patrick Pearse, Rossa's Funeral Oration.[1]

The above statement, made by Patrick Pearse during his funeral
oration for O'Donovan Rossa, has been interpreted as being
prophetic and indicative of the undercurrent of radical nationalism
in Ireland that would come to burst forth some eight to nine months
later in the Easter Rising. In this interpretation and hypothesis, the
forces of latent radical nationalism were biding their time, always
present though not quite manifest. Pearse's oration has been seen as
laying down a marker, a declaration of intentions. But what was the
state of radical politics in Ireland on the event of the Rising? Was the
Rising some sort of purgatory – an All Souls' Day with the spirits of
physical force nationalism passing through the contemporary Irish
world having completed their penance for past failures?

This chapter will point to some of the elements of radical
nationalist politics in the run-up to the outbreak of the First World
War, and the Easter Rising. In order to provide a comparative basis
for analysis, the chapter will examine radical nationalist politics,
concentrating on its effects, or lack thereof, on Irish society
immediately before the Rising. Towards this end, it will initially
examine Sinn Féin – attempting to understand its *raison d'être* and
impact. It will then look at the 'arming of Irish politics' through the

establishment of first the Unionist Ulster Volunteers and later the Nationalist Irish Volunteers. Both of these paramilitary organisations operated outside the official British political and institutional structure – and both relied on an ability to generate emotion and images rather than on their tactical abilities. The analysis of these Volunteer bodies also includes the different treatment of each by the British authorities. For Unionists, non-interference with the landing of weapons at Larne and the support inherent in the Curragh Mutiny seemed to suggest toleration of, if not tacit support for, their anti-Home Rule project. For Nationalists, the fiasco at Bachelor's Walk, with the death of street protestors in the wake of the Irish Volunteer's landing of arms at Howth, seemed to objectify the difference between British treatment of each body, especially in terms of the attitudes of the military and police. Such events pushed Ireland to the brink of civil war in 1914 – and intensified sectarian political tensions in such a way as to poison pro-British/Imperial war efforts on the part of moderate/constitutional Nationalists such as Redmond.

The Ulster Volunteers, the Landing of Guns at Larne and the Curragh Mutiny

The arming of Irish politics and drilling of Unionist and Nationalist Volunteer bodies added a new and explosive dimension to the sectarian Irish political scene. The Home Rule crisis dominated every aspect of politics in Ireland. It is difficult to overemphasise the scale of Unionist opposition to Home Rule, spilling out of Westminster and the pulpits of churches into the Orange Order, Unionist Clubs, the Ulster Volunteers and ultimately the streets of Belfast and the rest of Ireland.[2] Passions were running so high that even those who perceived themselves as the most loyal subjects of the Empire were prepared to jeer the national anthem – a previously unthinkable demonstration of 'disloyalty'.[3]

The organisation of the Ulster Volunteers in early 1913 was presaged by a protest march of over 100,000 Ulster Protestants in April 1912, two days before the introduction of the Third Home Rule Bill.[4] By early 1912 it had become inevitable that a new Home Rule Bill would be introduced, and there were clamours for an Ulster-based resistance to Home Rule 'if the quarrel were wickedly fixed upon them'.[5] The recently appointed leader of the Tories, Andrew Bonar Law, called on a force 'stronger than a parliamentary majority' and said that such strength should include 'no length of resistance to which Ulster can go that I should not be prepared to support them'.[6] By late September 1912, the Ulster Solemn League and Covenant was signed. It tapped into a rich historical vein, as a Solemn League and Covenant had been signed by Scottish and English opponents of Charles I, to preserve and advance the Reformation and ultimately establish Presbyterianism.[7] The Solemn League and Covenant of 1912 was signed by the vast majority of Ulster Protestant males, some of who signed in their own blood, with a similar document produced for and signed by women.[8] The Covenant called for the defence of 'our cherished position of equal citizenship in the United Kingdom and in using all means which may be found necessary to defeat the present conspiracy to set up a Home Rule Parliament in Ireland'.[9]

The Ulster Unionists were aided in the formation of a Volunteer body to oppose Home Rule by a close relationship with the British military, both active and retired. Former army officers assisted in the organisation and drilling of the Ulster Volunteers. The next step was to arm the members of the Ulster Volunteers, beyond a collection of antiquated Italian hunting rifles that had been imported during previous introductions of Home Rule Bills, in 1886 and 1893. Addresses by dignitaries such as Randolph Churchill and Lord Londonderry at mass rallies throughout 1913 helped to provide an organisational boost for the Ulster Volunteers. One account from a mass rally in late March 1913 talks of Lord Londonderry, 'In addition to the usual resolutions pledging resistance to Home Rule … the universal topic at these meetings was the Ulster Volunteer Force which all Unionists were urged to join …'[10] Such exhortations did not fall on deaf ears – by April the Ulster Volunteers numbered 41,000.[11] Even amongst radical nationalists, there was a recognition that with the formation of the Ulster Volunteers "armed men in the North have threatened – and without a shot being fired there has resulted panic and disruption'.[12] This recognition, certainly amongst moderate nationalists in the South, was of great concern. The Ulster Volunteers became a body of political leverage – with the *Evening Herald* espousing the opinion that 'Ulster is getting what she wants [partition and exclusion from Home Rule] simply because she has threatened to riot.'[13]

Weapons bound for the Ulster Volunteers were landed at Larne, County Antrim, in what was hailed as a publicity coup by Unionists. In reality, the bulk of the weapons were landed at several other, more secure and less public locations. However, the landing of guns at Larne was carried out with an eye for publicity, and it was not coincidental that this event fundamentally transformed Irish politics and the Home Rule question.[14] Even prior to the landing of guns at Larne, the Ulster Volunteers had shown their desire to become an armed body. The Dublin Metropolitan Police Special Branch, illustrating a keen awareness of the potential for arming the Ulster Volunteers, had already sought a legal opinion from the Attorney-General by March 1912 on what to do if they caught Unionists trying to import arms. The response from the Attorney-General was that:

> The importation of the arms under a false description and in quantity so large as not to be explained by any legitimate purpose than in connection with speeches inciting rebellion may afford very strong evidence of sedition ...[15]

The arms arrived in late April, 1914, almost two years to the day before the outbreak of the Easter Rising, comprised of some twenty-five thousand rifles and three million rounds of ammunition having been shipped from Germany. While the above statement likens the landing of arms to sedition, the official British stance on the arming of the Ulster Volunteers is difficult to pin down. At one of the landings of these weapons, the RIC was called in, but instead of interfering, the detachment

> ... beyond noting the proceedings ... took no steps to interfere with the illegal landing of the arms under their eyes ... they did not even warn the persons of the illegality of their actions or enter a protest at the threat ... that any action on their part would meet with resistance.[16]

Such actions on the part of the Royal Irish Constabulary (RIC) caused some consternation in Britain as well as in Ireland. When taken in combination with the dedication shown by former British military officers to drilling and organising the Ulster Volunteers, the inaction of the RIC was perceived as indicating the links between the Ulster Volunteers, Unionism and the ruling and military classes of the Empire. Even amongst the higher echelons of traditionally conservative institutions such as the Catholic Church there was a recognition that in this situation 'constitutional methods to achieve reform were utterly useless'.[17]

By the time of the gun-running at Larne, the Ulster Volunteers were around 85,000 members strong, so the landing of weapons in Ulster did not put a gun in the hands of each member. In fact the Ulster Volunteers were not a great fighting force, their tactical ability and proficiency being in many ways secondary. They were subject to absenteeism and at times suffered from apathy amongst Unionists, who tended to show up at 'grand marches' and to meetings on public holidays rather than to regular meetings.[18] Indeed, intelligence estimates of arms in the Ulster Volunteers' possession were only at 17,051 at the end of 1913, and by the beginning of April around 25,000 weapons, so less than 30 per cent of the Volunteers were actually armed.[19] The formation of the Ulster Volunteers, and the gun-running at Larne served rather as Unionist propaganda, loudly proclaiming a broader Unionist agenda to the British government and public as well as a declaration of intent in Ireland. One caption in the *Daily Freeman* refers to the Unionists having formed a unit and armed it with cameras, saying that the camera was their best weapon.[20] Such humour at the expense of the 'theatrical' Ulster Volunteers was quite common in the pages of the the *Daily Freeman*. The gun-running at Larne served to put the Home Rule question at the top of the British and Irish political agendas, and heighten sectarian tension in Ireland. The Volunteers' formation and agitation were seen and recognised by Irish nationalists in the context of earlier events, such as the signing of the covenant – an event previously described as 'theatrical rather than dramatic'.[21]

Rumours abounded that the army would be used to forcibly disarm the Ulster Volunteers, and to shut them down. Newspapers were full of reports of troop movements at this moment, fuelling rumours and speculation as to the army's moves and tactics.[22] Regular comparisons were made between contemporary events and the beginning of the war in South Africa.[23] The government perceived the situation to be so grave as to see it as an undeclared state of war.[24] In March 1914, 60 cavalry officers stationed at the Curragh resigned their commissions *en masse* rather than face the prospect of enforcing orders to disarm or quell the Ulster Volunteers. Debates raged as to the rationale behind the movements of officers and troops at the Curragh base – was it a simple exercise, or the decisive order to disarm and quell the Unionist threat?[25] Bonar Law made a dramatic political point in the Commons out of this confusion, pushing the government to explain what had happened, and what their intentions had been – its ultimate impact being to place further strain on sectarian fears and tensions in Ireland.[26] General Paget, the Commander-in-Chief of forces in Ireland, in a response to the War Office, stated that any movement of troops would 'precipitate a crisis' in Ulster, such were the existing tensions.[27] In fact officers from regiments throughout Ireland had demonstrated their sympathy with the officers at the Curragh. When the army was about to be deployed, the Commander-in-Chief gave the order that officers domiciled in Ulster would be permitted to disappear rather than take part in the actions that they found to be so distasteful.[28] The result was convoluted. The War Office refused to accept these resignations, and it gave an undertaking that the army would not be used to disarm or quell the Unionists in Ireland. This assurance was given without the permission or knowledge of the Prime Minister, resulting in the resignations of the Secretary of War and Chief of General Staff. Although this assurance was rescinded by Prime Minister Asquith, the army was rendered a non-option in terms of operations against the Ulster Volunteers in Ulster, and its loyalty to Asquith's government and overall intentions had been called into doubt. The event was reported as demonstrating a struggle which in reality was between 'Tory Officers and the Liberal House of Commons'.[29] The Ulster Volunteers had achieved their objective, and Unionists could now apparently act as they wished in Ireland with little concern for any ramifications in the broader British political context. By May 1914, not only had the ranks of the Ulster Volunteers swelled, as well as the membership of Unionist clubs, but the situation was described in the intelligence reports as being a 'very grave' one, on account of organised and developed Unionist opposition to Home Rule.[30]

The pages of the *Irish Catholic* in early May of 1914 reveal the fact that the Ulster Volunteers were receiving weapons from Germany, and their purpose was of clear importance and concern. These events 'fully warrant[ed] grave suspicions as to sinister possibilities in the future'.[31] The historical parallels of the landing of arms were not lost either, as there are clear and repeated references to the landing of arms prior to the Rising of 1798.[32] Even amongst the intelligence reports of the period, there is a recognition that with the Home Rule question 'being to a large extent a religious one aroused a very bitter sectarian feeling', such feelings were heightened and made manifest by the close relationship between the Ulster Volunteers and the Orange Order.[33] In this way, then, the formation and arming of the Ulster Volunteers not only heightened distrust of

British authority, in terms of the inaction of the RIC, the participation of ex-military officers in the Ulster Volunteers, and the Curragh mutiny, but also heightened and highlighted pre-existing sectarian tensions. The rise of the Ulster Volunteers was meteoric, from non-existent in 1912 to their height of almost 85,000 members immediately prior to the outbreak of the First World War. The fall in numbers to just over 60,000 by the spring of 1915 is indicative of its members heeding Kitchener's call to enlist in the British Army. Before the events of the war overshadowed events in Ireland politicians throughout Britain and Ireland, were alarmed at events in Ulster.

The formation of the Ulster Volunteers had three main effects on the Irish political scene. The first was that it indicated the extent to which Unionists rejected Home Rule, and the lengths to which they would go to fight against any kind of Home Rule solution. The second is that the Ulster Volunteers were an extremely effective tool of political propaganda rather than a strategically effective (para)military organisation. This is not to detract from the great effect that this propaganda had, or from the well-organised nature and huge resonance of the Ulster Volunteers. Third, the events of the Curragh, the questions hanging over the army's willingness to actually confront the Ulster Volunteers, the inaction of the RIC at Larne, the assistance of retired military offices in drilling the Ulster Volunteers and the broad support of the Tory Party demonstrated, or at the very least were perceived by nationalists as demonstrating, the close relationship between the British authorities, the Tory Party and Unionists. The perception of these strong ties created fear on the part of Irish nationalists, as well as for the Liberal government, who were unable to estimate accurately the strength of this relationship and the lengths to which the Unionists might actually go to prevent Home Rule. In this way, Carson's claim that Ulster had a 'strong right arm' rings true – as Ulster Protestants, in so far as they desired exclusion from any Home Rule settlement, looked fearsome and threatened to 'regardless of the consequences go on ... to the end with their policy of resistance'.[34] Overall, the formation of the Ulster Volunteers would have big and tangible effects on the Irish political scene prior to the Rising, and played into perceptions and fears about what would actually transpire after the war with the implementation of the Home Rule Bill. This means that the formation of this paramilitary body was a fact that would have coloured and contextualised the events of the Rising and their interpretation.

Sinn Féin and Radical Nationalism

Sinn Féin was the radical nationalist party established by Arthur Griffith and Bulmer Hobson in November 1905 as an umbrella organisation for radical political groups and individuals who fell outside traditional political parties and organisations in Ireland. Its stated purpose was to achieve 'National Self-Determination through the recognition of ... the rights of citizenship ... and not looking outside of Ireland for the accomplishment of their aims'.[35] By design and coincidence, Sinn Féin was a party that served as an umbrella for those who felt that the Irish Party was not radical enough, and for others who did not fit into the 'politics as usual' of Ireland.

Sinn Féin took in and amalgamated disparate radical nationalist organisations, such as the Dungannon Clubs.[36] These were clubs formed by Bulmer Hobson in 1905 to promote 'advanced' or radical nationalism, and were particularly involved in campaigns against recruiting into the British army.[37] The emergence of Sinn Féin mirrors the fate of contemporary radical nationalism in Ireland, especially in the wake of the double failure of Home Rule, in 1886 and 1893. While Parnell, as leader of the Irish Party, had been able to unite the disparate forms of Irish nationalism, Redmond was unable to unite radical and moderate nationalists under a single institutional structure. This was in no small part a relic of the unfinished land revolution, and may be understood to reflect regional and/or class differences in terms of land reform and nationalist politics in Ireland.[38] The failure of this 'Redmondite–Feinian' nexus meant that by as early as 1900 splits in Irish nationalism were becoming deeper and more explicit.[39] Radical Nationalists were increasingly being forced to 'go it alone' – not unlike their moniker of 1905, 'Sinn Féin'.[40] Prior to this split, although these factions of Irish nationalism may have differed in their objectives and methods, there was a degree of solidarity in their efforts to achieve a devolved Ireland. The collapse of the nexus could be seen as resulting in the emergence of a younger, more vehement, aggressive and independent and initially less popular strain of radical nationalism.[41]

Sinn Féin was distinct from its moderate counterparts in the promotion of an 'Irish Ireland' platform. Cultural nationalists, political nationalists and radical nationalists, amongst others, made up the radical fringe of Irish politics, and it was this radical fringe that fell under the umbrella of Sinn Féin. Some scholars have attempted to differentiate the constitutional politics of the IP and the radicalism of

Sinn Féin by assigning Sinn Féin a cultural/romantic nationalist ideology and purpose distinct from the Irish Party's constitutional/ moderate and/or pragmatic approach. However, two things become clear about Sinn Féin – at first it had no singular policy ambition (other than an 'Irish Ireland') and its approach was opportunistic. By 1906, John Dillon, deputy leader of the Irish Party, amongst others, was well aware of Sinn Féin's ability to make political headway at the expense of the Irish Party.[42] Nor can Sinn Féin's roots be traced neatly or simply without the various land agitation movements, under the auspices of the United Irish League and/or other organisations.[43]

Arthur Griffith was considered the founder and leading member of Sinn Féin, and he was the intellectual engine behind the party, giving voice and shape through his journalism to ideals such as the support of a dual monarchy of equals, between Britain and Ireland, and the promotion of an economically and industrially independent Ireland to foster this equality. A policy of passive resistance was to be deployed to bring about the conditions under which the 'sovereign independence of Ireland' could be regained.[44] This policy included the abstention from Westminster of Irish MPs, the rejection of British institutions, such as the courts, on the part of the people, and in both cases the establishment of Irish alternatives. In order to foster his nationalist agenda, Griffith not only used his position as a journalist, but understood that the creation of Sinn Féin meant its emerging as an umbrella organisation under which 'the disparate forms of advanced nationalism' could be amalgamated.[45]

Sinn Féin found especially fertile ground amongst those who rejected the Irish and Liberal Party's propositions of a 'step by step' approach to the Home Rule question.[46] Such statements could be motivated by personal encounters with this type of approach and a rejection of its outcome – as happened for some in Galway.[47] This was what made it radical. This step-by-step approach was reliant on piecemeal legislation on issues such as the land question, a labourers' housing act, the repeal of coercion, changes to the personnel of and attitudes to the Land Commission, action to aid evicted tenants, and financial and official promotion of the Irish language in education.[48] Sinn Féin promoted and was active on a variety of agrarian and cultural issues, allowing it, as a small, fringe political body, to develop its own political niche. This niche broadly consisted of opportunistically attacking Redmond and the Irish Party on different fronts at different times. The issues surrounding the university question, the Land Commission, appointments to Dublin

Castle, evicted tenants and the scuppering of the Local Government Act provided Sinn Féin with political ammunition.[49] It was recognised by contemporaries that Sinn Féin, as an amalgamated party of radical politics, was unified in its political views or opinions. Key players, such as Griffith, promoted and supported disparate social issues – feminism and suffragism, for example – as long as they did not affect the one element that bound Sinn Féin together – an 'Irish Ireland' a brand of Irish radical nationalist politics.[50] For other activists, such as Countess Markievicz, there was no difference between the social issues of suffragism and national freedom – with the first step towards national freedom being 'to realise ourselves as Irishwomen – not just as Irish or merely as women but as Irishwomen, doubly enslaved with a double battle to fight'.[51] One observation states that:

> ... the term Sinn Féin denoted every shade of Nationalism, from innocent enthusiasts for Gaelic literature and Gaelic sports at one end to red-hot Feinians at the other; so that to call a man a Sinn Féiner established nothing about him, until one knew to which section of Sinn Féin he belonged ...[52]

In this way, there was a sense of confusion as to what Sinn Féin really stood for, and whose voice and vision were really driving the party.

   In part, the confusion over what Sinn Féin 'stood for' resulted from its opportunism – it stood for what the Irish Party could not or would not. In part, this stemmed from a sense of hopelessness and disappointment with the Liberal Party's inability to produce meaningful reform and/or Home Rule and the Irish Party's inability to push the Liberals along in this direction. In this way, Sinn Féin hoped to attract small tenant farmers in the west, because of a commitment to land reform and cultural nationalists committed to an Irish Ireland approach – and the ability to create an umbrella for these strands of pragmatic and cultural nationalisms was the party's niche. When Dolan ran as the Sinn Féin candidate in a 1908 by-election (their only electoral campaign until 1917), he specifically stated that his lingering belief in the Liberals was now 'smashed' and that continued attendance at Westminster meant 'deceiving constituents and betraying the cause of Irish nationalism'.[53] Furthermore, Sinn Féin and other opponents of the Irish Party political machine regularly and opportunistically attacked the close relationship between the Irish Party and the British authorities, especially the relationship between its leader John Redmond and the Irish Chief Secretary Augustine Birrell, in light of Irish Party patronage and appointment to jobs in Dublin Castle.[54] Of course their antagonism towards the Castle, and Dolan's assertion that participation in 'politics as usual' meant the betrayal of his constituents, dovetailed with Sinn Féin's policy of abstention. This was an opportunistic method by which to politically outflank the Irish Party's nationalist credentials. Abstentionism, non-participation in the British institutional rule of Ireland, would become a key plank of radical nationalism, leading to the ultimate establishment of the Dáil Éireann in 1918.

Radical nationalists in Ireland were a tiny minority in Ireland. Despite the fomentation and growth of the radical niche, and the disparate political organisation of Sinn Féin, the Irish Party retained its 'hegemonic role within the nationalist tradition'.[55] Yet their small size did not make them complete unknowns. They were a familiar political grouping and often a familiar focus of political enmity.[56] The existence of this radical political fringe, though in the shadows and manoeuvring behind the scenes, was by no means hidden from public view. Characters such as Griffith, Pearse, Yeats and Francis Sheehy-Skeffington were all familiar characters on the Dublin scene, and all were involved to varying degrees and at different times with the radical nationalism of Sinn Féin. They met at various reading groups and lecturing societies, imbibing intellectual ideals and nationalist myths on a regular basis with the rest of Dublin 'society'.

The relationship between Sinn Féin and cultural nationalist movements such as the Gaelic League or the Gaelic Athletic Association is apparent, if opaque and complex. They are linked not only by shared institutions and common individuals, but also symbolically in an 'Irish Ireland'/Gaelic Revival platform.[57] Intelligence reports from the period recognise the relationships and links between Sinn Féin and these organisations – especially as these nationalist bodies and their policies would affect recruiting into the British army during the war.[58] For an individual such as Griffith, who was not considered to be particularly gifted in the Irish language, and Pearse, who was fluent in the Irish language, the Gaelic League and organisations such as the GAA fulfilled a crucial purpose in their radical nationalist agendas. They were stepping-stones to another level of radical nationalism. At times these organisations served as channels, funnelling members and sympathisers from one to the other and back again.[59] However, the extent to which these organisations were explicitly channelling individuals towards radical nationalism is unclear. Individuals such as Douglas Hyde, founder of the Gaelic League, resigned as head of this organisation rather than allow the cultural nationalist movement to become what he considered to be too radical and/or political.[60]

With the outbreak of the war, Dublin Castle and the British military expressed concern over the potential of this radical fringe to disrupt their recruitment drives, a condition further exacerbated by the splits in the Volunteers. Diary entries and newspapers also express concern about this. The *Irish Catholic* proclaiming shortly after the outbreak of the war in early October 1914 that:

> If there be any persons crazy and criminal enough to imagine that they could in any degree benefit Ireland by creating a disturbance within our shores at a moment when the Empire is fighting for its existence, we can only say that small show of sympathy will be extended to them if they are compelled to pay the penalty of their folly.[61]

From such comments, it is apparent that radical nationalism was identified as a potential liability. This liability was not only pertinent because of the heightened tensions of the war, but also more broadly fit into concerns over the Home Rule question. Correspondence between Dillon and Sir Matthew Nathan, Irish Under-Secretary, demonstrates the variety of opinions on the Sinn Féin movement. Dillon asserted that as long as the British government did not acknowledge and act on the Irish Party's and moderate nationalists' suggestions for recruiting, he did not believe that 'Sinn Féiners and Pro-Germans are making any headway in Ireland'.[62] Nathan responded however by pointing out his belief that Sinn Féin leaders were active and recruiting new members – that the strength of the 'hatred party' may have been underestimated.[63]

The bulk of Irish opinion was concerned that these 'crazy and criminal' characters would jeopardise the political victory of Home Rule, with or without the exclusion of Ulster, which Redmond believed to be, and asserted, was dependent on Irish loyalty to the Imperial effort. A failure of Home Rule because of some form of 'disloyalty' would have had serious consequences. On the one hand it would lead to the political ruin of Redmond, whose entire personal political career depended on its full implementation. It also would have also meant ruin for his party – and perhaps even more symbolically potent, it would have meant the failure of Parnell's dream. The fear of radical nationalism was based not only on personal political concerns, but also on a sense that what the British authorities had given could always be rescinded. In light of these personal and political benefit and goals, and a real concern about the future of the Home Rule question, Redmond made his famous speech on 20 September 1914 at Woodenbridge, Co. Wexford, pledging the Irish Volunteers for the defence of Ireland, and made personal efforts on the part of the British recruiting drive after the outbreak of war.[64] This support for the war gave Sinn Féin an opportunity to attack and meaningfully distinguish itself from the Irish Party, and especially the political ambitions of Redmond. It would also make them a more attractive choice when fears of conscription and dissatisfaction over the war began to creep into Irish politics.[65] Participation, perhaps even sacrifice, it was hoped, would earn Ireland Home Rule. Redmond couched this new challenge as a 'test of men's souls' – as a war for the defence of the 'sacred rights and liberty of small nations' – and as a war that would bring about the union of Irishmen of different backgrounds on the battlefield and that would 'lead to a Union in their home so that their blood' may bring all Ireland together in one nation'.[66]

Despite the anxiety of moderate nationalists over the potential jeopardy to Home Rule, radical nationalists agitated against the Home Rule Bill, because of the proposed exclusion of Ulster. As the war progressed, Sinn Féin became more visible, both through its anti-recruiting efforts, and more broadly in terms of its ultimate political representation in the spectrum of nationalist politics in Ireland. As part of its political opposition, this anti-recruiting campaign was phrased in such a manner as to discuss where 'Ireland's quarrel' really lay – with Germany or with Britain. In this way, Sinn Féin, as Irish nationalists, had only one duty 'to strive for Ireland's interest, irrespective of the interests of England or Germany or any other foreign country.[67] The Irish Volunteers represented the only cohesive group remaining after both the Ulster and National Volunteers were decimated by recruiting. On important issues of the day, such as the potential extension of the Derby Act to implement conscription in Ireland, Sinn Féin regularly claimed that their agitation prevented its extension. Diaries at the time make light of this stating:

Of course the Sinn Féiners say they frightened Redmond into

opposing the application of the Derby act to Ireland. This section of our unhappy Island are praying for Germany to lick England; at the same time they hold that if Ireland is lost England smashes up automatically, and they therefore count on England hanging onto this isle and fighting for it like grim death ... one of the S.F.'s told me the other night that it would be a great thing for Ireland if the Germans had this country. There would be more work, more industry, and more prosperity ... we are a lazy bragging mean-spirited lot when it comes to doing anything real for our country.[68]

This statement demonstrates that Sinn Féin's claims were not broadly recognised as reflecting reality, and the way in which Sinn Féin and radical nationalists were not equated with 'doing anything real for our country'. Sinn Féin was not a viable political alternative to the Irish Party, nor could it break the hold of the Unionists and British government over politics in Ireland. Sinn Féin's message, aims and objectives were unpalatable and unpopular during the initial rush of imperial enthusiasm that accompanied the onset of war, but this fringe began to look not quite as unappealing, or even quite so radical, by the late winter/early spring of 1915/1916. Its political opportunism and pursuit of a radical 'Irish Ireland' form of nationalism began to look more palatable and appropriate when the alternatives became less attractive. Once an initial rush of enthusiasm for 'John Bull' and the British war effort had worn off, especially after high taxation, commercial restrictions, recruitment and the looming threat of conscription, the mainstream political outlook of the Irish nation became more sympathetic to the general direction of the radical fringe. Radical nationalists portrayed this as the Irish nation continuing to bear the imperial yoke for not much benefit – Home Rule with the exclusion of Ulster and a clear imperial sectarian bias that showed no real possibility for abatement. Within Irish nationalism as a whole, there emerged a binary opposition over these issues, ultimately meaning that there could only be one political victor – although which party and strand of nationalism would be victorious would not become apparent until well after the Rising, during the by-elections of 1917–18 and Sinn Féin's electoral victory in the general election of 1918.

Ultimately attitudes towards Sinn Féin were typified by a lack of popularity evident in the absence of explicit references in the contemporary sources to the radical nationalist movement. Sinn Féin as a party was not taken seriously, especially after its defeat in the 1908 elections. Redmond's success in the reintroduction of the Home Rule Bill, as well as in securing its passage on the eve of the war, helped to marginalise radical nationalists despite its delivery being marred by exclusion. The outbreak of the war 'distracted' attention away from radical nationalist politics and more generally the Sinn Féin agenda. Given then, all of the rising social pressures which typified the build up to the Rising, the looming threat of conscription, telegraphs informing families of the death of their sons, brothers and fathers, the passage but non-enactment of Home Rule, and the potential exclusion of Ulster and/or a return to an unappealing pre-war status quo, two key aspects of Sinn Féin and radical nationalism seem to stand out. First in terms of an official political capacity, the impact of this radical fringe was minimal, its organisation more ineffectual than efficient. There is a clear danger of retrospectively assigning more causal power to pre-Rising radical politics in Ireland, in the guise of Sinn Féin, than this movement and the party actually possessed. Second, it was these same mounting social, economic and political traumas that engendered a shift towards radicalism in the Irish nation as a whole. The initial inertia that prevented a political shift towards radicalism had already been momentarily surmounted during the Home Rule crisis when it appeared as though civil war in Ireland was about to break out. While this momentum had dissipated with the outbreak of war ensuring that mainstream Irish nationalism was firmly anchored to a moderate position, these boundaries had already almost been crossed.

The Irish National Volunteers and the Landing of Guns at Howth

In November 1913, the Irish National Volunteers were formed in Dublin at the behest of Eoin MacNeill. Their purpose was ostensibly to support Home Rule in the face of the armed opposition of the Ulster Volunteers. Between the threat of partition and fears over the Curragh Mutiny, the ranks of the Irish Volunteers had swelled to an excess of 150,000 by June 1914.[69] Through late 1913, Pearse had been calling for the arming of nationalists, stating that 'an Orangemen with a rifle is a much less ridiculous figure than a nationalist without a rifle' and that 'a citizen without arms is like a priest without religion'.[70] The manifesto of the Irish Volunteers called for their formation because 'the menace of armed violence [is] the determining factor in the future relations between this country and Great Britain'.[71] The ultimate goal of the Irish Volunteers was to 'secure and maintain the rights and liberties common to all the people of Ireland'.[72] The Irish Republican Brotherhood (IRB) was heavily involved in the initial formation of the Irish Volunteers, not just among the rank and file of the Irish Volunteers, but especially in terms of its leadership. The infiltration into the Irish Volunteers of radical nationalists, individuals who supported the physical force tradition of Irish nationalism, made it difficult for Redmond and the Irish Party to lend support to the Irish Volunteers from their inception. This was especially the case because Redmond's forerunners in constitutional nationalism had been so vehemently opposed to the use of violence to gain Home Rule, let alone other nationalist objectives such as land reform. The presence of this radical element was observed by intelligence gatherers in Ireland from the outset, with the realisation that:

> From the inception of the movement at the meeting in the Rotunda, the Volunteer Organisation was under the control of a self-elected Provisional Committee, the members of which, with few exceptions, belonged to leagues and Associations of an Anti-British character. The majority of the members of the Provisional Committee were hostile to the Irish Parliamentary Party, and lest their influence in the country might be detrimental to national interests, Mr. John Redmond, MP, in June 1914, addressed a letter to the Public Press, demanding a reconstitution of the Committee on representative lines ... [73]

There is clearly some sort of relationship between the Ulster and Irish Volunteer movements but the extent to which the formation of the one caused the formation of the other is debatable. The sectarian climate of the time served to heighten pre-existing tensions. MacNeill, often credited with coming up with the idea of the Irish Volunteers, did not see their formation as related to the Ulster Volunteers. MacNeill was viewed as someone who, though a committed radical nationalist 'deplored the foolish speeches of hot headed extremists' and as a result was not viewed as a firebrand in terms of the encouragement of others to rebel.[74] MacNeill's vision was one in which the Irish National Volunteers would come together with the Ulster Volunteers and the Irish Citizens' Army to form one unified Irish force, after the enactment of a Home Rule settlement.[75] Yet the sense on the ground was that it was being armed and trained to fight Ulster.[76] It is reported in 1914 that 'the feeling against Home Rule, and the determination to resist it were increasing [amongst Unionists] while on the other hand the Irish National Volunteers ... were alarmed at the attitude of the Unionists and were pushing on their movement so as to be able to resist any aggression'.[77] In this way the Irish National Volunteers, like Irish nationalism as a whole, were subject to multiple pulls and pressures. On the one hand they had to counter the perceived threat of the Ulster Volunteers, on the other there was pressure to be seen as an aggressive organisation prepared to strike a counter-blow Unionism in order to gain Home Rule. As opposed to the clear role of the Ulster Volunteers, the confused emergence of the Irish Volunteers and their muddled purpose made them appear as an also-ran organisation to politicians at Westminster, and they were not structurally an equal counterbalance to the Unionist threat.

Other examples of this perceived relationship between the organisations is evident in the constant descriptions of the Irish National Volunteers as following the example of the Ulster Volunteers in arming and drilling. Initial reactions, for example, on the part of the Archbishop of Dublin were not particularly supportive of the formation of the Irish National Volunteers. However, according to his personal secretary, the Archbishop recognised that there was substantial justification for the formation of the Irish National Volunteers since the arming of the Ulster Volunteers had 'frightened and coerced' the 'weak' English government.[78] His opinion of the Irish National Volunteers therefore fluctuated, but he never believed that the movement would amount to much or succeed in its objectives.[79] Both organisations were fundamentally opposed in their ambitions and actions and ultimately reactionary, mirrors of each other in their fears and concerns about the Home Rule question. Regardless of each organisation's tactical or propagandistic abilities, it is evident that the existence of these armed paramilitary organisations had considerably heightened tensions in Ireland at this time, permanently and fundamentally changing the Home Rule crisis.

The inclusion of members of the Irish Republican Brotherhood in the Irish National Volunteers, whom Redmond considered to be dangerous Feinians, some of whom had supported or participated in violent uprisings in the past, made it difficult for him to give his political blessing to this body, and therefore their popular appeal was initially checked by the Irish Party machine, despite simultaneously heightened sectarian fears on the part of the Ulster Volunteers. British intelligence reports make it quite clear that they perceived this radical nationalist element to be represented from the inception of the Irish National Volunteers, not only by members of anti-British associations such as the IRB, but also by the GAA, the Gaelic League and the Irish Transport and General Workers Union. In contrast, the intelligence reports note the absence of official representatives of moderate or constitutional nationalists, in the guise of representatives of the Irish Party, the United Irish League or the Ancient Order of Hibernians.[80] There was, in general, a concern about the direction and leadership of the organisation, with the realisation that without moderation 'the movement may lead to great trouble in the future'.[81] In fact, it was then the main concern that 'country people' were being encouraged to think that they were being armed and trained to fight Ulster.[82]

In the pages of the *Irish Catholic* in June of 1914 there were expressions of support from eminent members of the Catholic Church, such as the Archbishop of Tuam.[83] Such support, however, was tempered with expressions of concern, that while it was an organisation of 'great benefit to the National Movement' it should be organised 'under leaders whom the Irish people can follow'.[84] Leaders whom the Volunteers should follow meant Redmond and the Irish Party, rather than radical nationalists, such as MacNeill or members of the IRB, under whose leadership the Volunteers ran the risk of becoming 'an instrument of destruction of our national hopes'.[85]

Redmond, concerned about the intentions of the Irish National Volunteers, and caught by surprise at their rise, threatened to dismember the Irish National Volunteers unless he could appoint 25 members to its Provisional Committee – as many as were already sitting on the Committee. By late May and early June 1914, the absence of moderate nationalists had been addressed: after threatening to set up a rival volunteer organisation, Redmond had negotiated with the Volunteers to allow him to appoint these 25 additional members of his choosing to the Irish National Volunteers' Provisional Committee. This would now establish the Committee in such a way that it was considered, at least by Redmond and the Irish Party, to be along 'representative lines'. He believed that this would ensure his ability to monitor and moderate the activities of the Irish National Volunteers. In fact, this was a tried and tested tactic for the Irish Party – infiltrate and moderate – and they had tried to do the same with the United Irish League, the Land League and various other movements between the 1880s and 1916.[86] With this deal, Redmond threw the full weight of his personal support, as well as the political machine of the Irish Party and the Ancient Order of the Hibernians, behind the Irish National Volunteers, and their membership rose to a number in excess of 150,000. Archbishop Walsh, amongst others, viewed Redmond's manoeuvre to secure control of the Volunteers as 'dishonest and typical of the [Irish] Party's unconstitutional and underhand practices'.[87] Some observers thought there were other reasons behind the political manoeuvrings on the part of Redmond, believing that his involvement was based on a fear that 'they dare not remain aloof any longer, and that they were obliged to turn the movement to their own ends'.[88] Such concerns must have been double – to combat the growing political might of armed Unionists and to reign in radical nationalists – as both groups were a real danger to Redmond politically, and to Home Rule.

Just as the Irish Parliamentary Party and Sinn Féin had, each in their own way, struggled to create an umbrella under which to amalgamate disparate and distinct nationalist political tendencies, the Irish Volunteers encompassed different strands of nationalism and differing levels of military ability. There was some consternation in the press that Redmond and the Irish Party's support for the Volunteers came late in the day – with references to their (re)formation and Party backing for the Volunteers being in the nick of time, etc.[89] Such sentiments were an explicit expression of the fear that civil war could break out over the issues of the Home Rule crisis. Despite Redmond's efforts to infiltrate and control the leadership of the Volunteers, the organisation remained tinged with radicalism and became increasingly factional and divided. The intelligence reports refer to the fact that even after the appointment of Redmond's men to the Provisional Committee, the Irish Volunteers retained a 'character detrimental to nationalist interests'.[90]

The Bachelor's Walk Incident

In order to arm themselves, the Irish National Volunteers sent representatives to Germany to purchase 1,500 rifles and ammunition. These weapons were landed in two batches, the first in early August on the Wicklow coastline without incident, the second at Howth, in

North Dublin, on 26 August 1914. The timing of these landings is significant, as war had just broken out on the Continent, and tensions were running high, not only over the Home Rule crisis, but also over these events on the Continent. While the Unionist landing of arms was subject to little interference, the events at Howth would leave several dead and many wounded at the hands of the RIC and British army. For those organising these landings the arming of the Irish National Volunteers was not only a practical necessity, but was also needed to counter the success of the Unionists at Larne. The landing of arms at Howth was carried out with public knowledge of the landing beforehand, and was accompanied by popular expressions of support. It was planned in part as a propagandistic counter-strike to the Ulster Volunteers' triumphal achievements.

Unlike the Unionists at Larne, the police and army were dispatched to disarm the Volunteers. The weapons were landed and subsequently dispersed amongst groups of Volunteers. The initial actions of the Dublin Metropolitan Police and King's Own Scottish Borderers were initially ineffective and perceived as being heavy-handed, leading to tension and aggravation on the part of the Borderers and the crowds. The King's Own Scottish Borderers dispatched to disarm the Volunteers failed to do so, and as the regiment made their way back to the barracks after failing to disarm the Volunteers, they were subjected to 'aggravation' and taunts by the crowd. In response, the Borderers opened fire on the unarmed crowds at Batchelor's Walk, killing three and wounding thirty-eight. The intelligence reports do not describe the effects of this event on the population in detail; however, the events were deemed significant enough to necessitate an investigation by a Royal Commission.[91] Events at Howth, and the subsequent incident at Bachelor's Walk, are important in light of the sectarian competition between the Ulster Volunteers and the Irish National Volunteers, and evocative of the fears of Irish nationalists and the Irish Volunteers about the intentions of the British authorities.

The incident at Batchelor's Walk was perceived as demonstrating the heavy-handedness of the army, and the difference between the treatment of Unionists and Nationalists. One diary states that these events and the general treatment of the Irish National Volunteers, as opposed to the Ulster Volunteers, were indicative of the way that 'to trap a nationalist meant promotion; to trap a unionist meant perdition ... it accounts for a good deal of the irritation and the resentment against the existing system of administration and ...

England'.[92] The *Irish Catholic* reported the events in a matter-of-fact tone, blaming the crowd's incitement on 'rumours which had been circulating on [the King's Own Scottish Borderer's] conduct'.[93] Such rumours were possible in the context of the understanding of the 'usual' or expected conduct and policies of the army. The *Irish Catholic's* reporting of the events at Batchelor's Walk culminated with the announcement that all the bodies of the victims would be sent to the pro-cathedral for their funerals.[94]

The official government report into the events describes the behaviour of the crowd as being of 'insulting demeanour, language and behaviour', with 'some throwing of stones and other missiles'.[95] The report blames rumours 'accompanied by falsehood and exaggeration' of military intervention as the impetus to the gathering of the crowd, and the cat-and-mouse tactics of protestors and army as heightening the tensions between the two.[96] The Royal Commission reported that the soldiers involved were without 'great provocation', but, even so, they got 'out of temper and partly out of hand' going so far as to chase people into shops and 'in one case a soldier drove a bayonet through a shop door'.[97] The report found that the crowd itself was not excessively violent, but the commissioners did not believe that an occasion had arisen for using loaded firearms. The report found no fault with the officers or their men, believing the officers never to have issued an order to fire, and that their men, having been subjected to the provocation of the crowds, 'may have been productive in their minds of the misapprehension as to an order [to fire] having been given'.[98] The result was some degree of unpopularity, especially of the Borderers in Dublin. One diary entry, dated a few days after the shootings, mentions that soldiers on trams were greeted with 'boos and groans – an after effect of the shooting by the Scottish Borderers at Bachelor's Walk on the previous Sunday week'.[99] Boos and groans, though significant demonstrations of a Nationalist antipathy for the British army at this moment, do not constitute evidence of support for radical nationalism in Ireland.

Despite the attempts of Westminster to cool the situation, the Bachelor's Walk incident generated a great deal of tension between the residents of Dublin and the army. It was an issue that would later have effects on recruiting attempts.[100] It was also an event that retrospectively seems as though it could have potentially unleashed a great deal of popular nationalist unrest. Despite the high levels of concern about the incident, this unrest failed to materialise – meaning that while the event continued to ratchet up the pre-existing tensions between Nationalists and Unionists or the British government, it did not constitute an event that triggered a mass radical or violent nationalist movement.

The Split of the Irish National Volunteers

On the outbreak of the war, Redmond 'declared it to be the duty of the Irish Volunteers to take foreign service under a Government which is not Irish'.[101] This pledge did not sit well with the original and more radical members of the Provisional Committee, and it precipitated the split of the Irish Volunteers. British intelligence reports identify five different categories of Volunteers after their split into a radical Irish Volunteer section from the more popular and moderate Redmondite section. They are listed here in order of their size: 1) supporters of Redmond; 2) supporters of MacNeill – a group of radicals who would go on to form the Irish Volunteers and a category which was itself split in two, between those 3) in Dublin and those 4) outside Dublin, as well as the supporters of Connolly in the 5) Irish Citizens' Army. The analysis of the Archbishop of Dublin and his personal secretary, Monsignor Curran, was similar. They thought that the 'vast rank and file abstained from the dissensions, neither completely understanding these splits nor wanting to aggravate them further'.[102] The intelligence reports describe the way that there was no 'outward exhibition of disunion' on the Provisional Committee, that the original members were members of anti-British organisations, and that the split between Redmond's constitutional nationalists and these radicals had always been festering under the surface.[103] The damning verdict on the Irish Volunteers was that they were 'disloyal, seditious and revolutionary if the means and opportunity were at hand'.[104]

By mid-September 1914 the Home Rule Bill had been passed, placed on the statute book, and immediately suspended. The suspension of the Bill removed the prospect of an enactment of the controversial item of legislation, and therefore decreasing the prospects of alienating potential Unionist recruits into the army and Unionist support for the war and potential civil war, while the passage of the Bill was simultaneously believed to be a placating gesture to Nationalists, encouraging their participation in and support for the war effort. Redmond's support of the war may have been part of a strategy to ensure the enactment of Home Rule after the conclusion of the war. His pledge of the Volunteers and support of recruiting was intended, at least in part, to reassure the British army and government that the Irish nation was trustworthy and loyal.[105] It is into this overall context that the split of the Volunteers must be placed.

This split in the Irish Volunteers came to a head with Redmond's pledge of the Irish National Volunteers to the British war effort. Redmond had envisioned the role of the Volunteers to be one of home defence of Ireland, and he lobbied for the Volunteers to be taken as a whole division into Kitchener's new army, such as the Ulster Volunteers had been. Although Redmond pledged the Irish Volunteers to the war effort, and personally promoted army recruitment, his main aim was to ensure that 'the coast of Ireland will be defended from foreign invasion by her armed sons ... Is it too much to hope that out of this situation there will spring a result which will be good for, not merely the Empire, but for ... the Irish nation?'[106] Those who remained loyal to Redmond, the National Volunteers, were the vast majority of the original group, and many of those in the National Volunteers subsequently enlisted in the British army, though not in an Irish division as had been envisioned by Redmond. For Redmond's supporters, the split came as something of a 'relief' – the radical elements, being described as unreasonable, bitter and narrow minded, constituting a 'danger to the youth of Ireland'.[107] This role of home defence would prove that the Irish were capable of taking care of themselves within the confines of the imperial setting. The Ulster Volunteers had been accepted more or less *en masse* into the British army as the 36th (Ulster) Division, and would go on to fight in the trenches in Belgium and France – suffering particularly heavy losses at the Somme.[108]

Diaries of the time express a great deal of doubt about Redmond's plan for the entry of the Irish Volunteers into the British army, especially if such entry meant serving outside of Ireland.[109] This was not only because it was not popular amongst the Volunteers themselves, who were not keen on the possibility of service outside of Ireland, but also because Kitchener himself did not 'seem to be much enamoured with the volunteers; his requirements being soldiers ready for service anywhere, i.e. not just in Ireland.[110] This attitude is indicative of the high degree of distrust on the part of the British establishment against Irish nationalists – especially amongst the army's elite.[111]

With Redmond's pledging of the Irish National Volunteers to the British war effort, the organisation split into two. The split ultimately occurred over concerns about the diminution of Home Rule, the exclusion of Ulster, and the unwillingness to participate in 'foreign quarrels' and over antipathy towards Dublin Castle rule, especially in light of the events of Bachelor's Walk, with the radical Irish Volunteers calling for Castle rule to 'be abolished without delay and that a National Government be established forthwith in its place'.[112]

The heeding of Redmond's call to enlist accounts for the gradual fall in the numbers of moderate nationalist and Redmond-supporting National Volunteers, apparent in Figure 3. The radical nationalist Irish Volunteers, comprising followers of MacNeill, though also inclusive of some members of the IRB and the members of Connolly's Irish Citizen Army, would be the group that would go on to carry out the Easter Rising of 1916. In the second graph (Figure 4), we can see that while there is a gradual drop in membership of the National Volunteers, there is a gradual increase of membership in the Irish Volunteers. The drop in the numbers of the National Volunteers is due

Figure 3: Redmond vs. Radical Sections of the Irish Volunteers

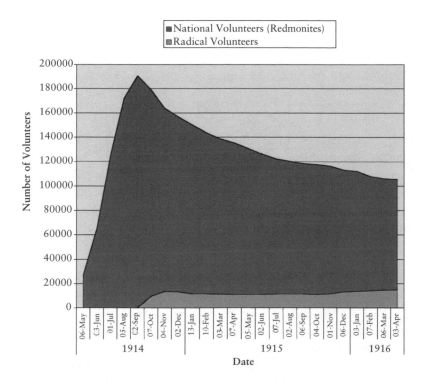

Source: Intelligence Reports, 1914-1916 CO 903/19 PRO Kew

Figure 4: National Volunteers vs. Irish Volunteers and ICA, May 1914–April 1916

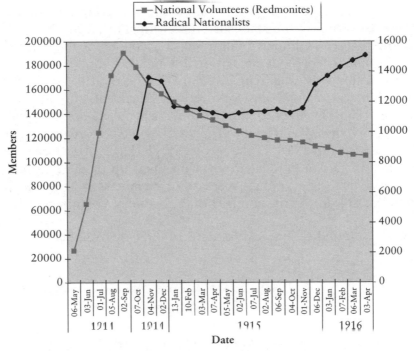

Source: Intelligence Reports, 1914-1916 CO 903/19 PRO Kew

to the enlistment of individual members into the British army dissipating the number of National Volunteers. The simultaneous increase in the membership of the Irish Volunteers may reflect a dissatisfaction with Redmond's support of the war and with the resolution of the Home Rule question with exclusion, a general sense of concern and anxiety about the progress of the war, and a concern that conscription would be introduced in Ireland.[113]

In terms of the indicative elements of the split in the Volunteer movement, Figure 6 helps to demonstrate the extent to which radical elements of the Volunteers were in the minority. Although they were clearly in the minority, they were a slowly growing group representative of nationalist concerns festering beneath the façade of the Irish National Volunteers and the nationalist movement in Ireland as a whole. In October 1914, shortly after the outbreak of the war, the split of the Volunteers, and Redmond's committing the organisation to the British war effort, the radical element of the Volunteers represented just over 5 per cent of the movement, according to contemporary British intelligence reports. This element grew steadily over the course of 1915, both in terms of an increase in its overall numbers (Figure 5) and as a percentage of the overall nationalist movement with members of the National Volunteers enlisting in the British army. The extent to which we can assign this growth to dissatisfaction with British rule, opposition to Redmond's leadership, an attraction to radical nationalism, and so on, is unknown. The ultimate consequence was that the more radical elements of the Volunteers not only became stronger numerically, but they also became a more visible and stronger element of Irish nationalism as a whole.

Figure 5: Percentage of Radicals as Segment of Irish Volunteer Movement, October 1914–April 1916

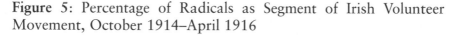

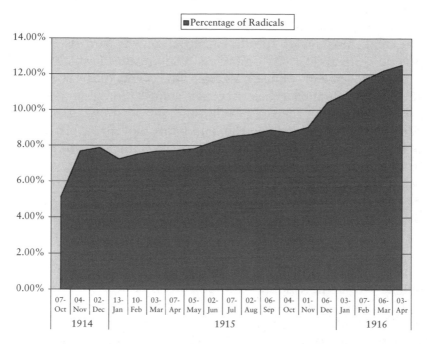

Source: Intelligence Reports, 1914-1916 CO 903/19 PRO Kew.

In retrospect Redmond's vision for the Volunteers suffered from two miscalculations. The first was the belief that the British imperial, especially military, establishment, would trust an Irish, Catholic and nationalist force to 'protect' Ireland, when it was representatives of this same establishment that had helped to support, organise, arm and drill the Ulster Volunteers. As the differences between the events at Larne and Howth illustrated, there was a clear institutional sectarianism in dealing with both communities. It would have seemed like leaving the children home alone with an open cookie jar. The second major fault was the assumption that nationalists would immediately and permanently support the British war effort. One diary suggests that Redmond's overestimation of support led him to be blind to the initial formation and purpose of the Volunteer movement. It suggests that had Redmond known of the ulterior reasons behind the formation of the Volunteers, he would not have felt compelled, or believed it politically expedient, to have made the concession of the exclusion of Ulster from Home Rule in March of that year.[114]

Diary entries describe the way in which the split dominated thoughts on events at the time – 'the one party submitting to Redmond, the other submitting to no control from him ...'[115] Diaries at the time also make specific mention of the surprise felt at Redmond's invitation to Unionists to join the Irish National Volunteer movement – shock because of the events of the formation of the Ulster Volunteers, their sectarian connotations, the events of Larne, Howth and Bachelor's Walk, and shock knowing that this would exacerbate the splits in the nationalist movement. There was also hostility to Redmond's support of recruiting efforts on the grounds that it was not a demonstration of an organic or grassroots movement, or of a personal moral stance, but rather that 'the Irish Party's recruiting campaign ... [was] an inevitable result of their parliamentary subservience to the Liberals'.[116] It demonstrated the weakness of Irish nationalism in Westminster, and the inability of the Irish Party to think beyond immediate political gains.

Various official British documents would later (after the Rising) detail the split in the Volunteer movement, not least the report of the Royal Commission on the Rebellion in Ireland. In these retrospective reports, as with the contemporary accounts, it was Redmond's attitude towards recruiting and the British army that was perceived as bringing about the public split between the Irish and National Volunteers. The Royal Commission later felt that the split ultimately led to a force of Irish Volunteers comprising an estimated 13,000 members, 2,000 of whom were in Dublin.[117] The Royal Commission's concerns over the ramifications of this split are evident in the reports presented by the Inspector-General of the RIC, from 15 June 1914, as quoted in their report. There was a recognition that the paramilitary phenomenon, constitutional and radical, Unionist and Nationalist, had altered 'the existing conditions of life' in Ireland.[118] This alteration was particularly problematic, as the Inspector-General had reported that:

> Obedience to the law has never been a prominent characteristic of the people. In times of passion or excitement the law has only been maintained by force, and this has been rendered practicable owing to the want of cohesion among the crowds hostile to the police. If the people become armed and drilled effective police control will vanish. Events are moving. Each county will soon have a trained army far outnumbering the police, and those who control the Volunteers will be in a position to dictate to what extent the law of the land may be carried into effect.[119]

So there was an explicit and conscious recognition that the Irish Volunteer movement was one that had the potential to force political issues and the Home Rule question to their ultimate end, and that the split in the leadership of this body, while not necessarily representative of the percentage of opinion of the members of the time, had the potential of forcing and implementing a radical nationalist agenda in Ireland. A Dublin Metropolitan Police Report, just after the outbreak of the war in early September 1914, expressing concern that radical elements of the Irish Volunteers in Dublin believed that they could 'establish control of the Government of Ireland before the present difficulties are over, and that they may attempt such an escapade before long'.[120] An Irish Volunteer handbill from July 1915 makes the urgency as suggested by the DMP report even more palpable, in so far as:

> Now, more than 1913, it is manifest that Ireland requires self-protection against 'the menace of armed force' from whatsoever quarter. The future prosperity, perhaps the very existence of the Irish nation, may depend on the country being in a position to offer effective resistance to the imposition of a ruinous burden of taxation for Imperial purposes.[121]

This handbill goes on to describe, in detail, the nationalist project to

attain a 'National Government 'free from external political interference' as well as 'resistance to any partition or dismemberment of
Ireland which would exclude a part of the people ... from the
benefits of national autonomy'.[122] The handbill ends by making the
point that the only rightful participation in the war is one made not
under duress, and that therefore the Irish Volunteers would struggle
in every capacity to ensure that conscription would not be brought
to Ireland. Of course all of these potentialities, the real and
exaggerated fears of radicals in Ireland on the part of Unionists,
Nationalists and the British government must be tempered by
attitudes such as that of Edward Grey on the outbreak of the war.
He claimed then that 'the one bright spot in the whole of this terrible
situation is that ... the Irish question [not being] now a consideration
which we feel we now have to take into account'.[123]

* * *

It is tempting to view the birth of Sinn Féin, and the formation and
eventual split in the Irish Volunteers as predictive of an emerging
popular radical nationalist movement but such an assessment would
not be entirely correct. The split is more indicative of a long-standing
antagonism in Irish nationalism – between the traditions of Grattan,
O'Connell and Parnell and constitutional and peaceful nationalism,
whereby change would be effected from within, and the radical
physical force traditions of Young Ireland and the Feinians. It
furthermore represented the failed outcome of an Irish Party strategy
to infiltrate and co-opt a potentially radicalising and/or threatening
nationalist institution. In the moderate/constitutional tradition, the
only ways which Ireland could make peace with its relationship with
England, and benefit from its role in the United Kingdom was
through a constitutionally managed political and economic relationship. The radical tradition saw the relationship between Britain and
Ireland as fundamentally flawed under any institutional
arrangement and therefore rejected it, whatever the proposals for
economic or political management. All the ills of Ireland – symbolic,
cultural and tangible, in terms of depravity, language and the Famine
– were blamed on the Union.

Radical Nationalists of this period felt as though they were the
true disciples of the Feinians, and that organisations such as the IRB
would get the Irish National Volunteers off the ground. Rather than
be indicative of an Irish predilection for radical nationalism, this
simply showed that 1) radicalism had some resonant and popularly
known antecedents, and 2) that although fewer than one in ten

supported radical nationalism, it had political and cultural potency beyond its direct adherents. This provides a context through which the Rising may later be understood. This weight of purpose, if not numbers, would have serious consequences when, in the power vacuum after the Rising, individuals in the Irish nation sought new ways to interpret these phenomena, and new institutions by which to express their political ideas and ambitions.

It was in the context of this long-standing split that Sinn Féin opportunistically sniped at the Irish Party and Redmond on a variety of political issues. Initially, Redmond's successful efforts to re-introduce, and the eventual passage of, Home Rule seemed to reduce the limited political appeal of Sinn Féin. This was the case even despite the unpopularity its of exclusion. Sinn Féin, however, had never been popular – its existence was marked by its inability to unite or be electorally effective, but this was balanced by its ability to offer a critique from afar. When Redmond's policies were ultimately viewed as ineffective or inappropriate, on Home Rule and the war, Sinn Féin, by its mere existence – and in the wake of the executions of the Rising's leaders – would provide a meaningful narrative and cohesive prism by which to interpret these events and organise effectively.

Overall, radicalism in Ireland can be said to be present before the Rising – evident to all if not popular. The Irish Volunteers and Sinn Féin would provide institutions and mechanisms in the aftermath of the Rising that would allow for the interpretation and organisation of radical violent nationalism. However, without the cultural trigger point of the Rising, and in light of the evidence provided herein, it is impossible to talk of the inevitability of the emergence of radical nationalism, and a pre-determination of popular support for the Irish War of Independence. The various pieces may have been in place – but a popular response had yet to be triggered.

NOTES

1   August 1915 in O'Clery, C., *Phrases Make History Here: A Century of Irish Political Quotations 1886–1986* (Dublin: O'Brien Press, 1986), p. 48.

2   As stated in the introduction there naturally follows from the discussion of Irish nationalist cultural trigger points, an analysis and discussion of Unionist ones – such that their opposition to Home Rule is 'rational and reasonable' to the same extent as the Nationalists' demand for it. This was especially the case as the Unionist community felt, and would come to feel even more strongly (after the Somme), that the contribution of their sons to the war effort merited a high degree of respect and deference from the British army and authorities.

3   County Inspector's Intelligence Reports, 1914, CO 903/17 PRO Kew.
4   Hepburn, A. C., *The Conflict of Nationality in Modern Ireland* (London: Edward Arnold, 1980), p. 75.
5   From Smith, Conservative MP, speaking in Liverpool, O'Clery, 1980, p. 37.
6   Bonar Law, quoted in Hepburn, 1980, p. 75
7   Connolly, S. J. (ed.), *The Oxford Companion to Irish History* (Oxford: Oxford University Press, 1998), p. 519.
8   Lee, J. *The Modernisation of Irish Society, 1848–1918* (Dublin: Gill and MacMillan, 1989), p. 6.
9   From the Ulster Solemn League and Covenant, in Mitchell and Ó Snodaigh, 1989, p. 136.
10 County Inspector's Reports, 1913, CO 903/8 PRO Kew.
11 Ibid.
12 *An Gaedal*, April 1914, No. 42.
13 *Dublin Evening Herald*, 18 April 1914.
14 See postcards of landing of weapons at Larne and other locations, in Rees, 1998 and at http://www.lol.1960.50megs.com/photo.html.
15 CSB Files, 3/716/24 NAI.
16 County Inspector's Intelligence Reports 1914, CO 903/17 PRO Kew
17 Statement of Monsignor Michael J. Curran to Bureau of Military History, MS 27728, NLI.
18 Bowman, T., 'The Ulster Volunteer Force and the Formation of the 36th Ulster Division', *Irish Historical Studies* Vol. XXXII, No. 128, November 2001, pp. 82–103; Bowman, T., 'Composing Divisions: The Recruitment of Ulster and National Volunteers into the British army in 1914', *Causeway Cultural Traditions Journal* Spring, 1995.
19 County Inspector's Reports, CO 903/19 PRO Kew.
20 *Daily Freeman's Journal*, 12 March 1914.
21 *Evening Herald*, 6 March 1914.
22 *Daily Freeman* and *Evening Herald*, March 1914.
23 See *An Gaedal*, March 1914, No. 41 as well as Redmond's speech, 15 September 1914, on the passage of the Home Rule act, comparing the way that Botha and Smuts were transformed from 'bitter enemies' into 'loyal comrades and fellow citizens ...' from Redmond's speech to Commons, in O'Clery, 1986, p. 48.
24 See *Evening Herald*, 21 March 1914.
25 Ibid.
26 Bonar Law as quoted in Mitchell and Ó Snodaigh, 1989, p. 156.
27 Paget, 14 March 1914, in O'Clery 1986, pp. 44–5.
28 Connolly, 1998, p. 130.
29 See *Evening Herald* 25 March, 1914.
30 County Inspector's Reports 1914, CO 903/8, PRO Kew.
31 *Irish Catholic*, 2 May 1914.
32 See *Irish Catholic, Evening Herald, Freeman's Journal*, etc., from March 1914.
33 County Inspector's Reports CO 903/8 PRO Kew.
34 Carson, February 1914 in Hepburn, 1980, p. 82.
35 'Invitation to join Sinn Féin', in O'Day, A. and Stevenson, J. (eds), *Irish Historical Documents Since 1800* (Dublin: Gill and MacMillan, 1992), p. 143.
36 Connolly, 1998, p. 513.
37 Ibid., p. 165. Their name referred back to the 'Dungannon Conventions' a series of public gatherings in the late eighteenth century where 'Volunteers' from Ulster sought a series of reforms in to secure Catholic rights and the primacy of the Irish Parliament's legislative authority.
38 Campbell, 2005.
39 See Fitzpatrick,1998; Garvin, T., *Nationalist Revolutionaries in Ireland 1858–1928*

(Oxford: Clarendon Press, 1987); Kelly, M., 'Parnell's Old Brigade: The Redmondite–Feinian Nexus in the 1890's' *Irish Historical Studies*, Vol. XXXIII, No. 130, November, 2002, pp. 209–34.

40 In this way Sinn Féin, variously translated as 'Us/We Ourselves' had a double meaning – on the one hand denoting radical nationalist aspirations of a split with the United Kingdom, but also as a separate entity in the pursuit of nationalist politics in Ireland.

41 Kelly, 2002.

42 Dillon in O'Day, A., *Irish Home Rule: 1867–1921* (Manchester: University of Manchester Press, 1998), p. 211.

43 Campbell, 2005.

44 Ó'Duibhir, C., *Sinn Féin: the First Election, 1908* (Nure, Co. Leitrim: Drumlin Publications, 1993), p. 15.

45 Jackson, A., *Ireland: 1798–1998* (London: Blackwell, 1999), p. 185.

46 O'Day, 1998, p. 209.

47 Campbell, 2005.

48 O'Day, 1998, p. 207.

49 See O'Day, 1998, Chapters 2, 4 and 9 for a discussion of the political issues of this period.

50 Jackson, 1998, p. 188. For an elaboration on the rejection of the 'step-by-step' approach see Monney's speech in Lyons, 1985, p. 249.

51 De Markievicz in O'Clery, 1986, p. 35.

52 Norway, M. L. and Norway, A. H., *The Sinn Féin Rebellion As They Saw It [1916]* (Dublin: Irish Academic Press, 1999), p. 92.

53 Dolan's 1908 by-election address, from *Sinn Féin* 22 February, 1908 in Mitchell and Ó Snodiagh, 1989, p. 125. This kind of support for abstentionism becomes common currency after the rising, in particular during Sinn Féin's by-election victories in 1917.

54 McBride, 1991, p. 148.

55 Jackson, 1999, p. 186.

56 See various reports in newspapers such as *Daily Freeman, Irish Catholic, Irish Times*, 1912–16.

57 See Chapter 4 on pre-rising cultural and religious nationalism, as well as Hutchinson, 1987.

58 See County Inspector's Reports 1914, CO 903/8 and CO 903/17 PRO Kew.

59 For more on this see Fitzpatrick, 1998 and Garvin, 1987 amongst others, and for the interplay between cultural and political nationalism see especially Hutchinson, 1987.

60 Connolly, 1998, p. 253.

61 *Irish Catholic*, 5 October 1914.

62 Dillon as quoted in Hepburn, 1980, p. 89.

63 Nathan as quoted in Hepburn, 1980, p. 90.

64 See Chapter 2.

65 See Chapter 2 for a description and analysis of issues concerning recruiting and the conscription crisis in Ireland.

66 Redmond's Manifesto on the War, *Freeman's Journal*, 17 September 1914, in Mitchell and Ó Snodaigh, 1989, p. 171.

67 'Sinn Féin Opposes the War' in *Sinn Féin*, 8 August 1914, in Mitchell and Ó Snodaigh, 1989, p. 168.

68 'A Dubliner's Diary by Thomas King Moylan', 1 March 1916, MS. 9620 NLI.

69 Lee, 1989, p. 20.

70 Pearse, November and December 1913 in *Irish Freedom*, in O'Clery, 1986, pp. 42–3.

71 From Mitchell and Ó Snodaigh, 1989, p. 148.

72 Ibid., p. 149.

73 County Inspector's Reports1914, CO 903/17, PRO Kew.

74 Statement on Character of McNeill by Archbishop in Walsh Papers: Special

Papers/Political Papers.
75 Letter from Eoin Mac Neill to Mrs Augustine Henry, 29 November 1913, in MS. 7981 NLI.
76 Carson, February 1914, in Hepburn, 1980, p. 82.
77 County Inspector's Reports, 1914, CO 903/17, PRO Kew.
78 Statement of Monsignor Michael J. Curran to Bureau of Military History, MS 27728, NLI.
79 Ibid.
80 County Inspector's Reports, 1914, CO 903/17 PRO Kew. Neither of these organisations were considered to be particularly placid or peaceful to begin with, however they tended to be the sharp end of the moderate nationalist stick.
81 Hickman to Moore, in Hepburn, 1980, p. 86.
82 Ibid.
83 Irish Catholic, 20 June 1914.
84 Ibid.
85 Ibid.
86 Campbell, 2005.
87 Statement of Monsignor Michael J. Curran to Bureau of Military History, MS 27728, NLI.
88 Ibid.
89 See An Gaedal, Daily Freeman's Journal, and Evening Herald from 21 June to 17 July 1914 for evidence of this sentiment.
90 County Intelligence Reports, CO 903/17 PRO Kew.
91 See Report of the Royal Commission on the Landing of Arms at Howth on 26th July 1914 available in The Irish Uprising, 1914-1921: Papers from the British Parliamentary Archive, 2000.
92 'Experiences in Belfast by G. F. H. Berkeley', MS. 7880, NLI Dublin.
93 Irish Catholic, 1 August 1914.
94 Daily Freeman 4 August, 1911.
95 Report of the Royal Commission on the Landing of Arms at Howth, 26 July 1914 in The Irish Rising, 1914–1921, 2000, pp. 11–12.
96 Ibid., pp. 12–14.
97 Ibid.
98 Ibid.
99 'A Dubliner's Diary by Thomas King Moylan', August 1916, MS. 9620 NLI.
100 County Inspector's Reports, 903/17 PRO Kew.
101 Redmond in F. X Martin as quoted in Hepburn, 1980, p. 87.
102 County Inspector's Reports, 903/17 PRO Kew.
103 Ibid.
104 Ibid.
105 Redmond's War Manifesto, in Mitchell and Ó Snodaigh, 1989, p. 171.
106 Redmond, 3 August 1914, Statement to Commons in Mitchell and Ó Snodaigh, 1989, 47; see Chapter 2.
107 Irish Catholic, 3 October 1914.
108 These heavy losses would become an important component of the Unionist repertoire of myths, memories and symbols, and underpin their belief that Home Rule in Ireland would be a betrayal of their sacrifice for the United Kingdom.
109 'A Dubliner's Diary by Thomas King Moylan' MS. 9620 NLI; 'Experiences in Belfast by G. F. H. Berkeley', Ms. 7880, NLI Dublin.
110 'A Dubliner's Diary by Thomas King Moylan', 12 August 1914, MS. 9620 NLI.
111 Denman, 2000.
112 Manifesto of Volunteers, in Mitchell and Ó Snodaigh, 1989, p. 178.
113 See Chapter 2.

114   'A Dubliner's Diary by Thomas King Moylan', 5 July 1914, MS. 9620 NLI.
115   'A Dubliner's Diary by Thomas King Moylan', 8 October 1914, MS. 9620 NLI.
116   Statement of Monsignor Michael J. Curran to Bureau of Military History, MS 27728, NLI.
117   *The Royal Commission on the Rebellion in Ireland, 1916*, in *The Irish Uprising*, 2000, pp. 86–7.
118   Inspector-General of the RIC as quoted in *The Royal Commission on the Rebellion in Ireland, 1916* in *The Irish Uprising*, 2000, p. 92.
119   Ibid.
120   Inspector-General of the RIC as quoted in *The Royal Commission on the Rebellion in Ireland, 1916* in *The Irish Uprising*, 2000, p. 93.
121   Handbill in Walsh Papers: Special Papers/Political Papers.
122   Ibid.
123   Grey in Mitchell and Ó Snodaigh, 1989, p. 167.

4

Religion and Cultural Nationalism

In order to establish the role of cultural and religious nationalisms, this chapter will examine cultural and religious nationalisms prior to the Rising. Cultural nationalism, with its distinctive philosophical and institutional elements, is related to Irish religious nationalism, and the chapter will examine both nationalisms in action, before concluding with several examples where little or no distinction can be made between the actions and sometimes actors in the cultural and religious nationalist movements. Both of these movements were concerned with the regeneration and restoration of the Irish nation, and this theme of regeneration demonstrates a sense of 'organic cultural distinctiveness' in the Irish nation at the time. While this is evidence of a latent sectarian tension in Ireland, in so far as sectarianism was demonstrably present, it did not manifest itself in any mainstream or popular forms of nationalism or political behaviour prior to the events of the Rising. Rather, the presence of these latent themes comes to account for emergence of popular radical nationalism after the Easter Rising.

Religion and Cultural Themes

Cultural and religious nationalisms in Ireland are often distinguishable by institutions and elites, actors and actions, but often indistinguishable in terms of means, aims and end results. Irish cultural and religious nationalists used a repertoire of myths, memories and symbols to achieve what they saw as the essential moral regeneration and expressions of the Irish nation in the wake of the devastation of the Famine.[1] They also sought to fight changes in the Irish nation due to 'anglicisation' – literally a process of becoming, or being made 'English'. Although these nationalisms were distinct from their political counterpart, each contributed to the underlying political development of the nation, and therefore were part of the ultimate rationale of nationalism as a whole – that is, that there existed a religiously and/or culturally distinct Irish nation which deserved political recognition and a form of national self-determination. This line of argument had dogged understandings of the role of Ireland in the Union since its creation in 1801 – and it was dominated by questions over the extent to which Ireland was an equal or junior partner in British affairs.

The difference between those who supported a *Sinn Féin Amháin* (Ourselves Alone) cultural nationalist outlook and those who sought the regeneration of the Irish nation through the practice of Catholicism lies in a belief in the inherent importance of an Irish organic cultural identity and expression versus the practice of the 'true' religious doctrine as the cornerstone of the Irish nation. The Famine, which loomed large in both cultural and religious nationalisms, had a great unifying impact for their forms, yet for both of these varieties of nationalisms it had distinct and separate ramifications for their practices. While the long troubled history of the relationship between England and Ireland, Protestant and Catholic, in terms of the disestablishment of the Catholic Church and the Penal Era always loomed in the background, it was the Famine that made these myths, memories and symbols come alive in the latter half of the nineteenth and beginning of the twentieth centuries. For cultural nationalists, the Famine triggered concerns about the loss of Irish culture, which they believed lay at the heart of the nation itself. This fear was not only a function of anglicisation, but also a result of the loss of cultural expression and knowledge that resulted from the literal reduction through death and emigration of the rural population of Ireland resulting from the Famine. For religious nationalists the Famine transformed the Catholic Church in its institutional form and religious content in terms of ritual and in terms of a massive church-building project in the latter half of the nineteenth century. Despite the fundamental and striking difference in the effects of the Famine on cultural and religious nationalism, and despite the creation of competing institutions, each of these Irish nationalisms sought to advance the nation through the pursuit of the Irish language, Irish cultural expression and the fundamental moral regeneration of a 'corrupted' and 'tainted' contemporary Irish nation, thereby restoring it to a mythical 'pre-English' golden age.

The Catholic Church and its institutions were a natural location for cultural nationalist narratives. Regeneration and redemption were shared themes in religious and cultural nationalisms, reinforcing the nation and harmonising with historical memory in Ireland and religious practice. Hutchinson clearly identifies the myths that were being projected from the past on to contemporary Ireland – the myths of migration, origin, settlement, a golden age, degeneration, regeneration and/or redemption.[2] Such myths, as espoused by cultural nationalist elites such as Eoin MacNeill, identified Ireland as an ancient nationality, superior to its 'British' counterpart, although, as the experiences of the Gaelic League suggest, these myths needn't be religious.[3] For religious nationalists, the religious element, as covenant and sacred communion, were obvious, but Irish nationalism based in and around the Church was not the politics of the state or a movement struggling for the congruence of the nation with political institutions. Rather it sought to reinforce, (re)create, and (re)discover the untainted moral community of Catholics in Ireland – that is, the Irish nation. In this way, its aims and ambitions were not dissimilar from the Gaelic Revival of the late nineteenth century.

Theologically and culturally, the themes of degeneration, redemption and regeneration were fundamental components of the practice of the Roman Catholic religion and cultural nationalist expression in Ireland. The lives of the saints, religious festivals such as Easter, concepts such as original sin and baptism, rites of reconciliation, and so on, are all marked by their emphasis on the moral corruption of the human condition. From this viewpoint, such moral corruption can be rectified and regenerated only through actions such as confession, communion and other religious rites practised through, and espoused by, the Church in its theological outlook and institutional rites. These themes were echoed in 'secular' cultural nationalism – Douglas Hyde, proponent of the Irish Language, and founder of the Gaelic League, ascribed Irish ills to the process of anglicisation.[4] The various invasions and incursions of 'outsiders', of Vikings, Normans, Old and New English, were all understood to have driven Ireland from its 'rightful Gaelic' path. There was a lamentation that Ireland had been driven from its path of 'national evolution' because before the 'commercial massacre of the Tudors [Ireland] had reached a high degree of industry and wealth ... a flourishing commerce, a considerable culture and a life tempered by the arts.'[5] After this 'massacre' Ireland necessarily became a colonial satellite of England, an evolution that culminated in the Act of Union of 1801.

The default identity of the Irish nation as Catholic not only had a myth of origin, but also had a clear myth of golden age, when Ireland had been a moral, untainted and uncorrupted land of Catholic faith – although to which period this golden age referred was always disputed (pre-Celtic, Celtic, Gaelic, Norman, and so on.) One history book from the time states that Catholics 'can be properly called the Irish people, the "natives"'.[6] Such was the devastation of the memories of the Penal Era that 'they are only but gradually freeing themselves from the idea that the Protestant is the master of Ireland ... that they are helots'.[7] The memories of the Penal Era were tainted by their perception as a 'persecution of religion ... an attempt to degrade and demoralise a whole nation'.[8] The Church could be understood to be the 'Mother of all the Catholic Churches in the Anglo-Saxon world'.[9] The parishioners of the Church are especially fervent, as 'few race characteristics are so profoundly marked as is the intensity of religious feeling in the Celtic races ... they would seem to have instinctively adopted the Catholic religion'.[10]

Degeneration, Debauchery and the Nation

Myths of degeneration are a prerequisite for myths of regeneration. These were rife due to the experiences of the Famine. Meetings of temperance societies, almost always sponsored by Catholic religious institutions, were often accompanied by a description of how outsiders viewed drunkenness in Ireland. Of course drunkenness, as an issue of morality, was associated with the moral degradation of pre-Famine Ireland. The intemperance of Irish society was described as being the result of 'the debasing examples and influence of the dominant class, who by force of arms had secured possession of all power and of all property in their midst'.[11] It was interpreted as part of the debasing effects of foreign interference and something that had to be put 'morally' right in order to gain national redemption. In this description of the reason behind drunkenness in Ireland, we see how even those who were against drink blamed not Irish drinkers themselves, but rather the Irish nation's experiences of colonial domination.[12] This is a good example of an historicist vision of contemporary ills in Irish society, utilising history and myth to explain and understand contemporary situations in Ireland in 1914. Yet the Irish nation's redemption was necessarily attached to cultural and religious practice. In this way, nationalists and Catholics were able to assess blame for their subservient position and the sectarianism that they were railing against, and to encourage a maintenance of ethnic boundaries in order to protect their own communities.

Cultural Nationalism

In the Irish case, cultural nationalism was particularly important in crystallising and disseminating national myths, memories and symbols, such as those of origin, golden ages, degeneration and redemption, and examining how they were disseminated and maintained.[13] Cultural nationalism, as a phenomenon, is a variety of nationalism independent from, though associated with, political nationalism.[14] It is a variety of nationalism that reinforces the role of historical memory in defining the community of the nation.[15] Cultural nationalists are sometimes described as 'inventors of tradition', but are better understood as 'challenging established social identities, [and promoting] a novel historical vision of an integrated and distinctive political community'.[16] Cultural nationalists contribute to nationalism by providing a repertoire for the crystallisation of the nation, providing the myths, symbols and memories that unite the rubric of the community of the nation cultural nationalists provide a framework for understanding and interpreting the nation's path of historical and cultural development, especially as this path of development renders their nation separate from other foreign, and often dominant, nations.[17]

For cultural nationalists, the state, its institutions and so on, are 'accidental' because the nation is an organic entity – a self which becomes clothed in the institutions and powers of the state as a result of the processes of modernity.[18] The institutional framework of the state grows around the distinct and pre-determined entity of the nation because 'nations are then not just political units but organic beings ... [founded on] the passions implanted by nature and history'.[19] From this perspective, it was thought that 'had Ireland been left to herself, [it] would have succeeded ... along a path of modern progress'.[20] Cultural nationalists are therefore engaged in efforts to document the pre-modern myths and memories of their organic unit, establishing national legitimacy and authenticity while attempting to achieve a state congruent to the nation. To remove external influences and/or to return to an organic status quo was perceived to lead to the expression of equality amongst the members of the Irish nation. Cultural nationalism, as with all types of nationalism, attempts to guarantee political rights for members of the nation through the (re)generation, (re)discovery, (re)emphasis and (re)creation of the moral community of the nation in the contemporary era.[21]

Irish Cultural Nationalism

An examination of cultural nationalism in Ireland prior to the Rising exposes basic assumptions of the Irish nation's 'givenness' and distinctiveness in this process of legitimising and authenticating. Irish cultural nationalist elites saw the Irish nation as tainted by factors such as modernity and 'anglicisation'. Cultural nationalism in Ireland repackaged and disseminated national myths, memories and symbols deemed by cultural nationalist elites to be simultaneously moral, popularly resonant amongst the nation, and given to the organic national self.[22] Cultural nationalists assert the perennial nature of the nation, but their actions represent active and conscious attempts to disseminate and crystallise the repertoire of national myths, symbols and memories that form the cultural content of the nation. In this way, for cultural nationalists, the nation is subject and object, creator and creation (though not *ex-nihilo*!).

Prior to the Rising, cultural nationalism in Ireland was a movement that stressed the distinctiveness of the Irish nation above everything else.[23] The contemporary phrase 'Irish Ireland' often appears as a political project of cultural means.[24] Cultural nationalism's main effect was to establish and maintain the primacy of an Irish and Catholic historical memory in the Irish nation prior to the Rising.[25] There exist many versions of the Irish national myths, memories and symbols, which have been (and continue to be) espoused by numerous competing cultural nationalist elites. The resonance and ultimate success of these competing visions were determined in part through processes of trial and error. Relevance and resonance were contextualised through a determination of political need and necessity, which helped to give shape and content to the myths, memories and symbols of the Irish nation.[26]

Cultural nationalism depends on 'resonance' – not necessarily contemporary instrumental political needs.[27] A myth, memory or symbol is resonant when it strikes a common chord in the nation, denoting a common or shared significance for members of the nation. Resonance occurs when the personal experience of individuals, whether real, vicarious or imagined, corresponds to these myths, memories or symbols in the repertoire of the community, in this case the nation. The emerging set of myths, memories and symbols held and disseminated by Irish cultural nationalists, which were widely resonant, accepted and understood by members of the Irish nation, need not have been expressed in a mirror image to the political nationalism of the Home Rule movement – and therefore need not have fulfilled contemporary and immediate instrumental political needs. Cultural nationalism was only broadly congruent with political nationalism, rather than being identical or derivative. Cultural nationalists in Ireland ultimately succeeded in their project – creating and reinforcing a strong sense of national distinctiveness.

The Three Stages of Irish Cultural Nationalism

Hutchinson identifies three stages in the crystallisation of cultural nationalism for the Irish nation. The first stage was a project carried out by Irish antiquarians in the mid-eighteenth century, and it was closely followed by the emergence of a movement of historical scholars and poets during the 1830s, culminating in a movement of poets and folklorists at the end of the nineteenth century.[28] In the Irish case, the emergence of the antiquarians, historians and poets of the 1830s was a consequence of the Anglo-Protestant population of Ireland trying to 'make sense of' or rationalise their position in Ireland and in the newly formed Union.[29] In the wake of the failure of Tone and the United Irish Rebellion of 1798, the movement which emerged was led by George Petrie.[30] This movement attempted to unite the disparate and divided religious communities in Ireland by projecting a Gaelic past on to the island's contemporary inhabitants in order to bring about the amalgamation and moral regeneration of a secular and artistic Irish nation.[31]

This phase of cultural nationalism was a reaction to contemporary events, such as the Act of Union in 1801. It was a movement seeking to distinguish an Irish nation from the newly forged British state.

This phase of cultural nationalism in Ireland was simultaneously involved in a dynamic relationship with contemporary politics. The politics of O'Connell, the repeal movement and mass meetings meant that cultural nationalism, to remain relevant, had to take into account and engage with the emergence of a Catholic landowning class in Ireland, and to a certain extent justify attempts to bridge the religious divide.[32] This second revival failed in the quagmire of the Great Hunger, and in the wake of the Young Ireland Rising of 1848. In light of these events, the popular projection of a new found Gaelic unity, encompassing Protestant and Catholic, rich and poor, in all of Ireland, rapidly dissipated.[33]

Cultural Nationalism and O'Connell's Legacy

The strength of the third phase of the Gaelic revival of the late ninteenth and early twentieth centuries lay in its popular resonance as a movement of regeneration. Ireland had been devastated by the events of the mid-ninteenth century, and there had been a national introspection in the wake of the Famine. The Gaelic Revival, after the fall of Parnell, was introspective, and it emerged as an alternative during a period when political nationalism seemed 'sterile' and 'bitter'.[34] This national introspection can also be thought of as an accommodation to the inability or lack of desire to politically, culturally or economically deal with 'modernisation'.[35] Irish cultural nationalism also emerged out of the frustration with constitutional nationalism in Ireland.[36] This process was mirrored in religious doctrine at the time. It is almost impossible to determine which factor – culture or religion – was more causal for initiating this process of introspection.

O'Connell's mass meetings for repeal and continued Catholic Emancipation, and the removal of the last vestiges of the penal era, had already forced the British government to restore some rights to Catholics in Ireland. Hutchinson argues that this was part of an 'assimilationist drive'. In the wake of these political gains, a cultural nationalist movement emerged. This projected Ireland as a 'superior rural Gaelic communalist civilisation exemplifying to a corrupt power-hungry world a higher synthesis of the spiritual and material'.[37] Almost twenty years later, when the momentum for this assimilationist drive had faded, there was a new expression of frustration with the political conditions in Ireland. The unsuccessful Feinian rebellion of 1867 'nudged' the British regime into carrying out some more 'assimilationist' reforms which addressed the grievances that lay behind its outbreak. Overall, these reforms did not adequately address the demands and rhetoric of Irish nationalists or match the hopes promised by the legacy of O'Connell.[38]

Indeed, O'Connell's repeal movements, land reform (culminating in the Irish Land Acts of 1903 and 1909) and the Local Government Act (1898) had only accomplished so much for the Irish nation since the Famine and fifty years after the Young Ireland rebellion. They were specific pieces of legislation answering diverse and not always allied nationalist political demands.[39] The emergence of the Feinian Brotherhood, and the failed Rising of 1867 – organised by Young Ireland exiles and Irish immigrants who had fled to America for economic and political reasons – sprang from a 'reservoir of hatred against the British state as a malign agency seeking the extirpation of the Irish people'.[40] This reservoir was found in the vast body of the Irish diaspora who had left in the wake of the Great Hunger. Even a political nationalist such as Redmond, who was not deeply involved in cultural nationalism, made political capital by appealing to these fears and the sense of frustration with contemporary politics, by stating that Catholics at the turn of the nineteenth/twentieth centuries were only just emerging 'from a state of absolute slaves and bondage ... those who profess the religion of the great majority of the Irish people are still in an inferior position'.[41] The result was that cultural nationalists in Ireland had created a complementary movement to political nationalism. The pursuit of Home Rule became, with this complementary movement, more than a return to a form of self rule in Ireland, but rather a return to a national golden age.

The Role of the Famine in Cultural Nationalism

Doubts and concerns continued to dog Irish cultural nationalists as to Ireland's role, politically and culturally, in the Union. Myths and memories of the Anglo-Protestant other, of the era of plantations, Penal Laws, stories about hedge schools and exile, had been kept alive in the glowing emotional embers of the Famine; kept alive in newspapers and ballads and on book covers.[42] In the wake of the Famine, there was a drive for tangible political gains, but now nationalism had an added role – to prevent the recurrence of the past. The 'glowing emotional embers' of the Famine help to explain the continuing popularity of the myths, memories and symbols of the Reformation and Penal Era. The Famine formed a key component of the repertoire of Irish national myths, memories and symbols, and they seemed particularly salient after its occurrence. Attempts to 'modernise' agricultural practices or to proselytise amongst victims of the Famine, providing food and shelter in return for religious conversion, helped to keep pre-Famine and pre-modern myths, memories and symbols of the Penal Era and beyond alive. They provided a repertoire of meaning by which survivors could apportion blame for the devastation of the Famine, and explain the vast repertoire of myths, memories and symbols of Irish historical suffering.

Blame for the Famine was often laid at the door of the Anglo-Protestant 'other'. The Famine had led to 'all joy [leaving] the people ... a hatred of England and Lords [sinking] deeper than ever into their souls'.[43] Commentators such as Mitchel laid the foundations for these interpretations, perceiving the Anglo-Irish relationship to be inherently exploitative.[44] These ideas were crystallised and disseminated in nationalist histories, stories, plays and poems written in the latter half of the nineteenth century and beginning of the twentieth century.[45] The fear of Anglo-Protestant malign intention was exacerbated and underpinned by the extant set of myths, memories and symbols of the disestablishment of the Catholic Church in Ireland, and of the Reformation. In fact it was contemporarily thought that the reason for the decline of 'piety, like morality [in the wake of the Famine] ... may be found in the brutally abrupt introduction of the elements ... foreign to the spirit of the race' – these brutal elements having been introduced in the sixteenth and seventeenth centuries.[46] The events of the Famine seemed to make these earlier myths, memories and symbols come alive in a contemporary era.

Institutional Dissemination

Cultural nationalism was organised through institutions such as the Gaelic League (Conradh na Gaeilge). The Gaelic League was founded in 1893 by a group of twelve, including Eoin MacNeill and Douglas Hyde. The League's purpose at its inception was not to espouse any political viewpoint, and it shied away from questions of political nationalism. Rather it attempted to 'provide fellow Irish-Language enthusiasts with a forum to help preserve the dieing Irish language'.[47] Hyde, the driving force behind the Gaelic League, set out many of his ideas in a speech he had delivered the previous year to the National Literary Society entitled 'On the Necessity for de-Anglicising the Irish People'.[48] As its title suggests, its *raison d'être* was that a return to the Irish language meant a return to the national and organic status quo that had been lost in the Anglo-Irish relationship: a return to a Golden Age of Celtic Ireland. In this speech, Hyde 'pointed out that the country which had once occupied a leading position among European nations because of its cultural achievements had now sunk to the very bottom ... due to a process of Anglicisation'.[49] As expressed by its slogan, 'A country without a language is a country without a soul', there was a belief amongst those who supported the Gaelic League that all the components that marked Ireland as a distinct and great nation were encompassed in its language, and that without this distinctiveness they were merely another set of participants in the Union.[50] Without its language, Ireland would become a nation of imitators.[51]

Despite Hyde's secular intentions, there was a clear interplay between religious identity and linguistic nationalism in the Irish case. At the time, historians such as Paul-Dubois compare the contrast of 'the profoundly religious spirit' of the Gaelic language to the 'materialistic and utilitarian character of the Anglo-Saxon tongue', and the 'spiritual idealism' of Celtic Catholics to the 'rationalist' Protestants.[52] He goes on to state that:

> To-day that living and fervent faith which is so different from the cold observance by the Anglo-Saxon of his utilitarian and secular religion would seem, in truth, to have become a portion of the race and of the nationality so that the one cannot be distinguished from the other. Her religion is in the blood of Ireland. It is a second nature, a hereditary and traditional instinct which has no need to be reasoned in order to be profound ... it has not ... reduced itself to reason ...[53]

This sectarianism, the link between culture and religious identity that manifested itself in various nationalist movements, meant that in practice a latent separation existed in the minds of the members of the Irish nation, between themselves and the Anglo-Protestant other.

An example of this is the Gaelic League, an ostensibly non-sectarian institution, becoming an umbrella institution fighting against the Anglo-Protestant establishment in Ireland. Discussions about the Gaelic League, in the pages of the *Daily Freeman* in March 1914, refer to the 'Irish Language Week' – important for the revival of Irish, and an event which encouraged not only broad expressions of 'nationality', but also 'the practical development of national resources in production and manufacture'.[54] In this way it deviated from some elements of Irish religious nationalism, as will be discussed later, in so far as it did not shy away from embracing 'modernity'. The week, according to the *Freeman*, provided an opportunity for every Irishmen, no matter his level of education, to 'do his share in the work of the revival'.[55] Again, in the pages of this moderate, pro-Irish Party, pro-Redmond and pro-Home Rule *Freeman's Journal*, there are regular statements to the effect that 'It is a truism that a national language is an essential element of nationality – that without it our claim to nationhood would be vitally impaired ...'[56] Ultimately, the Irish language, and more specifically the movement behind the language, not only served the general purposes of any national myth or symbol, but also cemented clergy to separatists, forming a broad platform for those broadly dissatisfied with the current state of affairs in Ireland, and particularly those worried about a march towards modernisation.[57]

Famine, Land and the Myth of the Golden Age

The experience of the Famine led to agitation for the redistribution of land in Ireland, especially in those areas most affected by its devastation, and the transformation of land tenure that occurred in its aftermath.[58] The land issue was an example of where cultural and political nationalisms acted in complementary fashions – where pre-Famine myths, memories and symbols came alive in contemporary politics. Myths, memories and symbols of eviction, emigration and suffering over the course of the nineteenth century and before were highly salient in light of the land question, as they had been in the Famine itself. The power of these issues amongst individual members of the Irish nation was due to their being along similar thematic lines to the Famine. This means that the repertoire of myths, memories and symbols which were attached to the land issue and the Famine both emphasised suffering and deprivation.[59] Popular phrases such as 'To Hell or Connaught' reinforced the set of myths, memories and symbols about the eviction of Catholics and their suffering under Cromwell and later the Penal Codes, yet the repertoire underpinned contemporary political debates and wrangling over land reform in Ireland.

Cultural and political nationalists were both concerned about the possession of land in Ireland. For political nationalists, land reform led to economic and political power for the Irish nation. For cultural nationalists, possession of the land would redeem and restore the nation. For both cultural and political nationalists, possession of the land meant preventing a recurrence of the deprivations of the past through a gain of symbolic and economic power in the present. It is interesting to note that for the *Daily Freeman*, 'nationality' and indeed cultural expression of the nation, such as linguistic nationalism, were bound up with the commercial endeavours of manufacture and production. As with the land question, economic power was seen as a cultural symbol of nationalism, above and beyond its clear political implications.

Both cultural and religious nationalist movements were frustrated by the slow and incomplete nature of land reform in Ireland, although each expressed this frustration in different ways. Cultural nationalists, in reaction, espoused the ideal of an 'Irish Ireland' which was thoroughly de-anglicised, notions crystallised in institutions such as the Gaelic League, the GAA and the Irish Literary Theatre.[60] For religious nationalists, this frustration led them to intensify their search for salvation in the practice of Catholicism, and to bolster, solidify and expand the institutions of the Church. In this way, the example of the land question demonstrates a practical example of the distinction between cultural and political nationalists. On the one hand, it was an issue that propelled Parnell and the Irish Party to political prominence in Ireland because it mustered votes. On the other hand it was a highly symbolic issue, the resolution of which was a key step in the very resurrection of the nation and the restoration of a national golden age and which underpinned a rejection of an anglicised Ireland.

Religious Nationalism

The relationship between nationalism and religion is traditionally viewed as one of status quo and usurper. In this view, nationalism, as secular ideology, replaces the religious system.[61] In modernist theories of nationalism, religion is viewed as a kind of fertile soil from which nations and nationalisms emerge. Nationalists compare their efforts against and construct their projects in light of religious antecedents; religion acts as a backcloth.[62] However, these approaches do not indicate the depth and dynamism of the relationship between religion and the Irish nation at this time. The political nationalism of O'Connell, Parnell, Redmond and others cannot, as Smith points out, be viewed in the context of 'secular political ideologies like liberalism and socialism' because their aims and the content of their message transcended the political quest for 'human autoemancipation'.[63] The movement of religious nationalists perceives the nation as a sacred communion, devoted to the cult of authenticity and the ideals of national autonomy, unity and identity in an historic homeland.[64] The following section, therefore very much follows in the footsteps of Smith's project in *Chosen Peoples*: 'to explore some aspects of the relations between certain elements within older belief systems ... and the sacred foundations of national identities.'[65] Establishing the role of Irish religious myths, memories and symbols helps to explain the process of radicalisation in Ireland at the beginning of the twentieth century, rather than to establish a continuity between ancient religious practice and identity in Ireland.

Religious myths, memories and symbols of the Irish nation were sectarian. The division between Catholic and Protestant in Ireland, and the way in which this division affected claims to membership in the Irish nation, were bound up with notions of religious truth and superiority, elements of divine election and communion, which were cemented by national 'suffering' at the hands of an Anglo-Protestant other. This suffering was 'remembered' through myths, memories and symbols of events such as the Penal Laws and the Famine. The dominance of an 'Irish Ireland' or a *Sinn Féin Amháin* outlook in Irish nationalism was tantamount to a sectarian declaration that the regeneration of the nation, or the achievement of a meaningful level of personal and/or national security, could occur only within an Irish *and* Catholic context. This outlook boils down to a romantic belief that the character of the Irish nation could be found only in the ordinary and not yet anglicised Irish people, rather than in a project of the cultural or political elites.[66]

Images of martyrdom and political struggle were consistently demonstrated and reinforced in Irish religious life prior to the Rising. The importance of martyrdom went beyond simple individual bravery or heroism, tapping into a broader cultural Irish national narrative of Christian martyrdom and sainthood, and of specific cases in the Irish past, recent and ancient, of those who had died defending their faith. The Manchester Martyrs demonstrations in Dublin over the latter third of the nineteenth century, with their peculiar mix of Feinian myth and Catholic ritual, made for an event where the Irish national narratives of sainthood and martyrdom were publicly and popularly apparent.[67] The demonstrations also became an opportunity for radical nationalists, especially the Irish Republican Brotherhood as opposed to Redmondites, to command attention and garner respect. Even in the aftermath of the Rising, the first comparisons and some of the first demonstrations of positive public opinion regarding and sympathy with its participants were held at the 'hastily erected' memorial next to the Manchester Martyrs memorial in Glasnevin Cemetery.[68]

Within the descriptions of the religious Irish nation, terms such as predestined or spiritual idealism were often used. St Patrick's day was a crucial day for the nation – a national festival – although it was considered to be more of a celebration for the political and cultural establishment, i.e. the Church and Irish Party, but again, the mix of religion, culture and politics was readily apparent.[69] The celebration of religious days, such as St Patrick's Day or the feast of St Columbcille, and symbols such as the shamrock, combined religious significance with the symbolism of the nation. Following a pre-modern golden age of Christianity in Ireland, there was a 'fall from grace' – a period of degeneration and 'suffering' which began with the disestablishment of the Catholic Church and the establishment of the plantations in Ulster (despite the fact that they were established by a Catholic monarch) and clear attempts to deny the Irish Catholics their 'organic' self in the Penal Era. In this way the Church fulfilled a necessary element of being the locus for cultural nationalism in Ireland, as Catholicism in Ireland had been 'implanted' by nature and history, and its organic character was reinforced by institutionalised rites of passage, such as baptism, first communion, etc. These were reinforced by the Church's monolithic role in the education of the young Irish and Catholic population of Ireland, especially as regards the role of Christian Brother education. Cultural rites and reinforcement, as mechanisms for crystallising and disseminating the cultural nationalist project of the Catholic Church in Ireland, ensured that the Church had a major role to play in the expression of Irish national myths, memories and symbols.

Catholicism and Distinctiveness

The impact of the Famine on the practice of Catholicism, on Irish national myths, memories and symbols, and on an individual's thoughts and beliefs was significant. Ireland's devastation as a result of the Famine was not unique, as other countries, like Belgium, were also hit hard and suffered the agricultural and demographic effects of this calamity.[70] The evolution or establishment of other nations had also been affected by the chaos and disruption that accompanied the Reformation. The Penal Codes, while marking the Irish case as particularly horrific, were, by the time of the Rising, two hundred years old. The 'Popery Laws' had forbidden Catholics from possessing weapons, leaving Ireland, purchasing land and inheriting property and money from Protestants, and from leasing land for more than 31 years, as well banishing the upper echelon of the Catholic clergy.[71] They were a set of rules that did more than attempt to force the assimilation of the Catholic population of Ireland – they reinforced cultural and economic boundaries between the communities in Ireland.

The events of the nineteenth century melded with earlier myths, memories and symbols of the sixteenth and seventeenth centuries, and in this way the myths and memories of a previous era came alive in contemporary minds. The degeneration of the Irish Catholic community in the nineteenth century was contextualised through the prism of the myths and memories of this earlier era, and the myths and memories of the Penal Codes, hedge schools and proselytising efforts on the part of Protestant missionaries became contemporarily manifest. The myths, memories and symbols of Irish and Catholic difference and distinctiveness from 'non-Irish' (or more accurately non-Catholic) Protestants, who had resided in Ireland for 200 years or more, were coming alive in this event that reduced the population of Ireland by as many as four million through disease, death and emigration.[72] The demographic effects of the Famine were extreme – it had emptied tracts of land in the west of Ireland, affected birth rates and the average age of marriage, and permanently altered the structures of Irish Catholic society throughout the entire island for over a century afterwards.[73] While memories of the Famine were as varied as the individuals that remembered them, universal images such as vivid descriptions of 'dead bodies strewn' along the roadside, and the opening of a front door to find a corpse of someone who had sheltered there, were widely disseminated and recognised.[74]

In the wake of the Famine, survivors apportioned blame for its devastation. These myths, memories and symbols of the Famine created a tangible sense of 'survivor's guilt,' leaving those who survived to seek reasons for the Famine in past immoral or irreligious behaviour, and with a sense of anger at the injustice of the experience.[75] A great deal of the blame was placed on the self, as if there was a variety of self-hatred for the culture that had led to this disaster.[76] This personal 'shame' accounted for the emergence of a new set of religious practices amongst famine survivors, culminating in the 'Cullenisation' of the Catholic Church.[77] It provided an institutional framework through which expression of guilt over past cultural practices – for example, sexual promiscuity accounting for high birth-rates and a society so dependent on a single crop – could be 'psychologically' worked through. The role of the Church in religiously proscribed actions became more important for individuals seeking to overcome their experiences. The Cullenisation of the Church was a 'devotional revolution', whereby a shift in theology, including a 'weaning of the people from an over-reliance on folk religion', was accompanied by the construction of new church buildings.[78] Cullen's key 'pastoral goal' in the wake of the Famine was to make the Irish Catholic congregation a church-going one.[79] This was accompanied by the end of practices such as the waking of the dead or the transformation of ancient festivals such as Bealtaine (1 May) from raucous, debaucherous, drunken celebrations to sombre occasions celebrating sobriety, morality and piety.[80] The Church, as a set of institutions, took on the role of 'moral arbiter' so that both state and nation needed its support to reinforce their claims of political legitimacy.[81] The emergence of new religious orders, temperance societies, and so on was a variety of introspection that assigned the cause of the calamity to the complete degeneration of society and the nation.[82]

The 'congealed' distinctions that emerged in Ireland between the Catholic and 'British/Protestant' populations led to resentments that, when coupled with religious fundamentalism, became an important source of separatist feeling.[83] Regular references appear in newspapers to 'Fighting the Soupers' and the proselytising efforts of Protestant missionaries in the Dublin tenements. In May 1914, the Irish Catholic began a campaign to deal specifically with this issue, describing Protestant missionaries as 'souper harpies ... plying their foul and monstrous traffic' in the slums of Dublin, meeting limited success, as the paper reported that 'at present less than 100 are to be found debased enough to deny their faith or to accept at the hands of soupers help which they can obtain from Catholics'.[84] These stories form part of an appeal for money to support Catholic charities, on the grounds that it is only through an equal or greater provision of charity on the part of Catholics that 'souperism' could be stopped. Such appeals supposed the 'organic' relationship between the Irish nation and Catholicism. There was a link between the prospect of souperism, and the loss of identity, whether it be religious or national, as the two were at the time inseparable.[85] These constant references to the tensions, contemporary and historical, between Catholics and Protestants served to demonstrate and reinforce sectarianism in Irish society at the time. The ethnic divisions that separated Catholic and Protestant in Dublin were clearly apparent.[86]

Blame for the Famine on the national 'self' and on the Anglo-Protestant other reinforced the role of Catholicism, as theology, as institution and as ethno-national identity marker in the Irish nation. As a devastating event and through an institutionally and elite engineered response, myths, memories and symbols of the Famine solidified the role of the Catholic Church in the Irish nation. These institutions allowed for the repentance of past sins, while marking the Irish nation as permanently and unalterably distinct from the ruling British regime. Like cultural nationalism, religious nationalism provided a mechanism by which the Irish nation was rendered distinct, organic and morally superior. Religious nationalism, through the Catholic Church, created solidarity and unity in the nation through a sacred covenant and communion. The existence of blame and guilt only served to reinforce the central role of Catholicism in the Irish nation and reinforced this covenant and communion.

Religious Nationalism in Action

After the initial disgrace and consequent death of Parnell, Irish political nationalism was in a shambles. Parnell had never been a particular favourite of the Catholic leadership, in part because of his initial support for 'obstructionist' tactics, potential support of physical force nationalism in the agrarian struggle and overall political agenda, and not least because of his religious persuasion (Protestant). With Parnell's fall, after he was named in a divorce proceeding, the Catholic Church, under the leadership of Archbishop

Walsh of Dublin, amassed all of its political might to defeat Parnell's supporters in the Irish Party.[87] Walsh attempted to create a political movement whose aims could be controlled and determined by the Church.[88] This action created schisms in the Irish Party and in Irish political nationalism which came back to haunt the Church in its efforts to suppress radical nationalists after the Rising.[89] This incident serves to show two important points, the first being that religious nationalists saw their religion as a 'launching' point from which to effect and determine political nationalism in Ireland. The second is that even where not 'explicitly' involved in Irish politics, religious nationalists in Ireland saw it as part of their moral duty to direct and influence its agenda and those who were participating in it. Despite the perceived moral duty of religious nationalists, the Church, as the set of institutions which religious nationalists used to accomplish their agenda, was limited in its scope for action by its precarious position between state and nation. Furthermore, it was constantly subject to the disparate and competing views of its elites, resulting in only occasional stands on political questions at the time.[90] The pressure on the Church, external and internal, meant that when it did take these stands they were moderate.

The expression of the will of the elite religious nationalists came not only from pronouncements from above, but from control of their message and institutions from below. At the grassroots level, priests played a prominent role in promoting the role of religion in Irish politics.[91] This was only natural, in so far as the day-to-day interaction between individual and Church was mediated by the priest. Exposure to the Church and its specific messages occurred at mass, led by the priest. If individuals disobeyed the will, rules or intents of the Church or its hierarchy, they were publicly shamed by the priest, in so far as they were denied the sacrament. Furthermore, there was the sense that the priest was part of the community itself and that 'the priest suffered with the people'.[92] The local priest was understood to be not only 'spiritual shepherd' but also 'guide and counsellor in temporal affairs' and as 'usually the only person in the village who has any education ... the only leader who is obeyed'.[93] In various situations, 'the response of ecclesiastics to any public issue was governed by a combination of their ideals and the interests of their institution'.[94]

The message of regeneration espoused by religious nationalists was located in the pastoral care of the Church, and emotionally in a process of 'recalling the sorrows ... traversed [renewing] confidence and strength and vitality of a race which no ruin has until now destroyed'.[95] Even though there was financial difficulty in Ireland at the time, priests encouraged their parishioners to stay in Ireland because 'even if the wages were small in Ireland there were compensating advantages ... at home in "holy Ireland" there was an atmosphere of faith and piety ...'[96] Although there was a recognition that Ireland suffered from its lack of modernisation and industrialisation, and that this increased levels of emigration, one bishop believed that these industrial conditions led to 'physical decadence ... those hives of industry ... [were] destroyers of the morals of the people ...'[97] One bishop gave a sermon in which he insisted that 'the average Irishman or woman is never so happy as in his Catholic Irish home, where the air is pure, and where there is a feeling of religion and sympathy around him'.[98] The link between religion, culture and national identity was a strong one, and it was the correct balance of all three that would bring about the fulfilment of the aims of cultural nationalists.

Priests were under pressure to toe the Church line on various issues. If a priest became too active in radical nationalism, for example by encouraging radical or violent agitation, these actions were often dealt with severely.[99] The Church did take a position on land agitation, and especially on land reform, believing that the redistribution of the land away from the Protestant landlords 'is the essential condition for the prosperity and happiness of Ireland'.[100] If a priest was under the leadership of a bishop who was unsympathetic to his particular political outlook, however, he was often disciplined and/or transferred.[101] There was a real attempt on the part of the Church elites to concentrate political power under the auspices of its institutions, quashing those individuals and institutions that it deemed did not adequately recognise or adhere to its ultimate authority.[102]

Religion and Education

Interactions with the Church were not limited to religious practice. The Catholic Church also dominated the Irish educational system. The Christian Brothers schools have been considered by many scholars to have been the factories in which a generation of young Irish nationalists were cast and refined, and the correlation between Christian Brothers education and participation in post-Rising 'radical' nationalism is

apparent.[103] Several key political struggles elucidate the position of the
Church and its attempts to control politics in Ireland, such as the
university question and its involvement in the Home Rule Bill.[104]

The university question shows the extent to which the Church sought
to control social and political power outside of the confines of a strictly
religious pastoral sphere. The foundation of a national university in
1908 meant the Church gained 'effective control on all levels of what
was now really a system of denominational education financed by the
state'.[105] In practice, this meant that from primary schooling through to
university, the Catholic Church controlled the education system, its
curricula and staffing. The university question had been a key plank of
Irish nationalist political debate since the establishment of the Queen's
Colleges in 1845. It was an issue that was particularly salient amongst
the rising Catholic middle class and nationalist elites – and it would
come to be an issue that was highly symbolic to the entire Irish nation.[106]
The university question was of particular import first to the Church,
and later to Irish-language supporters (such as the Gaelic League), both
of which deplored what they perceived as the anglicising influence of
the Queen's Colleges and Trinity.

At the time, it was thought that the university question made the
nation 'the football of Church and State', as the Church and Parliament
each sought to control the outcome on this issue.[107] The Church, as a
religious nationalist institution, determined that 'whomever controls
the education of the rising generation is the conqueror of the future'.[108]
The Catholic Church, under Cullen's leadership, had condemned
religiously mixed education. As part of the assimilationist drive of the
British government, the Church formed a Royal University in response
to Catholic demands – as an examination body – a fact that did nothing
to satisfy religious nationalist demands.[109] Archbishop Walsh dropped
the demand for a solely Catholic institution, and sought to establish a
university which was 'Catholic in atmosphere and administration'.[110]

With the passage of the Irish Universities Bill in 1908, the Queen's
Colleges in Galway and Cork and University College Dublin were
established as two new universities. Questions as to their official
theological outlook and about the official role of the Irish language
dominated the discussions over their foundation Augustine Birrell, in
drafts of the University Bill, had included a clause that denied
ecclesiastics guaranteed representation in the administration of these
new universities. This caused anxiety amongst the Catholic hierarchy,
but it was unfounded.[111] The role of the Catholic Church, in terms of
official ecclesiastical participation and in terms of the Catholic

character of these universities, would be in little doubt.[112] It was ultimately the Church that had the political power and national credibility to fight the British state for nationalist gains, and it created a moderate and powerful institutional umbrella under which most nationalists could happily fit.

Religion and Language

The Gaelic League, a cultural nationalist institution, recognised that the only institution capable of initiating and leading the regeneration of the nation after the devastation of the Famine was the Catholic Church and clergy.[113] This is a perfect example of the interplay apparent in nationalist visions – secular cultural pursuits of language, literature and archaeology, and so on, were inseparable in their moral purpose from the 'upright', 'untainted' and 'incorruptible' institutions of the Catholic Church. In this way, the self was Catholic, the nation was self, and the nation was Catholic. Contemporary advertisements and notices for religious festivals, such as that of the Feast of St Columbcille, described them as being appropriate for 'those who are in sympathy with piety's own tongue should attend'.[114] Indeed, the service was described as being for 'every Catholic who pays more than a mere lip-homage to the language of his country'.[115] This particular celebration was also described as 'showing how the feast of a typical Irish saint should be celebrated in a Catholic City which looks forward to the Crown of nationhood'.[116] Even in less explicitly religious papers, such as *An Gaedal* or the *Evening Herald*, there were regular references to religious festivals and Church politics. In this way, the inherent religious element in Irish nationalism is apparent in the apparently secular pursuit of the Irish language.

The debate over the role of the Irish language in the university question, a row which had started over the perceived neglect of the language at Trinity College, Dublin also demonstrated some of the interplay between nationalisms in Ireland.[117] By the time of the Rising, the Irish language, due to agitation on the part of the Gaelic League, had been made compulsory at the national universities.[118] One commentator went so far as to frame the debates over religion and language as 'the decisive battle between Irish and West Briton'.[119] Congruence between religious and cultural nationalisms could occur despite their often contradictory goals or orientation.

Even for moderate nationalists and 'Home Rulers' the inseparability of religion, identity and nationalist politics was apparent, in so far as the first two to three pages of every issue of the *Daily Freeman's Journal*, the organ of the moderate and constitutional nationalist Irish Party, contained regular references to meetings of the 'Father Mathew Union' (an abstinence congress), 'Christian Brothers Past Pupils Union' or indeed committees being formed or meeting regarding 'The Religion of Children'.[120] These meetings, as examples from the *Daily Freeman's Journal* over the course of 1914 show, go towards demonstrating the meshing of religion, culture, politics and civil society at all levels of Dublin society, and amongst all degrees of nationalist persuasions in the run up to the outbreak of the First World War.

At times religion and culture came into conflict. In one diary, a description of Douglas Hyde, administering Casement's fund for feeding schoolchildren in the fever districts of the west, in Lettermullen, was greeted with anxiety by priests, fearful that this was souperism in a new guise.[121] This is because the relief was attached to education in the Irish language, rather than more broadly to the institutions of the Church. Also Hyde, as an individual, was viewed as a secular nationalist rather than as a staunch 'religious' nationalist.[122] Ultimately, however, the competition for dominance amongst Irish nationalists, even for non-religious groups of elites, had to be couched in terms of the history, myths and themes of the nation, and viewed within the symbolic context which was resonant amongst the nation.

* * *

Irish national myths, memories and symbols were a mix of politics, religion, language, literature, and art. They were ultimately inseparable, although at times they may well have been opposed or in competition. These cultural themes are the canvas for later interpretations of the Rising, the filter through which these later events and actions were understood and carried out. The intertwining of religion and culture with national myths, memories and symbols created the context in which the events of the Rising would be understood. Despite occasionally competing claims to the 'true identity' of the nation, each served to reinforce the Irish nation's distinctiveness from the 'Anglo-Protestant' other.

Each of these nationalisms also reinforced a latent sectarianism in Irish nationalism. The myths of organic distinctiveness, moral rectitude and superiority existed in the religious sacred communion of the Irish nation, and its cultural pursuit of de-anglicisation. Martyrdom and the suffering of the Famine defined the Irish nation in so far as it distinguished its members from the Anglo-Protestant other. Despite the varying philosophies on the Irish past, the Famine served to reify the sets of shared and competing myths, memories and symbols of cultural and religious nationalisms – solidifying a belief in the victimisation of the Irish nation. Both cultural and religious nationalisms were laden with assumptions of national 'predestination.' Both varieties of nationalism focused on restoring an 'untainted' golden age of the Irish nation, but this vision serves to betray their assumptions of what the 'organic' status of the Irish nation was – either Catholic or not Anglo-Protestant. There may have been competing nationalisms, but they were constantly coming together, and the institutions of the Catholic Church and cultural nationalism served to perpetuate these popular sets of myths, memories and beliefs.

The debates over Home Rule and the university question are evidence of the way in which political issues, or power struggles between institutions (the Catholic Church and the British government) rapidly became nationalist issues. In this way religious and cultural nationalisms can be seen as complementary phenomena, at times in competition but quite obviously in broad sympathy. The power of both movements, and the myths, memories and symbols that each brought to bear, are harnessed under the rubric of the Irish nation. In the same ways in which Hutchinson has suggested that political and cultural nationalisms reinforce and reinvigorate each other, so too can we begin to see evidence for a similar relationship with cultural and religious nationalisms, such that each serves to energise and invigorate the other, so that the feast of St Columbcille or celebrations of St Patrick's Day are more symbolically potent than their religious or cultural significance alone would suggest. Despite the general lack of support for in radical political nationalism, it may be said that there was a clearly sectarian orientation to the Irish nation at this time. The existence of this latent sectarianism will help to explain why a process of radicalisation occurred in the wake of the Rising.

NOTES

1   I have used the word 'Famine' deliberately in this chapter and throughout the book despite the controversy over its use to define this event. A famine, by definition, refers to a time when there was lack of food due to a failure to produce enough to eat for a given population. In the Irish case, there was enough agricultural production to have fed the population of the island of Ireland, but much of the food was exported and

withheld. The crop which failed, the potato crop, was the one on which an entire section of the Irish population was dependent for economic survival (see Edwards and Williams, 1957) and accounted for demographic growth in Ireland, while the production of other crops and livestock continued unabated. In this way, the combination of the failure of the potato crop, British reactions to its failure, and various proselytising efforts exchanging relief with religious conversion constituted what some have described as a form of 'ethnocide' rather than famine.

2   Hutchinson, 1987, pp. 124–9.

3   Ibid., p.127.

4   McCartney, D. 'Hyde, D. P. Moran and Irish Ireland', in Martin, F. X. (ed.), *Leaders and Men of the Easter Rising: Dublin 1916* (London: Methuen and Co. 1967), p. 44.

5   Green, A.S. *The Making of Ireland and its Undoing 1200–1600* (London, 1908), p. 463.

6   Paul-Dubois, L. *Contemporary Ireland* (Dublin: Maunsel and Co., 1911), p.462.

7   Ibid., p. 463.

8   Ibid., p.39.

9   Ibid., p.480.

10   Ibid., p.491.

11   *Irish Catholic*, 4 July 1914.

12   For a discussion of drunkenness, especially in light of the puritanical nature of radical nationalists, see Garvin, T., 'Priests and Patriots: Irish Separatism and Fear of the Modern, 1890–1914' *Irish Historical Studies*, Vol. xxv, No. 97, May 1986, pp. 67–81.

13   An entire book could be written on cultural nationalism in Ireland in its various forms and guises, and how countless institutions and individuals played a role in its dissemination and reinforcement in Irish society. For reasons of brevity, this chapter has identified three archetypal cultural nationalist institutions in Ireland: the Catholic Church, the Gaelic League (*Conradh na Gaeilge*) and the Gaelic Athletic Association (GAA). It is intended that despite the brevity of the analysis herein, it will provide a benchmark by which the reader may be able to judge pre-Rising attitudes towards the Irish cultural nationalist movement.

14   Hutchinson, 1987, p. 9

15   Ibid. p. 9

16   Hutchinson, 1987, p. 20; for a further discussion on cultural nationalists as inventors of tradition, see Hobsbawm, 1992.

17   Hutchinson, 1987, pp. 38–40.

18   Ibid., p.13.

19   Ibid., p.14.

20   Paul-Dubois, 1911, p. 13.

21   Hutchinson, 1987, p. 15.

22   Of course this raises the problem that if these components of the nation are organic, popular and timeless, why do they have to be actively repackaged and disseminated by cultural nationalist elites and their movements? This section does not deal with this question; rather it accepts this as the process as it appears to occur on the ground.

23   Pesata, S., *Before the Revolution: Nationalism Social Change and Ireland's Catholic Elite, 1879-1922* (Cork: Cork University Press, 1999), p. 3.

24   Paul-Dubois, 1911.

25   Smith, 1998, p. 178 Catholic here refers to an ethno national identity rather than a set of theological beliefs or practices; see Coakley (2002).

26   Smith, 1998, p. 178.

27   Ibid., p.178.

28   Hutchinson, 1987, p. 50.

29   Ibid.

30   Ibid., Connolly, 1998, pp. 439–40.

31 Hutchinson, 1987, p. 79.
32 In this case, Catholic is used to describe a constituent element of the Irish nation, rather than a form of religious practice or theological outlook.
33 For a much more detailed discussion and analysis of these events, see especially Hutchinson, 1987.
34 Boyce, D. G., *Nationalism in Ireland* (London: Routledge, 1995), p. 259; Hutchinson, 1987.
35 See Drumm, 1996.
36 See Hutchinson, 1987.
37 Ibid., p.115.
38 Ibid., p.115.
39 Campbell, 2005.
40 Hutchinson, 1987, pp. 114–15.
41 Redmond's speech at Mansion House, 4 September 1907, in Redmond, J., *Some Arguments for Home Rule: Series of Speeches by John Redmond* (Dublin, 1908).
42 Mitchell, 1983; Reilly, 'Beyond Guilt Shamrock: Symbolism and Realism in the Cover Art of Irish Historical and Political Fiction, 1880-1914' in McBride, L., *Images and Icons and the Irish Nationalist Imagination* (Dublin: Four Courts Press, 1999).
43 Paul-Dubois, 1911, p. 73.
44 Mitchel, 1983.
45 Morash, C. and Hayes, R. (eds), *Fearful Realities: New Perspectives on the Famine* (Dublin: Irish Academic Press, 1996), p. 115.
46 Paul-Dubois, 1911, p. 492.
47 Grote, G., *Anglo-Irish Theatre and the Formation of a Nationalist Political Culture between 1890 and 1930* (Lampeter: The Edwin Mellen Press, 2003), p. 86.
48 Ibid., p. 89.
49 Ibid., p. 89.
50 Grote, G., *Torn Between Politics and Culture: The Gaelic League, 1893–1993* (Munster: Waxman, 1994), p. 47.
51 Grote, 2003, p. 90.
52 Paul-Dubois, 1911, p. 492.
53 Ibid.
54 *Daily Freeman's Journal*, 17 March 1914.
55 Ibid.
56 Ibid.
57 Garvin, 1986, p. 74.
58 Campbell, 2005.
59 Moran, 1999, p. 44; *Connaught Telegraph*, 3 January 1880; *Annual Report of the Local Government Board for Ireland*, 1880, p. 136.
60 Hutchinson, 1987, p. 115.
61 Smith, 2003, p. 9.
62 Ibid., p. 10.
63 Ibid., p. 18.
64 Ibid., p. 254.
65 Ibid. p.257.
66 McCartney, 1967, p. 44.
67 Owens, G. 'Constructing the Martyrs: The Manchester Executions and the Nationalist Imagination' in McBride, L. (ed.), *Images and Icons and the Irish Nationalist Imagination* (Dublin: Four Courts Press, 1999); McGee, O., 'God Save Ireland: Manchester Martyr Demonstrations in Dublin, 1867–1916' *Eire-Ireland,* Fall/Winter 2001, pp. 39–66
68 McGee, 2001
69 Alter, P. 'Symbols of Irish Nationalism' in, O'Day, A. (ed.), *Reactions to Irish*

Nationalism, 1865–1914 (London: Hambledon Press, 1987), p. 9.
70   Connolly, 1998, p. 228.
71   Connolly, 1998, p. 438.
72   Miller, D. W., *Church, State, and Nation in Ireland 1898–1921* (Dublin: Gill and MacMillan, 1973), p. 18.
73   See Mokyr, J., *Why Ireland Starved: A Quantitative and Analytical History of the Irish Economy, 1800–1850* (London: Allen and Unwin, 1983) amongst others. See also the discussion of Cardinal Cullen's reforms of the Catholic Church in the wake of the Famine (i.e. the Cullenisation of the Church) and the debate over the devotional 'evolution' or 'revolution' in the practice of Catholicism after the Great Hunger in Larkin, E. 'The Devotional Revolution in Ireland', *American Historical Review*, Vol. 87, 1972, pp. 625–52, Drumm, 1996, and McGrath, T. G. 'The Tridentine Evolution of Modern Irish Catholicism, 1563–1962: A Re-examination of the "Devotional Revolution Thesis"', in O'Muirí, R. (ed.), *Irish Church History Today* (Dublin: Cumann Seanchais Ard Mhacha, 1992).
74   Paul-Dubois, 1911, pp. 71–4.
75   Drumm, 1996.
76   Garvin, 1986.
77   Drumm, 1996; Kerr, D. A., *The Catholic Church and the Famine* (Dublin: Columba Press, 1996).
78   Baily, M. 'The Parish Mission Apostolate of the Redemptorists in Ireland, 1851–1898', in Gallagher, R. and McConvery, B. (eds), *History and Conscience: Studies in Honour of Sean Ó Riordan* (Dublin: Gill and MacMillan, 1989).
79   Drumm, 1996, pp. 88–9.
80   Drumm, 1996; Kerr, 1996.
81   Miller, 1973, p. 3.
82   Kissane, B. *Explaining Irish Democracy* (Dublin: UCD Press, 2002), pp. 81–2; Drumm, 1996.
83   Garvin, 2002, p. 3. This, of course, held true for Protestants as well as Catholics, although remains unexplored in this book.
84   *Irish Catholic*, 9 May 1914.
85   Drumm, 1996.
86   Garvin, 1989.
87   Miller, 1987.
88   For an extensive discussion of this situation see Miller, 1973.
89   Miller, 1987.
90   See Miller, 1973.
91   Paul-DuBois, 1911, p. 481.
92   Ibid., p. 493.
93   Ibid., p. 495.
94   Miller, 1973, p. 27.
95   Green, 1908, p. 493.
96   Father Guinan in Miller, 1973, p. 70.
97   *Freeman's Journal*, 6 January 1902, as cited in Miller, 1973, p. 72.
98   *Irish Catholic*, 4 November 1905 as cited in Miller, 1973, p. 72.
99   Miller, 1973, p. 20–4
100 *Record of the Maynooth Union*, 1898–99, pp. 31–2 as cited in Miller, 1973, p. 75.
101 Miller, 1973, pp. 20-4.
102 Ibid., p. 53.
103 See Fitzpatrick, 1998; Garvin, 1987; Augusteijn, J., *From Public Defiance to Guerrilla Warfare* (Dublin: Irish Academic Press, 1996) amongst others.
104 De Weil, 2003.
105 Larkin, 1976, p. 1267.

106 Paseta, 1999, pp. 5–6.
107 Hackett, 1918, in Paseta, 1999, p. 6.
108 Bishop O'Dwyer in *Freeman's Journal*, 26 February 1906, cited in Paseta, 1999, p. 7.
109 Paseta, 1999, pp. 12–13, 15.
110 Ibid., p. 18.
111 Miller, 1973, p. 142.
112 Kissane, 2002, p. 105.
113 McCartney, 1967, p. 45; Hutchinson, 1987, p. 127.
114 *Irish Catholic*, 16 May 1914.
115 Ibid.
116 Ibid.
117 Garvin, 1986, p. 73.
118 Kissane, 2002, p. 105.
119 *Hiberian Journal*, Vol. iii, 1909, p. 3, in Pesata, 1999, p. 21.
120 See *Freeman's Journals*, 1912–14.
121 Diary of Mrs Augustine Henry, MS 7981 NLI.
122 Ibid.

5

The Rising as Cultural Trigger Point

The Rising set the immediate context in which a sea-change in popular Irish nationalism occurred – a context of rumour and anxiety. The cultural trigger point is an event or series of events that triggers a radicalisation in identity, a sense of injustice and perceptions of agency which accounts for a shift from a popular sympathy for and participation in constitutional nationalism to radical nationalism in Ireland. This chapter aims to establish the Easter Rising 1916 as a cultural trigger point for the Irish nation. The chapter will provide a very brief outline of the immediate events of the Rising, then some initial examples of popular reactions to the Rising before the executions of its leaders. However, though full of historical references, the chapter does not constitute a history of the Rising. Rather, it serves as a survey of some contemporary perspectives on this event. This will allow for a comparison of the changes in reactions to the Rising resulting from the British responses. The moment of the cultural trigger point was in the shift in the outlook of popular Irish nationalism between the executions of the leaders of the Rising, the failure of Home Rule and the series of Sinn Féin by-election victories in the run- up to the general election of 1918. The three chapters which follow this one will then examine the evidence for the extent of this radicalisation throughout Irish society, focusing on how it was that this radicalisation was expressed in popular politics in the wake of the failure of Home Rule and the rise of Sinn Féin.

This chapter is split into three sections. In the first I present a brief précis of the events of the Rising itself. In the second the events of the executions that followed the Rising will be described. The third section will examine initial reactions to the Rising. These reactions demonstrated confusion, anxiety and outrage. It is not surprising that the Rising did not stimulate a simple shift in the popularity of radical nationalism. Radical nationalism was not only unpopular, but, as we have seen in previous chapters, was actively discouraged on the part of nationalist elites and institutions in Ireland. It will become apparent that a state of confusion, anxiety and outrage dominates the contemporary initial reactions to the Rising.

This entire situation was intensified by the circulation of rumours which heightened tensions and anxieties, and is not only evident after the fact in the interpretation of the Rising, but also remarked upon at the time.[1] Rumours dominated the reporting of events during Easter Week and they were rife in its aftermath. Rumours as to the intentions of the British government were used to mobilise radical nationalists, and fears over the secret or surreptitious introduction of conscription in Ireland served as a tableau on which the events of the Rising unfolded.[2] Rumours circulated about the intentions of the entire Volunteer movement, and as to the scale of the Rising. Rumours circulated concerning the response of the British, culminating in rumours of mass executions after the Rising.[3] Confusion, anxiety and outrage, exacerbated by rumours, when later combined with the loss of legitimacy for Redmond and the Irish Party, and in the climate of distrust of the British forces in the aftermath of the Rising, would foster a climate in which myths, memories and symbols of latent sectarianism came to form the foundation for interpretation of contemporary events and a basis for national action. The following brief précis of the aftermath of the Rising will not provide any evidence for the cultural trigger point, but will signpost the direction in which these events were headed after the initial shock of the outbreak of the Rising.

Context of the Rising

As the previous chapters have shown, the myths and memories that lay at the heart of the ideology of the Rising had roots going back decades, if not centuries. For practical purposes, the roots of the Rising can be traced back at least to the split in the Volunteer movement at the outbreak of the First World War. This split was mirrored in the split in radical and moderate political nationalism, as detailed in Chapters 2 and 3.[4] By the spring of 1916, specific concerns had emerged over Ireland's role in the imperial war effort. Elements of the Irish nation felt themselves estranged from the

British political establishment, which they perceived as dominated by the Tories and the military especially after incidents such as the Curragh Mutiny. When Kitchener accepted the Ulster Volunteer Force *en masse* into the British army as the 36th Ulster division, the long delay in the creation of an equivalent Irish Division for the National Volunteers seemed to illustrate this estrangement even after the outbreak of the war, and the passage of Home Rule.

Despite this estrangement, Ireland had managed to avoid most of the worst hardships of war. Although there was a threat of conscription, it had not been enacted in Ireland. The rural population had benefited from the war as suppliers of various agricultural goods to the war effort. The urban population, especially the Dublin poor, had also benefited from the war. The war industry created new job opportunities and many men enlisted. It seemed as though Catholic Ireland could grow fat off the conflict without indiscriminately contributing its sons to the trenches. It wasn't only poor Irishmen, seeking an escape from urban destitution, who were fighting in the British army. All classes of Irishmen heeded Redmond's call to enlist, in part through the National Volunteers. This was, however, participation in a British war on Irish terms, a practice which suited the moderate Home Rule nationalists and their Home Rule mentality, but which infuriated the Tory–army establishment, and which threw Unionists into 'fits of rage'. The opaque and ambiguous role of Ireland in the war served to illustrate a deeper problem. The events of Easter Week must be seen within the context of the lack of clarity about Ireland's position in the United Kingdom as colony or home nation. The unsettled issues of the 'exclusion' of Ulster in the Home Rule settlement and the uncertainty surrounding its implementation heightened the ambiguity that defined the Anglo-Hibernian relationship. The outbreak of the war intensified this ambiguity.

Planning the Rising

Plans had been put in place by radical nationalists to foment a rebellion since the outbreak of the war. The infiltration of IRB men on to the executive committee of the 'pre-split' Volunteers had been carried out in order that physical force nationalist would be able to control the movement's potential early on. This infiltration had forced Redmond into affiliating the Irish Party with the Irish National Volunteers in 1914. Redmond did so to control the radical nationalists who would have otherwise used the Volunteers for their own purposes. Various rumours had been circulating throughout the autumn of 1915, such as the possible implementation of conscription in Ireland and the disbandment and disarmament of the Volunteer movements. While Ireland had done quite well out of the war, and while its effects on the island and amongst Catholics and Nationalists were limited, conscription would, by its very nature, change this. Radical nationalists began to capitalise on the concerns over conscription, and thought them real and urgent enough to begin preparations for their Rising. With their normal drive to radicalism and with a belief that this was an opportune moment to strike, announcements were made concerning an Easter exercise for the Irish Volunteers in April 1916.

The strategic aims of the Rising remain unclear, and are a matter of great dispute amongst historians. The choice of Easter was highly symbolic, with its resonant imagery of sacrifice, regeneration and resurrection. The leaders of the Rising sought to link the Rising with this potent symbolism and imagery. They may have also sought to link the Rising to a continuum of Irish rebellion against foreign rule. It was their ultimate intention to 'impel moderate nationalist opinion' towards a more radical stand.[6] Some suggest that the leaders of the Rising had never envisioned a military victory but that they rather sought a form of blood sacrifice: an action to awaken the sleeping radical passions of the Irish nation.[7] The lack of any potential tactical chance for victory would have become especially clear after the failure of Roger Casement to land German weapons to arm the Rising, and in the confusion over the orders for mobilisation of the Volunteers. Even the particularly rational James Connolly expressed a similar sentiment, despite his espousal of pragmatic agitation and socialist nationalism, stating in February 1916 that 'without the shedding of blood there is no redemption'.[8] The Rising would constitute the means by the masses would be impelled to support radical nationalism, though how or why remains unclear.

For the Volunteers, an important aspect of their strategy was that their conduct be deemed above reproach and 'civilised'. Their strategy, to impel the Irish nation's support for radical nationalism, hinged on gaining the support of the people, and therefore they were imminently concerned with creating the conditions which would garner this support. The actions of the Volunteers were noted by prisoners who were held by groups of Volunteers, who generally commented on the 'civilised' nature of their treatment, a sentiment echoed in the Under-Secretary of Ireland's comments on the Volunteer's actions in the Rising.[9] For the British forces, this was not as high a priority, something which makes sense given the context in which they were acting – they needed to restore order and snuff out a military threat on the home front, i.e. their priorities lay elsewhere. Although this distinction in attitude does not fully play out in the reactions to the Rising, as a basis for political behaviour it would come to impact greatly on this situation and the way in which the Rising and the executions were interpreted.

The Castle Document and the Rising Commences

On 19 April 1916 a document which had been circulating behind the scenes for several days, and was known as the 'Castle Document', was published by a Dublin alderman.[10] The Castle Document described a British plan to disarm and disband the Irish and National Volunteer movements, and to arrest their leaders.[11] At the time debates raged as to the authenticity of this document – however, many felt that it was authentic. It has been suggested that it was forged by radical nationalists to provoke support for the Rising amongst sceptics.[12] It did have this effect in some contemporary accounts, some of which supplemented its publication with rumours of simultaneous and secret attempts to enact conscription in Ireland, seeing the two as steps in a broader conspiracy.[13]

Eoin MacNeill, leader of the Irish Volunteers, was one of the inner cadre of radical nationalists who had to be convinced of the necessity of the Rising. He had not been advised or consulted on the plans for the Easter Rising, nor did he support them once he got wind of the plot, although the Castle Document did force him to consider this position seriously. While MacNeill supported radical nationalism, he was described by one contemporary as not being a 'hot headed extremist'.[14] The document had also been given to the Archbishop of Dublin, via Sean T. O'Kelly to his personal secretary, some nine days before its publication.[15] Whether this was done with the intention of trying to get the Archbishop to intervene on behalf of the Volunteers, or whether in order to 'soften' the Archbishop up for the impending Rising, is unclear.[16] The Archbishop's personal secretary, Msgr Michael Curran, and O'Kelly had been boyhood friends, and it is therefore unclear to what extent O'Kelly was trying to keep a friend informed or to what extent he was attempting to exploit this relationship to create Church support for the impending Rising. The document was accompanied by rumours such as of an officer who told a dance partner that 'he had not taken his clothes off for 48 hours' because he and two hundred men were on standby to attack the volunteers.[17] O'Kelly later indicated to Curran that it had been possible that the document was drawn up 'in case of invasion' rather than for its immediate implementation.[18] Regardless of the veracity of the Castle Document, and regardless of its intended audience, it served as a curtain raiser for the Easter Rising, and demonstrates the context in which the events of the Rising must be understood, and the high degree of tension over war issues that dominated Ireland, even before the Rising.

Casement and German Guns

Over the three days following the publication of the Castle Document – 20–22nd April – German arms shipments were intercepted on the South Coast of Ireland. These shipments had been arranged by a former British civil servant, Sir Roger Casement. Casement had already tried to establish a German–Irish link, attempting to raise an Irish brigade amongst Irish soldiers in German POW camps to fight on behalf of the Germans. These efforts mirrored those of previous Irish nationalists such as the formation of an Irish brigade that had fought on behalf of the Afrikaners against the British in the Boer War. Casement's efforts were not successful, as the captives were mainly those who had been inspired by Redmond to enlist in the British army in the first place, generally marking them as supporters of moderate constitutional nationalism. When Casement landed off the west coast of Ireland from a German U-boat, the consignment of German weapons had been spotted, and the ship bearing the weapons, the *Aud*, had been scuttled. The men who were sent from Dublin to meet Casement and the arms shipment mysteriously drove off a pier on their way to meet him.

There has been a great deal of debate as to how the landing of weapons failed so spectacularly. Whether it was atrocious weather, misfortune, or the superiority of British intelligence, the attempt at landing arms was an unmitigated failure. Had the landing of the arms been successful, the method by, and areas to which, they would have been distributed remains somewhat unclear – although a large portion would have more than likely been distributed in Dublin amongst the participants in the Rising. As a preliminary act of the Rising, the landing of the weapons was a spectacular failure, serving only to reinforce British fears that the Rising was a German plot to destabilise the British home front.

Even though the British authorities were aware of Casement's activities, the outbreak of the Rising caught the authorities completely off guard. The Volunteers had shrouded their initial actions as Easter Monday Volunteer exercises and manoeuvres. These exercises were a 'cover' to conceal their real intentions. MacNeill wasn't the only Irish Volunteer kept unaware of the actual intent behind these exercises, as many of the rank-and-file members were also unaware of the full meaning of their orders, learning the real purpose of their mission only at the last minute, and often given no choice to back out.[19] MacNeill attempted to countermand the order for mobilisation once he had caught wind of the actual intention of the leaders of the Rising, despite his misgivings about the Castle Document. This led to a 'fraught' meeting at Liberty Hall on the Easter Sunday, at which it was decided that the Rising would go ahead despite the high degree of confusion over what was to happen.[20] However, MacNeill's countermanding orders, issued on Easter Sunday, served only to delay the start of the Rising rather than prevent it, throwing the entire operation into confusion.

The effect of this confusion was that the number of Volunteers who set out on Easter Monday was smaller than expected.[21] On Easter Monday, 24 April 1914, around 1,600 members of the Irish Volunteers took several key objectives in Dublin, including the approaches from the Kingstown harbour to prevent British reinforcements from landing and marching unimpeded on the city, as well as some locations of political significance, such as the General Post Office. The Volunteers also took possession of the railway depot at Amiens Street, the Jacobs biscuit factory and St Stephen's Green.[22] Trenches were dug in St Stephen's Green to defend these positions. Unfortunately the trenches were overlooked by all the buildings surrounding the Green, rendering the trenches too vulnerable to British sniping from surrounding roofs. The Volunteer strategy was a static one, seizing a location and holding it until relieved or defeated. This made some immediate strategic and symbolic sense in so far as 'territory' could be claimed, but it made little long-term tactical sense as it meant that the Volunteers were committed to various positions from the outset rather than using mobile guerrilla tactics. This left them unable to maximise the small amount of manpower which they possessed. Simultaneous supporting actions throughout Ireland were limited, due in large part to the publication of MacNeill's countermanding orders in the *Sunday Independent*. While simultaneous risings at Ashbourne, Athenry and Enniscorthy enjoyed some success, there was no contact or coordination between them.

The rationale behind the choice of the General Post Office as headquarters is debated. It was a centrepiece and symbol of British rule in Ireland. Its geographic location, near the Dublin tenements, was also important as it was, perhaps, chosen to cause 'maximum bloodshed ... in the hope of resuscitating Irish Anglophobia'.[23] After seizing the General Post Office, Pearse read a proclamation that declared the establishment of an Irish Republic. Pearse was credited with the drafting of the proclamation, which linked this event to the continuum of Irish insurgency against British rule, and emphasised its chivalrous character, thereby representing Pearse's 'greatest aspirations'.[24] Although he was leader, Pearse never fired a bullet. He was later credited with keeping morale up by talking with the participants about the future of the Irish nation, mapping out a detailed national destiny and its links with a mythic past.

Although they captured most of their objectives with limited forces, the Volunteers were unable to take possession of Trinity College. A small cadre of members of the Trinity Officer Training Corps (OTC) was able to repel the Volunteers, and the failure of the Volunteers to overcome the small force of eight who were guarding Trinity College was to have tactically deleterious effects for the Volunteers. Trinity was a location of major strategic significance, providing a base of operations for the British forces in the centre of the city, and providing a vantage point from which to snipe at and 'worry' the men who were in the General Post Office.[25] It was also an important symbol of the Anglo-Protestant community in Ireland. By Tuesday afternoon the small guard of the OTC had been reinforced by more than 140 British soldiers, including artillery, which it was decided would be used commencing on the Wednesday morning.[26] In the meantime, despite the relative ease with which the Volunteers took various positions, the first blood was shed. The Volunteers fired on a group of British Lancers, killing a soldier and a horse.[27]

Although they were initially caught off guard, the British authorities had organised their response by the second day of the Rising. Reinforcements were being brought in from the countryside

and from England by ship. On the first day of the Rising, the Lord
Lieutenant had made a proclamation enjoining all 'loyal and law-
abiding subjects to abstain from ... conduct which might interfere
with the action of the Executive Government'.[28] On this second day,
Dublin Castle made a proclamation officially declaring the city and
county of Dublin under martial law. The proclamation of martial
law was also accompanied by the decree of a curfew. In a move that
would foreshadow later events, Section I of the Defence of the Realm
Act, which provided the right to trial by jury, was suspended.[29]

There was not only artillery amongst the reinforcements in Trinity
– the gunboat HMS *Helga* was also sailed down the Liffey to
prepare to shell the Volunteer positions. The decision to use artillery
may have made military sense, but its use resulted in the razing of
central Dublin. The dilemma is apparent from today's perspective,
but the decision must be placed in its historical context. There were
real fears that the Rising was the first act in a German invasion of
Ireland and therefore had to be put down at any cost. There were
broader concerns, as well, over the fate of the French at Verdun – an
outcome which was not yet certain, during a period of Russian
defeats, Austrian victories over the Italians and the defeat of British
and Commonwealth forces at Gallipoli, all of which had led to 'vast
losses and grave deterioration in prestige'.[30]

Belligerents under Pressure

On the second day of the Rising another event occurred which would
come to have particular significance in the shaping of public opinion
on the Rising. Francis Sheehy-Skeffington, Thomas Dixon and
Patrick McIntyre were arrested in central Dublin by Captain Bowen-
Colthurst of the Royal Irish Rifles. Bowen-Colthurst had only
recently returned from action on the Continent and was described as
being 'by nature excitable and eccentric'.[31] On the Wednesday
morning after their arrest, these men were summarily shot by a firing
squad organised and commanded by Bowen-Colthurst. This was
done without trial, ostensibly because they had violated the
conditions of martial law on the previous day. Sheehy-Skeffington, a
vegetarian pacifist, had been engaged in posting signs to organise a
committee to prevent the looting of Dublin shops.[32] He was described
in one contemporary account as being 'outspoken' but 'harmless',
'being too sincere to have any following' and 'antagonistic to the

forcible methods for which the Volunteers stood'.[33] Dixon had been the editor of a weekly publication called the *Eye-Opener*, and McIntyre the editor of an 'anti-Larkinite' paper called *Searchlight*, neither of whom supported the Irish Volunteers or physical force nationalists.[34] From today's perspective, a reasonable conjecture may be that Bowen-Colthurst was suffering from post-traumatic stress disorder. After the Rising, Bowen-Colthurst was court-martialled for his actions, found insane and incarcerated in Broadmoor prison until 1922. This dramatic and emotive event conveys the context of confusion that dominated the Rising.

While there were other incidents where innocent individuals became caught up in the conflagration, the deaths of Sheehy-Skeffington, Dixon and McIntyre were not easily explained away at the time as being the simple result of 'confused and desperate fighting'.[35] Other incidents included a group of corpses, unarmed civilians, found on North King Street, apparently concealed on purpose amongst building rubble. This discovery raised some questions as to the conduct of the British forces, with some claiming that the men had been held as prisoners of the British troops. This was in direct contrast to the explanation given by the British authorities, that the men had been armed and active combatants. The coroner's report stated that these men had been 'unarmed and unoffending' and that the 'explanation given by the military authorities is very unsatisfactory'.[36] It was ultimately the execution of Sheehy-Skeffington that would have the greatest significance.

By Wednesday 26 April, shelling had commenced from Trinity on to the rebel positions in the General Post Office. The effect was to shatter all glass in the buildings of O'Connell/Sackville Street, and to 'wreathe [the surrounding buildings] in dust and smoke ... throwing open Northumberland House, and making the others mere empty shells'.[37] Wednesday also saw the largest and bloodiest single engagement of the Rising, when the Sherwood Foresters, who had just sailed in from England, marched from the port at Kingstown and were shredded by the defensive posts held by Eamon de Valera to prevent just such an advance. In this single engagement four officers were killed and fourteen wounded, and 216 men of other ranks were killed or wounded.

By the Thursday, the strategic failure of the Rising had become apparent. The shelling of central Dublin had rendered General Post Office a smouldering shell and an untenable position. The green 'Irish Republic' flag which had been raised outside of the General Post

Office at the same time as the proclamation was read on the Easter Monday was now 'scorched a deep brown by flames'.[38] By Thursday, the shelling came not only from the grounds of Trinity College, but also from the gunboat *Helga*. The Volunteers were forced to retreat, attempting to hold a new position not far from the General Post Office. This change of location did not bring about a change in fortune – by this point the Rising was more or less finished. Redmond, who had been previously warned by his deputy, Dillon, that a Rising was afoot, also publicly condemned the Rising on the Thursday.[39] In part, this was because he thought the Rising constituted an attack against the Irish Party as much as against British rule.[40]

Executions, Internment and Aftermath

By Friday, the number of British troops had increased to 18,000–20,000 from roughly 400–500 on Easter Monday. By Saturday afternoon Pearse was forced to accept terms and unconditionally surrender. The captured Volunteers were arrested and marched to temporary holding areas, such as Richmond Barracks. Those whom the British authorities identified as leaders were segregated, interrogated and tried. Over the course of the week, Dublin had suffered 'an almost complete paralysis', with banks closed, no trams, no gas supplies, no postal services, and almost no newspapers (save for the *Irish Times*, which had its own gas supply).[41] Central Dublin had been razed by fire and British shelling. The tactical importance of artillery had increased after the Sherwood Foresters suffered many casualties using 'traditional' infantry tactics. By the end sixty-four participants in the Rising had died. The British forces lost 134, with some 381 wounded, and out of these thirty-five were members of Irish regiments, five members of the Irish Voluntary Defence Force (the Gorgeous Wrecks, so named for the GR, an abbreviation for the royal insignia – George Rex – found on their uniforms) and seventeen who were part of the Royal Irish Constabulary (RIC) or Dublin Metropolitan Police (DMP). Civilians suffered the most in this conflict, with some 220 killed and in excess of 600 wounded.[42]

Even before the Rising had ended, John Dillon MP, deputy leader of the Irish Party, had been in contact with Redmond urging him to lobby Prime Minister Asquith that the punishment of the Volunteers be kept to a minimum lest Irish passions be aroused.[43] He did not urge this policy of mercy out of sympathy with the Volunteer cause – rather, he did not want the actions of the British forces to undermine the Irish Party's political legitimacy and dependence on Home Rule by creating a climate of martyrdom for the radical nationalists. Dillon and Redmond realised that one or two of the leaders were bound to be executed, but they were concerned that there would be wholesale executions as part of a policy of retribution for the Rising. As will become apparent later, it is difficult to assess the success of the entreaties of Redmond and Dillon to this effect. While fifteen men were executed for their actions in the Rising, countless others had their sentences commuted to penal servitude.

Once arrested the leaders of the Rising were tried by field-general courts-martial at which defendants did not have counsel, and with prosecution by a practising barrister.[44] The suspension of the Defence of the Realm Act (DORA) and the imposition of martial law meant that rights to trial by jury were suspended. There was no appeal against a decision made by the courts-martial; sentences, once pronounced, were 'simply carried out'.[45] The man in charge of this process was General Maxwell. Maxwell had been charged with taking 'all such measures as in his opinion may be necessary for the prompt suppression of an insurrection in Ireland' and was 'granted a free hand ... in regard to such measures as may seem to him advisable'.[46] Maxwell described his task in sorting out the aftermath of the Rising as being particularly distasteful, but he applied military precision to what he saw as a dangerous distraction and a potential new battle front in Ireland.[47]

By 3 May the executions had begun, with Pearse, MacDonagh and Clarke all being shot at dawn. Despite earlier promises from the authorities, these men were executed without a priest being present.[48] Maxwell refused to release Pearse's body for burial in consecrated ground for fear that 'Irish sentimentality will turn these graves into martyrs' shrines'.[49] When Clarke was being detained prior to his court-martial and before his execution, he was singled out for derision, with one officer declaring 'This old bastard has been at it before ... he's an old Feinian', after which he was reportedly made to strip and parade naked before nurses in the adjoining hospital.[50] The myths generated in the reporting and retelling of these events did little to delay the process by which Pearse and the others were nationally and symbolically canonised, or dampen the process by which radical nationalism would become more popular amongst the Irish nation.

On 4 May, four more participants were executed: Joseph Plunkett, Edward Daly, Michael O'Hanrahan and William Pearse. 'Willy' Pearse, who was Patrick Pearse's younger brother, was not a leader in the Irish Volunteers, and had had little to do with the planning of the Rising – his fate appears to have been sealed by his family ties. Daly, too, had had little to do with the planning or organisation of the Rising, but he was the son of a prominent Feinian, so questions emerged as to whether his execution was some kind of 'revenge' for the 'sins' of his father.[51] O'Hanrahan was a clerk in the Volunteers, whose execution was interpreted as meaning that if he could be executed then 'the indications were of a massive number of executions to be made'.[52] Plunkett had been heavily involved in the planning and leadership of the Rising. The night before his execution, Plunkett had been allowed to marry his fiancée, in a ceremony held by candlelight in the prison chapel. This story was prominently reported on the front pages of the Dublin newspapers, even those not sympathetic to or supportive of the Irish Volunteers.[53] As these four men were executed, sixteen had their sentences simultaneously commuted to penal servitude. But as Robert Kee points out, it was not these acts of clemency which were remembered or commented on at the time.[54]

After these initial executions Prime Minister Asquith telegraphed General Maxwell, telling him that there should be no more. This was after Redmond had approached him to ensure that no more executions would be carried out. However, on 5 May John MacBride was executed. MacBride had been a rank-and-file member of the Volunteers, and had had no part in the planning of the Rising. He had, however, led an Irish Brigade against the British in the Boer War – an endeavour that had marked him as a prominent radical nationalist, even if not a prominent leader in the Rising.[55] On 6 May, eighteen death sentences were commuted to penal servitude, including a life sentence for the Countess de Markievicz. The tide had seemingly changed. Then, on 7 May, despite the pleas of Redmond and Dillon and the orders of Prime Minster Asquith, four more men were executed: Con Colbert, Eamonn Ceannt, Michael Mallin and Sean Heuston. By 11 May, Redmond and Dillon had become increasingly desperate to stop the executions, and receiving reports of the changing mood in Dublin, they moved for the adjournment of the House of Commons. On 12 May, James Connolly and Sean MacDermott were both executed. Connolly, who had been shot in the ankle during the Rising, was tied to a chair to facilitate his execution – an image which would become increasingly iconic in the pantheon of the myths and memories of the Rising. MacDermott wrote, in his last letter 'the cause for which I die has been rebaptised ... by the blood of as good men as ever trod God's Earth'.[56] While these executions were occurring, it was unclear whether Connolly's was indeed the last. Rumours were circulating of 100-foot-long mass graves being dug outside Richmond Barracks, and the fate of the participants was far from secure.[57]

In the end, there were over three thousand individuals arrested, and over half of these would be imprisoned or interned in British Jails. Fifteen leaders, and later Roger Casement, were executed for their parts in the Rising. Seemingly the Rising had been crushed, the German plot foiled, and radical nationalism dealt a fatal blow. However, two major problems emerged – in light of these events, what power did Redmond and the Irish Party actually possess? And what was to become of Home Rule in Ireland?

Contemporary Interpretations

It is not surprising that initial reactions to the Rising were typified by confusion about what was going on.[58] The pro-Redmond *Freeman's Journal* proclaimed: 'When we search for the motive of it all we are baffled'.[59] When Pearse read the proclamation there was 'no enthusiasm ... the people were unwilling to see ... a person of great significance to the country' and no one saw this as a particularly significant event.[60] Even the storming of the General Post Office was initially greeted with disbelief.[61] There were some subdued expressions of satisfaction that the Volunteers had not succumbed immediately to the British forces, but this was as far as the support went.[62] Initial reactions were, for the most part, confined to shock and disbelief, with some openly wondering 'what sort of city will we have in the morning?'[63] Part of the shock of these events was due to a sense of distance between the war on the continent and life in Dublin.[64] Some reactions to the Rising also indicated not only personal shock at the events, but a disbelief at the 'utter unpreparedness of the Government ... [who] in the face of a huge body of ... openly revolutionary men ... had taken no precautions for defence'.[65] Some were initially perplexed, in so far as they could not understand how the rebels were carrying out these actions unchecked by the military.[66] There was a pervasive sense that events were spinning out of control.[67]

This sense of confusion rapidly turned to outrage. As the Volunteers took the Jacob's biscuit factory, there were accounts of 'howling mobs' screaming at the Volunteers to 'Come out to France you lot of so-and-so slackers'.[68] The shock and curiosity of the crowds became increasingly disapproving and angry as the events of Easter Week unfolded.[69] There were regular accounts of the Volunteers being attacked by civilians.[70] By the end of the Rising, not much had changed when the Volunteers had surrendered and were marched to captivity by a guard of British soldiers. On this march, they were greeted by 'jeers and rotten fruit and vegetables from hostile crowds' and were given little sympathy and a hostile reception.[71]

Beyond shock and outrage, there was also a palpable sense of fear. This fear was not only expressed in general concerns about what the future might hold for Ireland, but some personal letters make allusions to personal arrangements, such as what should happen to their children should anything happen to them.[72] Events that affected family members or loved ones took on a new significance, and perhaps as a manifestation of personal fear, or perhaps as a reaction to witnessing the events around them, rumour and fear led to an expectation of death and disaster at every turn.[73] There were fears about whether or not there would be enough supplies to last through a long siege. Shops were not stocked over the course of Easter Week, and in light of myths and memories of the serious deprivation of the Famine, many contemporary commentaries and histories written in the immediate aftermath of the Rising are contextualised in terms of these concerns.[74] This only heightened the sense of being 'absolutely cut off' from the rest of Ireland, let alone the rest of the United Kingdom, especially as there was a clamp-down by the censors on any news being printed, and in light of the mail boats being prohibited from travelling back and forth from England to Ireland.[75]

The trajectory of opinion over the course of Easter Week, from shock to outrage, was fuelled by fiction as much as by fact. For some contemporary observers, part of the power of the rumours was that they coincided with actual tragedies occurring during the Rising, making dramatic but real events even more potent and terrifying.[76] One individual stated that 'the rumour of war and death was in the air', having started on the first day, and that there would be 'many a year before the rumours cease'.[77] Msgr Curran, who was at the centre of Dublin life as secretary to the Archbishop of Dublin, even comments that he was noting rumours in his accounts, not just to show the 'sensational and varied' nature of the stories that were being reported to him, but also to show the stories which 'the people were fed and which they swallowed'.[78]

With little knowledge of events on the ground 'nobody knew how serious the situation might be' and as a result 'there were rumours of Rising here, there and everywhere'.[79] One rumour had it that conscription was going to be debated the same night as the Rising began.[80] The *Freeman's Journal* asserted that the entire endeavour was an 'insane German plot' and that 'the hand of Germany could be seen in the whole lamentable business'.[81] Towards this end there are many highly detailed descriptions of British army soldiers and officers interrogating participants in the Rising as to the location of German agents and snipers, as to when and where the German army was landing.[82] Other rumours claimed that Verdun had fallen to the Germans, that Zeppelins were on their way to Dublin, and that the German fleet was preparing a landing to invade England.[83] These rumours were powerful enough to make one witness believe that members of the Dublin Metropolitan Police in their tunics and 'pointy hats' were German soldiers who had just landed in Dublin.[84] Other rumours included one that said that the Germans were planning to land in Dublin, from a fleet of troop transporting U-boats submerged off the coast, and there were various other rumours that all of Ireland was subject to revolution or general invasion, or under arson attacks.[85] There were also 'wild rumours' of insurrection in Cork and other places.[86] It was said that as the Sherwood Foresters arrived in Kingstown they were unaware of where they were being sent. These troops had almost no combat experience, virtually none had training in urban combat techniques, and they arrived in Dublin without the bulk of their supplies.[87] Before arriving in Dublin Bay there was a real concern that the Volunteers had captured the port, which would necessitate a proper combat landing, and even at this point many soldiers were still unaware of where they were being shipped, believing that they were about to arrive in France.[88] In fact some, upon disembarking from their ship, started shouting '*merci*' at the crowds there to greet them.[89] Rumours even circulated as to what was going to happen to central Dublin – that gas shells were going to be used to drive the rebels out of the General Post Office.[90] All of these rumours had the effect of 'maddening the Irish people' – something that was perceived as spreading insurrection, popular disaffection and bitterness.[91]

Contemporary accounts are marked not only by rumour, but also by the expression of mixed and often contradictory emotions. This must have been in part due to the effect of the shock of witnessing the violence and destruction accompanying the Rising. For some, there was a sense of ambivalence towards the Rising and towards the participants, with a 'reluctance to express much more than curiosity or astonishment'.[92] The killing of five and wounding of nine members of the Irish Volunteer Defence Corps, the 'gorgeous wrecks' inspired by Redmond and consisting of 'middle class Irishmen over military age', on the first day of the Rising, had been viewed in a particularly negative light, especially given that these men had been on a route march through the Irish countryside, and, though carrying weapons, had no ammunition.[93] Those who had witnessed the death of the British lancer at the start of the Rising had considered it to be no less than an act of murder.[94] These emotions were further exacerbated by the shooting of a civilian trying to extricate a cart from a Volunteer barricade, something which transformed the crowd's mood from 'bewildered curiosity [to] one of hate for the Volunteers.'[95] There were various stories of motorists having their cars confiscated to be placed in barricades in a menacing and violent manner, and these stories did little to endear them to their audience.[96] The facts in all stories like these, either favourable or unfavourable to the Volunteers, were consistently exaggerated in the telling, such that a report of a single individual being shot and killed was rapidly exaggerated into several, or several dozen.[97]

Senses of outrage, however, must be balanced with the feeling that the reactions of the British forces were not entirely commensurate with the actions of the Volunteers, however unpopular. There was a sense that the shelling of the entirety of central Dublin was an extreme reaction. Blame for the shelling, and the death and destruction by Irish and British forces, was placed on the Volunteers and their 'irresponsible' actions. The shelling was greeted with open shock and horror, giving one woman 'cold shivers' and when the *Helga* shelled Liberty Hall, that 'nest of sedition', it made her feel 'quite sick'.[98] Even the *Irish Times* described the shelling as 'reverberating with nerve-wracking explosives'.[99] This shelling was also contextualised within the reported imagery of the war on the continent, and therefore it seemed to the contemporary observers that the war had now arrived in Ireland.[100]

Comments on the actions of the Volunteers and British troops indicate this mixed reaction and ambiguity. One letter describes the Sherwood Foresters as blazing 'wildly away at everyone indiscriminately ... [having become] hysterical with panic and [taking] everyone for a rebel'.[101] In this same letter, however, the actions of the soldiers are described as being typified by kindness and gentleness, leading to a good reception by the people. As word spread of Bowen-Colthurst's execution of Sheehy-Skeffington, there was a negative feeling about the actions of the British forces, a negative feeling that would later be compounded and became exponentially greater as news of the executions trickled out. These stories, however, must be balanced against accounts emphasising the decency of the British troops and officers – one Volunteer, who was particularly young, was given a clip round the ear, and told to 'get the hell home' when surrendering.[102] Another Volunteer, who had given his age as nineteen, was told by a British officer that he should have lied and said that he was younger so that he would be released.[103] In fact most accounts mention that, despite several notable exceptions, 'the British officers and troops treated [the volunteers] with all the kindness and consideration their own position permitted'.[104] Such stories contrast with popular accounts of British soldiers firing at drunks and others who were clearly non-combatants in the streets, such that they 'showed them no mercy at all'.[105]

The actions of the British forces were contrasted with depictions of Volunteer 'savagery'. One man described a prisoner of the Volunteers, who was shot while trying to escape, being 'a terrible case'.[106] Civilian casualties were also often blamed on the actions of the Volunteers, for example – old ladies being shot and having to have legs amputated, and a servant who mistakenly flashed an electric light being 'instantly shot through the head' by a Volunteer sniper.[107] Even where the wounds were incidental or caused by ricochet, etc., the accounts of the day place the blame squarely on the Volunteers.[108] Other stories were of Volunteers luring British troops with the raising of a white flag, only to fire on them upon approach.[109] Of course such stories directly contradicted the impression that the Volunteers hoped to give. Whether these stories were based on fact is immaterial.

Even though the actions of the Volunteers were described in some quarters as savage, in others their actions were praised. In particular the leaders of the Rising were described as being noble,

even by those who were not necessarily sympathetic to the radical
nationalist cause. These leaders were described as good men who
'died like saints ... mystics who kept the light burning'.[110] In this
vein, there were descriptions of the Volunteers which marked them
with a 'common feature' of acting like regular soldiers, with great
self-control, discipline and honour.[111] Their objectives were
described as creating a momentum for the Irish nation to fall into
line behind them.[112] They were seen as having 'brought great and
terrible trouble' but having meant to do the exact opposite.[113] There
were stories of British officers being captured after mistakenly
entering the General Post Office wishing to buy stamps, and not
being shot but rather being forced to peel potatoes for a meal which
they would later share with the Volunteers.[114] Various accounts also
emphasised the discipline of the Volunteers in the General Post
Office, not looting cash registers despite them being full of
money.[115] This story was cast as an example of the high degree of
morality amongst the participants in the Rising, despite their
misguided actions over Easter Week.

A high degree of moral rectitude and civility were important aspects
of the Volunteer strategy, and these were contentious issues in the
immediate aftermath of the Rising. From the viewpoint of today,
while the executions of some participants might have been expected
and not entirely unjustified given the context, stories such as that of
Plunkett's wedding were public relations coups for the Volunteers.
The Volunteers were desperate to maintain order after reading the
proclamation outside of the General Post Office, but looting soon
followed as word spread of their actions. They attempted to prevent
the sacking of Sackville Street without harming the destitute, who had
spilled out from the tenements to loot the candy stores, hat shops and
department stores. Towards this end, Connolly had instilled a policy
that the Volunteers were not allowed to shoot looters, even if they
themselves felt that this was the best way to prevent the looting.[116]
However, this again became a point of contention in making sense of
the Rising, as there were various accounts of the Volunteers shooting
looters in order to prevent their actions.[117]

Ultimately, the accounts of the Rising were marked by as many
claims of kindness as of atrocities on all sides.[118] One commentator
mentions the peculiarity of the scene of the arrival of the soldiers
from England into Kingstown, where 'the whole population turned
out to cheer them', but when this group of Sherwood Foresters
marched into Dublin, they quickly found themselves in the

bloodiest and deadliest episode in the conflagration.[119] For every report of friendly women supplying the arriving troops with tea and biscuits there were counter-stories of the civilians of Dublin being complicit in ambush tactics against British soldiers, or that the tea and biscuits the women were providing were laced with poison to kill them.[120] For British troops, let alone non-participants in the Rising, it must have been confusing, perplexing and exhausting to regularly encounter both extremes of the Irish sentiment towards the British and Volunteers, and this must have especially made these troops weary and untrusting. Despite the confused picture about these events, generally speaking opinion hardened against the Volunteers over the entire course of the Rising, but especially after the British began shelling central Dublin.[121] This animosity though has to be tempered with the disbelief that this could be occurring in Dublin and in Ireland, rather than on the continent.[122] Such confused outlooks were, in part, due to the shock of witnessing scenes such as a man with 'all his lower jaw blown away' through machine gun fire.[123] When the Volunteers had withdrawn from the trenches in Stephens Green, young boys had tried to jump the fence and explore them. However, the Green had become a kind of no man's land between the Volunteer and British positions, and the boys found that 'bullets were quickening their feet … small boys do not believe that people will really kill them, but small boys were killed.'[124]

Amongst women the hardening in attitudes towards the Volunteers was particularly apparent, with regular assertions that these actions constituted a 'civil war' and that the participants should be shot.[125] This was especially true for the poorer women who lived in the tenements neighbouring the General Post Office, many of whom had husbands and relations fighting for the British on the continent, and who depended on pensions for survival. The urban poor had economically benefited from the war.[126] The reaction amongst 'the lower classes' were thought generally to be 'necessarily more complex and uncertain … there was a divided allegiance in that some of their relations and friends were fighting in the rebel ranks, while others fought in … Irish regiments'.[127] While they may have facilitated a 'negative support,' such as aiding an escape, they 'extended no active support … the mass of popular opinion manifested itself as unmistakeably not with the rebels'.[128] This group in particular felt that the Rising, in its entirety, was a German plot.[129] Indeed, for Dublin's poor, the war had produced

financial gain in that it 'provided relief for a congested labour
market through enlistment ... and by the prosperity of industries
concerned with war work'.[130] These benefits, though, were
precarious, not least because this wartime prosperity was dependent
on the weekly payments of salaries and allowances to wives of
soldiers. This group had already felt that their position and their
access to these resources were under threat prior to the Rising,
when in January 1916 it had been reported that these payments
were leading to increasing levels of drunkenness and moral
debauchery.[131] When this money was not available, on account of
the events of the Rising, and with the concern that such payments
could or would be cut off in retaliation for perceived Irish
disloyalty, anxieties ran high amongst the working class of Dublin,
and in particular working-class women.

The reactions amongst the upper and middle classes were typified
by a belief in the British soldiers as 'deliverers from the regime of
anarchy'.[132] Of course, it wasn't just poor Irishmen who had joined
the British army – Redmond had pledged the National Volunteers to
the war effort, and encouraged young men to enlist in the British
army so as to, in a sense, earn Home Rule. By the time of the Rising,
rich and poor, urban and rural had heeded this call, so that for every
one Irishman who participated in the Rising there were eighty
serving in the British army.[133]

*   *   *

From start to finish the actions of the Volunteers, and the way in
which they were perceived, were confused and lacked the necessary
organisation, manpower and tactics to succeed. Beginning with the
debacle of landing Casement's arms, with the digging of trenches on
Stephens Green, and ending in the destruction of central Dublin,
none of their military objectives was achieved. Even in its symbolic
aims and objectives, the Rising initially failed. As an exercise in
public relations, the Volunteers were accused of as many atrocities
as acts of kindness. There certainly is no evidence of a spontaneous
impulsion of the masses to the radical nationalism of the Irish
Volunteers – no mass rush to take up arms in sympathy with the
Volunteers. The moments of greatest symbolic significance, such as
Pearse's reading of the proclamation, perplexed those who
witnessed them. Reactions to the Rising are universally
characterised by a sense of bewilderment. Observers could not quite
believe their eyes. Violence and war occurred on the Continent, not
the cosy confines of Dublin. Ireland in general and Dublin in

particular had gained from the war, and although there were real fears of conscription, it had been, thus far, a British war fought on Irish terms.

Soon after the outbreak of the Rising, the confusion tended to turn to outrage. There were accounts of Volunteer and British atrocities. In the reactions to the Rising, no blame for the Rising was initially apportioned to the British. Even if rumours had it that conscription was to be secretly debated, perhaps enacted, even if the Castle Document was perceived as being a real and imminent threat, it was a more or less universal perception that the Volunteers had picked this quarrel with the British. Therefore, despite some evidence of grudging respect for their bravery and civility, their defeat was never doubted, and the fact that they should be punished was not in question. What would later come to haunt the British authorities was how it was that this ultimately sympathetic attitude could be squandered in the aftermath of the Rising – how fifteen executions demonstrated too much brutality, and was not perceived as showing enough sympathy or respect for the Volunteers. This miscalculation would lead directly to the cultural trigger point and the transformation of popular Irish nationalism. It is, however, important to recognise that this entire process exponentially heightened tensions amongst all individuals in Ireland. Anxiety and confusion now reigned supreme, and when it came time to interpret and make sense of the executions and rumours of the executions in the aftermath of the Rising, these anxieties and confusions led to a great deal of pressure and concern for individuals in the Irish nation. The ground had been fertilised for the eventual moment of the cultural trigger point, and this would lead to the absolute and definite transformation of the Irish nation, from moderate to radical. Although the Volunteers had initially failed to impel support for radical nationalism, the actions of the British authorities would complete this action for them.

NOTES

1   Stephens, J., *The Insurrection in Dublin [1916]* (Buckinghamshire: Colin Smythe 1992), p. 62.
2   Papers Relating to Alphonsus Sweeney, MS. 35454 NLI; 'A Dubliner's Diary by Thomas King Moylan', 1916, MS. 9620 NLI.
3   Norway, 1999, p. 54.
4   See contemporary accounts in *Weekly Irish Times*, 'A Dubliner's Diary by Thomas King Moylan', 1916, Ms. 9260 NLI and in Walsh Papers in Dublin Archdiocese.

5   'A Dubliner's Diary by Thomas King Moylan', 1916, MS. 9620 NLI.

6   Jackson, 1998, p. 203; Augusteijn, 2003, p. 4.

7   See Kee, 1982 and 1983; O'Dubhgaill, M., *Insurrection Fires at Eastertide* (Cork: Mercier Press, 1966); Moran, S. F., *Patrick Pearse and the Politics of Redemption: The Mind of the Easter Rising, 1916* (Washington, DC: The Catholic University Press, 1997) and 'Images, Icons and the Practice of Irish History' in McBride, L. (ed.), *Images and Icons the Irish Nationalist Imagination* (Dublin: Four Courts Press, 1999); Edwards, R. D. *Patrick Pearse and the Triumph of Failure* (London: Gollancz, 1977).

8   Connolly's Editorial in *Worker's Republic* of February 1916, in Kee, 1983, p. 272.

9   Foy, M. and Barton, B. (eds), *The Easter Rising* (Gloucestershire: Sutton, 1999), pp. 177–81.

10   *Weekly Irish Times* in *1916 Rebellion Handbook*, 1998, p. 2.

11   Kautt, W. H., *The Anglo-Irish War, 1916–1921: A People's War* (London: Praeger, 1999), p. 37.

12   Ibid., p. 37; Jackson, 1998, p. 203.

13   'A Dubliner's Diary by Thomas King Moylan', 1916, MS. 9260 NLI 68–9.

14   Letter from Walsh to Maxwell, June 1916, Walsh Papers, Ref No. 385/7.

15   Statement of Monsignor Michael J. Curran to Bureau of Military History, MS. 27728, NLI.

16   For further elaboration on this point see Walsh Papers, and Statement of Monsignor Michael J. Curran to Bureau of Military History, MS. 27728, NLI.

17   Statement of Monsignor Michael J. Curran to Bureau of Military History, MS. 27728, NLI.

18   Ibid.

19   Foy and Barton, 1999, p. 165.

20   Jackson, 1998, p. 202.

21   O'Dubhgaill, 1966, p. 181.

22   Kautt, 1999, p. 38.

23   Fitzpatrick, 1998, p. 60.

24   Jackson, 1998, p. 205.

25   O'Dubhgaill, 1966, p. 233.

26   Ibid., p. 234.

27   Kautt, 199, p. 38.

28   Wells, W. B. and Marlowe, N., *A History of the Irish Rebellion of 1916* (Dublin: Maunsel, 1916), p. 157.

29   Wells and Marlowe, 1916, p. 157.

30   Falls in Martin, 1967, p. 212; Stephens, 1992, p. 63.

31   Kee, 1983, p. 271.

32   Stephens, 1992, p. 51–3.

33   'A Dubliner's Diary by Thomas King Moylan', 29 April 1916, MS. 9260 NLI; Stephens, 1992, p. 50.

34   Wells and Marlowe, 1916, p. 207.

35   Ibid.

36   *Weekly Irish Times* in *1916 Rebellion Handbook*, 1998, p. 25.

37   Sinn Féin Rebellion Handbook, in O'Dubhgaill, 1966, pp. 234–5.

38   Kee, 1983, p. 273.

39   For a full description of Redmond's actions see Coogan, T. P., *de Valera: Long Fellow, Long Shadow* (London: Random House, 1993); Gwynn, D., *The Life of John Redmond* (New York: Books for Libraries, 1971); Finnan, 2004; and Wheatley, M., *Nationalism and the Irish Party: Provincial Ireland, 1910–1916* (Oxford: Oxford University Press, 2005).

40   O'Day, 1998, p. 269.

41   Wells and Marlowe, 1916, p. 158.

42   Kee, 1983, p. 274.
43   Kee, 1982, p. 1.
44   Kautt, 1999, p. 48.
45   Ibid., p. 48.
46   Instruction to John Maxwell in *Weekly Irish Times*, in *1916 Rebellion Handbook*, 1998, p. 43.
47   Falls in Martin, 1967, p. 206.
48   Kee, 1982, p. 2.
49   O'Broin, L. *Dublin Castle and the 1916 Easter Rising* (Dublin: Helicon, 1966), p. 130.
50   Sweeney's Account in Griffith and O'Grady, 1998, p. 79.
51   Kee, 1982, p. 2.
52   Ibid., p. 3.
53   Edwards O. D. and Pyle, F. (eds), *The Easter Rising* (London: McGibbon and Kee, 1968), p. 242.
54   Kee, 1982.
55   Ibid., p. 3.
56   Phillips, W. A. *The Revolution in Ireland 1906–1923* (London: Longmans, Green and Co. 1920), p. 108; Kee 1982, 6.
57   Accounts of Easter Week and After, by Sean T. O'Kelly MS. 27697 NLI.
58   Jackson, 1998, p. 206.
59   *The Freeman's Journal*, 26 April–5 May.
60   Pamphlet from Eyewitness, quoted in Ellis, 2000, p. 25.
61   Norway, 1999, p. 56; Stephens, 1992, p. 7.
62   Stephens, 1992, pp. 39–40.
63   'A Dubliner's Diary by Thomas King Moylan', 24 April 1916, MS. 9260 NLI.
64   Stephens, 1992, p. 1.
65   Norway, 1999, p. 41.
66   Redmond-Howard, Norman, and O'Malley as cited in Kautt, 1999, p. 39.
67   Redmond-Howard and Norman as in Kautt, 199, p. 40.
68   Walton's account in Griffith, K. and O'Grady, T., *Curious Journey: An Oral History of Ireland's Unfinished Revolution* (Dublin: Mercier, 1998), p. 58.
69   See accounts of Comerford, Harling, Kavanagh and Walton in Griffith and O'Grady, 1998, pp. 55–9.
70   Walton's and Thornton's Accounts in Griffith and O'Grady, 1998, p, 58; see also Norway, 1999; Stephens, 1992.
71   O'Day, 1998, p. 269; Sweeney's Account in Griffith and O'Grady, 1998, p. 79.
72   Norway, 1999, p. 46, Stephens, 1992, p. 35, Lyons Account in Griffith and O'Grady, 1998, p. 60.
73   See 'A Dubliner's Diary by Thomas King Moylan', MS. 9260 NLI; Norway, 1999; Stephens, 1992.
74   Redmond-Howard in Kautt, 1999; O'Duibhgall, 1966; Kee, 1982; Wells and Marlowe, 1916; Letter in Edwards and Pyle, 1968, p. 202; Norway, 1999, p. 55; Stephens, 1992, p. 55.
75   Norway, 1999, p. 42, Stephens, 1992, pp. 21–3, 34, Lyons account in Griffith and O'Grady, 1998, p. 59.
76   Norway, 1999, p. 53.
77   Stephens, 1992, pp. 14, 21.
78   Statement of Monsignor Michael J. Curran to Bureau of Military History, MS. 27728, NLI,
79   Wells and Marlowe, 1916, p. 158,
80   *Irish Times*, 24 April 1916.
81   *Freeman's Journal*, 26 April–5 May, p. 1.
82   Kautt, 1998; Brennan-Whitmore, W. J., *Dublin Burning: The Easter Rising from*

Behind the Barricades [1916] (London: Gill and MacMillan, 1996).

83   'A Dubliner's Diary by Thomas King Moylan', 29 April 1916, MS. 9260 NLI; Foy and Barton, 1999, p. 176; Stephens, 1992, pp. 23, 63, 69.

84   Thornton's Account in Griffith and O'Grady, 1998, p. 71.

85   Foy and Barton, 1999, p. 176; See also Butler's 'Extracts from Lord Oranmore's Journal' 1995; Stephens, 1992, pp. 22–3.

86   Norway, 1999, p. 44.

87   Foy and Barton, 1999, p. 165.

88   Ibid., p. 165.

89   Foy and Barton, 1999, p. 165.

90   Norway, 1999, p. 49.

91   Redmond-Howard, L. G., *Six Days of the Irish Republic: A Narrative and Critical Account of the Latest Phase of Irish Politics* (London: Maunsel, 1916), p. 61.

92   Stephens in Kee, 1983, p. 272.

93   Kee, 1983, p. 271.

94   Redmond-Howard, 1916, pp. 3–4.

95   Kee, 1983, p. 27; Stephens, 1992, p. 17.

96   Stephens, 1992, p. 13.

97   Statement of Monsignor Michael J. Curran to Bureau of Military History, MS. 27728, NLI.

98   Norway, 1999, pp. 43–4, Stephens, 1992, pp. 38–42.

99   *Weekly Irish Times,* in *1916 Rebellion Handbook,* 1998, p. 7.

100   Norway, 1999, p. 66.

101   Letter in Edwards and Pyle, 1968, p. 203.

102   Harling's Account in Griffith and O'Grady, 1998, p. 76.

103   Sweeney's Account in Griffith and O'Grady, 1998, p. 80.

104   Brennan-Whitmore, 1996, p. 114.

105   Sweeney's Account in Griffith and O'Grady, 1998.

106   Norway, 1999, p. 45

107   Ibid., p. 51.

108   *Weekly Irish Times*, in *1916 Rebellion Handbook,* 1998, p. 12.

109   Norway, 1999, pp. 54, 56.

110   Letter in Edwards and Pyle, 1968, p. 205.

111   Kautt, 1999, p. 45, Stephens, 1992, p. 79.

112   Letter in Edwards and Pyle, 1968, p. 204.

113   Ibid., p. 205.

114   Stephens, 1992, p. 28.

115   Brennan-Whitmore, 1996, p. 68.

116   Ibid., p. 70.

117   Walton's and Thornton's Accounts in Griffith and O'Grady, 1998, p. 58; Norway, 1999; Stephens, 1992.

118   Foy and Barton, 1999, pp. 177–80.

119   Norway, 1999, p. 45.

120   Stephens, 1992, p. 27 Norway, 1999, p. 45, Foy and Barton, 1999, pp. 178–81.

121   Kee, 1983, p. 272.

122   Stephens, 1992, p. 45.

123   Norway, 1999, p. 44.

124   Stephens, 1992, p. 33.

125   Kee, 1983, p. 272; Stephens, 1992, pp. 24, 36.

126   Wells and Marlowe, 1916, p. 159.

127   Ibid., p. 159.

128   Ibid., p. 159.

129   Lee, 1989, p. 155.

130   Wells and Marlowe, 1916, p. 160.
131   Codd, 1986, p. 25.
132   Wells and Marlowe, 1916, p. 159.
133   Falls, C. B., 'Maxwell, 1916 and Britain at War' in Martin, 1967, p. 213.

6

The Transformation of Perspectives on the Rising

O but we talked at large before
The sixteen men were shot,
But who can talk of give and take,
What should be and what not
While those dead men are loitering there
To stir the boiling pot.

From *Sixteen Dead Men* by W. B. Yeats

Religious, cultural and political nationalism, as expressed in the myths, memories and symbols of the Irish nation, provided the repertoire by which the sixteen executions in the wake of the Rising were contextualised. This context reinforced the notion of Irish organic distinctiveness and victimhood. The previous chapter demonstrated the states of confusion, anxiety and outrage which pervaded initial reactions to the Rising, prior to the fifteen executions after the Rising, and the later execution of Roger Casement.[1] These executions and the policy of retribution on the part of the British authorities triggered a radicalisation in popular perceptions of the Rising, evident in the new popular attitudes towards radical nationalism, through the change of the Irish view of the Anglo-Irish relationship, and the transformation of the reputation and depiction of those who participated in the Rising and were executed after Easter Week.

This chapter comprises two sections. The first will establish the role that Irish national myths, memories and symbols played in contextualising the accounts of these events in the immediate transformation of the perceptions of the executions. The second will examine how accounts of these events *triggered* action on the part of individuals in the Irish nation – literally how perceptions of these events spurred individuals to participate in or demonstrate support for radical Irish nationalism.

Sectarianism and 'Organic Distinctiveness'

The Rising was an attempt by radical nationalists to revive Gaelic culture and to return Ireland to the former glory of its mythical Golden Age through physical force – it was ultimately a movement of restoration.[2] Even though this vision was unpopular, not particularly resonant, and considered radical in the extreme, as a position it was familiar to members of the Irish nation. Nationalism in general, and radical nationalism in particular were predicated on the assumption that Ireland was distinct from its English counterpart. In the aftermath of the Rising, when the executions were perceived to be an over-reaction, comparatively unjust, and carried out in an unfair manner, and at a time when martial law was being applied in such a way as to exacerbate these issues, the radical nationalist restorative project returned to the fore.

The antipathy towards the executions was contextualised within 'cultural truisms' and British behaviour. On the one hand, it was observed that the Rising generally had had the effect of 'stirring up the old bad feeling which all patriotic men hoped the Great War would kill out'.[3] In this context it was reported that 'the feelings of the people became hostile to the Government'.[4] On the other hand, some contemporary commentators more explicitly blamed the process of radicalisation on British policy – and especially contradictions in its application. It was felt that the government had 'made no attempt to explain the real gravity of the Rebellion' encouraging a belief that it had been 'merely a sort of street riot on an extensive scale'.[5] This then 'threw into disproportionately high relief the punishment inflicted on the leaders of the rising'.[6] Denying legitimacy to the Rising and radical nationalists, a reasonable and strategic reaction on the part of the British authorities, posed the question – why then did the signatories and others deserve to die?

One simple aspect of British reactions to the Rising that caused them to be perceived as inflammatory was that they were veiled in secrecy. Rumours of British savagery and over-reaction flourished because the courts-martial and executions were carried out in secret. Secrecy led to a context in which all British actions were subject to exaggeration and made more horrific than they actually were.[7] The dominance of rumour and confusion in the immediate aftermath of the Rising had led to a situation in which exaggeration was rife. It was believed that British policies after the Rising, in so far as they were secret, accounted for the 'the wildest rumours in circulation ... exciting popular apprehensions'.[8] This secrecy, in combination with what was perceived as the summary nature of these trials, did little to inspire confidence in British institutional reactions to the Rising, and this course of action was said to be 'inflaming public opinion'.[9]

Secrecy also contributed to the levels of uncertainty and fanned rumours and exaggerations of British belligerence and cruelty, in so far as no one definitively knew the boundaries of acceptable behaviour under this regime. The result was to make punishment seem random and arbitrary rather than just and transparent. There were reports of prisoners having been often arrested because they were known to speak Irish at home.[10] Others noted in their personal diaries that it was 'not quite safe to be too free with the pen as the most innocent expressions are liable to cause trouble'.[11] Others told stories of individuals being arrested and sentenced to long prison terms despite holding no rank or office in the Irish Volunteers.[12] Eoin MacNeill, who had not known of the planning of the Rising, and had done everything in his power to stop it, despite his misgivings about the Castle Document, was found guilty by the British authorities and sentenced to life imprisonment in Dartmoor.[13] This created confusion as to how far the executions would go. One story went so far as to say that MacNeill faced execution unless he implicated Dillon, who abhorred radical nationalism and was a moderate constitutional nationalist and staunch supporter of Redmond, in the organising of the Rising.[14]

In this context, no one knew what the British policies or reactions were, or why they might be carried out. This led to a situation where it was 'persistently stated that a large number of prisoners were secretly massacred'.[15] Dillon himself alluded to the manner in which the secrecy of the trials and executions was 'poisoning the mind of Ireland'.[16] Further exacerbation of this insecurity occurred because of the perceived injustice regarding the trials of the participants in the Rising. For those accused, there was no defence counsel, on the grounds that it would give them a platform for 'grandstanding', and there was no appeal against their sentence.[17] Accounts of these trials did leak out. Plunkett's 'Pathetic Wedding' was especially heralded in the *Freeman's Journal* being summarised as 'a touching element of pathos and romance', and with the events being described as 'buying a ring, married that night, executed that morning'.[18] These stories served to further inflame rumour and insecurity, heightening the fame of and sympathy for the participants in the Rising, who were now being popularly rehabilitated as 'lads' whose actions were misguided but brave and selfless. As events in the aftermath of the Rising were carried out in secret, without recourse to appeal and in a retributive manner, it seemed that 'normal' political interaction and behaviours had completely broken down. This, in turn, served to heighten concerns in Ireland that the British army, no friend of moderate constitutional Irish nationalism, let alone the radical variety of nationalism, was being given a free hand to govern and bring retribution for the Rising as it saw fit.[19]

Cultural nationalism and the latent expression of Irish organic distinctiveness were creeping into the vacuum of interpretation created by these events. The resultant process of radicalisation is evident in references to 'hundreds of years of difference' and the 'inherent' differences between Irishman and the English/British. These references, in the aftermath of the Rising, were as likely to come from moderate constitutional nationalists as they were from radical nationalists. For example, Dillon was 'thoroughly sympathetic' to the change in opinion while 'filled with indignation' about the executions and the rule which was being put on Ireland by the military administration in Dublin Castle.[20] In a speech to the Commons, he stated that the actions of the British authorities were 'letting loose a river of blood ... between two races who, after three hundred years of hatred and strife, we nearly succeeded in bringing together'.[21] This same speech also drew a clear distinction between Irish 'insurgents' and 'your soldiers' in so far as 'it would be a damned good thing for you if your soldiers were able to put up as good a fight as these men did in Dublin'.[22] Indeed, Dillon, in his extreme frustration with the treatment of Ireland and the participants in the Rising, stated that 'it's our country, though you seem to look upon it as a kind of backgarden of this country that you can trample into the dust without any consideration at all'.[23] For such a prominent member of the Irish Party to express these culturally loaded sentiments indicates exactly how dramatic the contemporary transformation was.

Even for Augustine Birrell, under-secretary in Ireland, there was a belief that the newly popular radical nationalism was 'composed of the old hatred and distrust of the British connection ... always there was a background of Irish politics and character ... this dislike is hard to define but easy to discern'.[24] Other contemporary accounts make reference to the 'old suspicion and dislike of the British army which the War seems to have destroyed gain[ing] a new lease of bitter life.'[25] Local councils passed resolutions to 'press' the authorities to release men who 'have been respectable, peaceable, and law abiding citizens and ... were in no way connected with disturbances'.[26] This sentiment was also observed at an institutional level, with RIC reports noting that 'it must be remembered that hostility to England has always been more or less ingrained in the Irish character'.[27]

Contemporary observers referred to 'English' soldiers as 'reared to regard every Irishman as a rebel'.[28] One woman commented in a letter that when trying to shoot a sniper, the British had used as much ammunition as 'would wipe out a German regiment ... But then the British don't hate the Germans the way they hate us.'[29] The treatment of the Irish belligerents was compared to that of German prisoners, such that 'they don't shoot German Prisoners although they call them "Huns" and "baby-killers" they only shoot brave Irish boys'.[30] Martial law became identified with 'odious memories of *regimes* of "Coercion" which had been fading into the forgotten backgrounds of Irish history'.[31]

There are many examples of how the actions of the authorities helped to fuel rumour and stirred up antipathy and distrust of 'Castle' rule. For example, the murder of Sheehy-Skeffington (detailed in the last chapter) had occurred during 'what was euphemistically called "The Rounding Up of the Rebels" and "House to House Visitation,"' a situation that it was noted was occurring 'while the citizens of Dublin were confined to their own houses under penalty of death if they stirred'.[32] The further persecution of Hannah Sheehy-Skeffington, after the murder of her husband, did little to inspire confidence in the justness and impartiality of the British forces.[33] Even the official British accounts of these events stated that 'Mrs. Skeffington and her boy had bayonets pointed at them and were ordered to hold their hands above their heads' while rooms in their house were 'thoroughly ransacked'.[34] This treatment was being meted out to a woman just widowed and who was popularly known throughout Dublin to be a feminist vegetarian pacifist – recognised as not being a radical nationalist. This harassment was carried out soon after her husband's murder, during a search for evidence. The authorities searched her house twice, the second time arresting and holding the maid for a week. When the house of Thomas Dickson, who had been murdered by Bowen-Colthurst with Sheehy-Skeffington, was similarly searched, a bag full of documents was removed from his house and placed in the house of Alderman Kelly – the same Alderman Kelly who had published details of the aforementioned 'Castle Document' – and it was suggested by some that it was done 'with the object of attaching suspicion to Alderman Kelly'.[35] The effects of such incidents must be understood beyond their immediate context – because the veil of secrecy meant that stories such as these rapidly became wildly exaggerated rumours, and this had the effect of making these stories greatly distressing to the public at large.

Another example of how Irish conceptions of distinction were reaffirmed is evident in the perceptions of Ireland's treatment as being different after the Rising compared to the reactions to similar events in other parts of the Empire. The fate of the participants in the Rising was compared to the fate of participants in the Boer War some twenty years before the Rising.[36] The executions were considered to be particularly unfair when they were compared to the British reactions to the 'more wicked and dangerous rebellion in South Africa'.[37] The *Freeman* alluded to the way that 'men are pointing to the contrast with South Africa where the victorious general who put down the rebellion ... proved to be a wise and prudent statesman ... People are asking, what is the difference?'[38] This level of comparison was common, so that even when the Archbishop of Dublin tried to explain to the Royal Commission what he saw as the causes that lay behind the Rising, he made specific reference to Ireland's political position *vis-a-vis* South Africa, Canada and Australia.[39] This comparison would later become important when, during the negotiations over the treaty to establish the Irish Free State, the British would draft in General Smuts to encourage the Irish to accept the terms.

Popular Beatification

As latent sectarianism and a sense of organic Irish distinctiveness emerges, it becomes apparent that British policies were having a radicalising effect on Irish nationalism. These men, who were at first reviled for their participation in the Rising, were now starting to be reinvented and rehabilitated as 'misguided' but brave and selfless. Their reinvention and rehabilitation were complete when this was combined with religious images of martyrdom and with their popular beatification. This was already evident in the comments of politicians such as Matthew Keating, an Irish Party MP, that the Rising, and in particular the alliance of the volunteers with Germany was 'between an angel and a demon in the cause of virtue.'[40] For the *Nation* this moral rectitude meant that, though they considered 'these men to be deeply guilty ... they were not hard, cynical or self seeking'.[41] Dillon refers to those being executed not as murderers but as 'insurgents who have fought a good clean fight, however misguided.'[42] When Keating's comments appeared in the *Kilkenny People* the paper responded that if public men had 'nothing to say in favour of brave if misguided men who fought and fell, let them be sparing of their censure'.[43] Some papers opined that although they found the pursuit of the Rising insane or abhorrent, the fate of the leaders was a 'sad one' worthy of sympathy, especially for those who had participated after having been 'gulled and poisoned by pro-Germanism' and were ultimately worthy of mercy.[44]

The first stage of resurrection of the participants in the Rising was typified by a belief that they were poorly led and misguided. This depiction soon gave way to other depictions of the morally upstanding characters of the leaders of the Rising, their love of the Catholic faith, and their 'Gaelic' bravery. For one commentator, the men who were executed were 'good men ... who willed no evil, and whose movements of body or brain were unselfish and healthy' and that it was 'mournful to think of men like these having to take charge of bloody and cursed work'.[45] The sense of moral rectitude therefore extended out from a personal trait to the way in which the participants in the Rising fought, so that 'from every quarter we have the same account; that the poor foolish young fellows made a good clean gallant fight ... hence a great wave of sympathy has gone out to their memory from every true Irish heart'.[46] This sense of upstanding moral character and rectitude facilitated the translation of sympathy for the executed into an expression of cultural and religious nationalism. Even amongst moderate nationalists there was a recognition that 'they died like saints though they had brought great and terrible trouble on Ireland'.[47] Other contemporary observers report that the executed men were 'passing into legend' and that a key part of this legend was their 'scrupulously upright characters' and that the 'posthumous fame of Pearse and his comrades tended to encourage pietism throughout Ireland'.[48]

The process of rehabilitation for Pearse and his companions is evidence of the power of the combination of cultural and religious nationalisms in Ireland. In the imagery of this synergy, the restorative project of radical nationalism becomes evident. One example of this can be found in contemporary popular religious expression. The role of the Catholic Church in this radicalisation in the aftermath of the Rising was not its traditional one of providing stability and moral political direction, an outlet for emotional expression of guilt, or mechanisms for prescribed forms of social and political organisation. Instead, the Church was used by the members of the Irish nation in a 'bottom-up' fashion, to express their distress at the aftermath of the Rising – a function of mass emotional expression which had been engineered as part of Cullen's devotional revolution.[49] This process can be observed where religious and cultural practice was curtailed by the British authorities. In order to bury the civilian dead during Easter Week, families were forced to apply for a permit and a pass, and then, at Glasnevin cemetery, 'every coffin passing was opened and the remains examined ... the gruesome duty was ... carried out by plain clothes officers of the police force'.[50] This meant that even beyond the myths and symbolism of the executions, it appeared that the British authorities, in their imposition of martial law, were interfering with the sacred moral and religious duty of dignifying and burying the dead.

However, the link between Irish organic distinctiveness extended beyond the mortal treatment of the participants in the Rising, to their immortal souls as well. There was an explicit juxtaposition between the 'slaughtered Irish recruit' sent to certain death and murder so that 'England might live', and the 'slain Irish Volunteer' proudly dying for the Irish nation.[51] The recruit was depicted as a restless ghost, the Volunteer as 'at peace and blessed by Jesus Christ'.[52] In popular depictions, skeletons and graves 'characterised' the fate of the Irish recruit, whereas the separatist martyr was instead immortal, being 'destined to rise again in the heart of the Irish nation itself'.[53] This was not the traditional institutional role of the Irish Catholic Church, but the expression of a popular and resonant 'folk' Catholicism. The juxtaposition was not just of the fate of the soul, but of the 'anglicised' nature of the recruit, and the Gaelic Irishness of the Volunteer – a distinction which made the portrayal of the Rising as a spiritual triumph more potent and more resonant than a mere political victory.[54] This meant in contemporary imagery that Jesus accompanied the Volunteers into martyrdom –

and this imagery was then tied the deaths of Pearse and his companions, to notions not only of martyrdom, but of resurrection, which was inherent in the core restorative project of radical nationalism. The mix of religious and cultural imagery, of martyrdom and self-sacrifice, discipline and moral rectitude, meant that the Volunteers were perceived by contemporary observers as part of a national tradition based on an 'inherent righteousness and sanctity of a cause hallowed by the blood of the martyrs'.[55]

These sacred depictions of the Volunteers indicated a process that unofficially but popularly beatified those who had been executed, a process that not only recounted their miracle, Easter Week, but also their strong moral characters before their sacred act. References were regularly made to the executed as being 'good men ... they died like Saints ... mystics who kept the light burning'.[56] This was part of a greater 'patriotic cult' which rose up around the Rising, which lent itself to the 'flood of rebel memorabilia, of postcards, mass cards, song sheets, pamphlets, flags, badges'.[57]

This was not a novel use of these particular myths, memories or symbols in Ireland. During the latter half of the nineteenth century, the Manchester Martyrs had been depicted as the 'noble-hearted three', with prayers and the recitation of the Rosary playing a central role in public commemorations of their executions.[58] Indeed, these commemorations explicitly linked death in the Fenian cause with early Christian martyrdom.[59] In the wake of the executions of the participants in the Rising, a temporary structure to commemorate the 'martyrdom' of Pearse and his companions was erected by the side of the Manchester Martyrs memorial in Glasnevin cemetery, despite General Maxwell, commander of the British forces in Ireland during the period of martial law, holding back the physical remains of these men. The extent to which the propagation of this imagery was intentional on the part of those participants in the Rising who were not executed, or whether it emerged as a function of radical nationalist 'propaganda' in its wake is unclear. However, it is apparent that these comparisons were 'conjured' in the wake of the executions in the full knowledge of their potential resonance.[60]

With the process of rehabilitation for participants in the Rising almost complete, all that remained was to link the institutional reorganisation of radical nationalism with the institutional power, legitimacy and authority of the Church. This was accomplished by asserting the 'traditional' Catholic credentials of the 'Sinn Féiners' through their regular and faithful participation in the rites and rituals of the Church. Accounts of participants who were arrested and interned in the wake of the Rising emphasise their religious character, such that they were always saying the rosary, attending mass, and so on.[61] One of the first letters the Archbishop received from internees at Knutsford, drew his attention to the fact that '95 per cent of the men detained here are Catholics' and that there were no arrangements to hear mass, with internees generally being 'treated more like dogs than like Christians and [being] unable to see a priest'.[62] From the internees themselves, there are regular references to the importance of religious practice, such as the saying of the rosary while being shipped in British merchant vessels from Ireland to Britain, and regularly on arrival at the internment camp 'for the repose of the souls of those poor fellows who lost their lives in the rebellion'.[63] Upon their arrival in the camps one internee remarked that 'it was impressive to look over row after row of kneeling men many of them saying a fervent prayer for our latest Irish martyrs who gave their lives in a glorious cause'.[64]

The process of transformation which led to radicalisation was therefore highly dependent on the rehabilitation of Pearse and his companions. The myths, memories and symbols of Irish cultural and religious nationalism provided a well-trodden, accessible and ready-made repertoire to aid in this process. The executed and still living participants in the Rising went from being booed, to being misguided, then misguided but selfless and brave, to morally strong, to finally undergoing a process of popular beatification which lent these figures a sacred quality. The flipside to this process was the demonisation of British actions. This helped to develop the perception, at an individual level through the myths, memories and symbols of the nation, that British reactions to the Rising were inherently unjust and retributive.

Trigger Action

Prior to the executions, before the full effect of the Rising became evident, the Chief Secretary in Ireland, Augustine Birrell, had written 'It is not an *Irish* rebellion … it would be a pity if *ex post facto* it became one'.[65] Birrell was picking up on the apparent and general lack of initial resonance of and support for the Rising by the Irish nation. However, this *ex post facto* process was exactly what was commencing as he wrote these words. The news of the executions began a process of transformation in the Irish nation, causing 'bitter feelings', with the imposition of martial law serving to 'intensify' this feeling.[66] Contemporary accounts of actions which were particularly 'strong' and unwarranted regularly featured in popular depictions of the imposition of martial law in Ireland. Various RIC reports allude to the fact that while martial law provided a 'prompt, ready and effective instrument for the repression and punishment of crime and disorder', it did not take away from the fact that under the surface and despite martial law 'there [was] a strong current of hostility towards England and sympathy with Sinn Féinism'.[67]

While radical nationalism had been a weak force in Ireland before the Rising, after the execution of the leaders of the Rising their message was disseminated far and wide, and heard by those who previously would have rejected them out of hand. The initial condemnation of the Rising was observed as being a function not of 'patriotic motives or the injury done the Empire' but rather that the actions of the 'Sinn Féiners' had damaged the prospects of Home Rule.[68] Though their actions had failed, British reactions created a social context in which their message began to resonate. Though broadly unknown before the Rising, these men would become famous in death.[69] This was noted by contemporary observers, such that on execution those who had been 'without any wide public influence in their lives, became popular heroes and martyrs' after their execution.[70] In RIC intelligence reports from 1916, there is a recognition that 'the shooting of the rebels and the speeches of Dillon have *created* sympathisers with the Rising arousing people outside the Sinn Féin Party ... even though they desired to see the Rebellion put down, they did not approve of the shooting of the rebels'.[71] In RIC memos there was regular reference to the momentum now enjoyed by these 'rebels'.[72]

Contemporary accounts emphasise the cumulative effects that the courts-martial had in raising Irish pulses and transforming opinion. Information emerged day by day in a 'piecemeal' fashion, only serving to heighten concerns and anxieties over these actions.[73] Even the staunchly moderate and constitutional nationalist newspaper, the *Daily Freeman* had identified the 'wholly disastrous' effect that this set of policies was having on popular sentiment, arousing sympathy 'with the victims where nothing but indignant condemnation of their criminal enterprise previously existed'.[74] For Dillon, there was a belief that the British authorities were 'doing everything conceivable to madden the Irish people ... and to spread disaffection and bitterness from one end of the country to the other'.[75]   One contemporary observer stated that mistakes in the implementation of martial law were serving to 'add fuel to the fire against the *régime*'.[76] In light of this, when there were hundreds being arrested every day, it was hardly surprising that there was fear and antipathy towards British reactions to the Rising.[77]

Sir Roger Casement's execution is another case where the perceived implementation of a policy of retribution exacerbated the situation. Whereas Pearse and his companions had been executed in the immediate, and confusing aftermath of the Rising, Casement was executed in a more sober period when the full effects of the Rising were beginning to become apparent, in July 1916. While there was some expectation, even initially some excuse, or even amongst some a desire, for the executions of Pearse and the other signatories to the proclamation, Casement's execution came in a now transformed situation. Casement's fate, however, was sealed. As a member of the British Imperial establishment, as a civil servant, his 'betrayal' of and 'disloyalty' to the Crown were even more pronounced than those of the others. In this way, the situation had a certain inevitability about it – the British authorities could not afford to be lenient, but a lack of clemency further exacerbated and triggered the process of radicalisation in Ireland, fuelling a popular sense of martyrdom for Ireland.[78] Contemporary public petitions make specific mention of this dilemma, claiming that the transformation in public sentiment regarding the execution 'was undoubtedly caused by the punishments inflicted' and the belief that 'another execution so long after will rouse popular feeling'.[79]

The transformation of the Irish nation engendered by the aftermath of the Rising was so complete that it was regularly remarked upon. However, the power of the transformation lay not just in the shift of public opinion, but also in the manner in which it created a sense of agency and urgency. Dillon commented that 'It would really not be possible to exaggerate the desperate character of the situation here ... the executions, house searching throughout the country, wholesale arrests ... *savage* treatment of prisoners, including those that who had no more sympathy with Sinn Féin than you have, have exasperated feeling to a terrible extent'.[80] Those who had welcomed the British troops when they arrived to quell the 'insurrection' were now criticising their use of overwhelming force, and their methods of maintaining the peace in the wake of the Rising.[81] This fostered a belief, suggested by both rumour and outrage, that the rebels were 'patriots, heroes, and martyrs murdered by the "cowardly" British'.[82] The participants in the Rising were being transformed from 'being objects of contempt and derision [to] heroes.'[83] The trigger effect was so thorough that one observer hailed the 'success' of Pearse and his companions during Easter Week, because Ireland had already been 'bled white with emigration and starvation ... if the Sinn Féin Rising cost a few hundred noble Irish lives, it saved hundreds of Thousands'.[84] These feelings were not 'limited to Sinn Féin', noted one RIC intelligence report, but the 'punishment inflicted on the leaders of the rebellion aroused widespread sympathy ... embraced by all nationalists'.[85]

The events of the Rising, and especially the events of its aftermath, forced an elite and institutional reassessment of the role of religion in Irish nationalism. Initially the vast majority of Irish prelates had remained silent about the Rising, or expressed mild condemnation emphasising the extenuating circumstances behind the brave but misguided actions of the Irish Volunteers.[86] But now the Church was forced to accommodate popular 'grassroots' religious expression. Correspondence between Bishops suggested that amongst those who supported moderate nationalism, and even amongst others who were openly hostile to all nationalisms in Ireland, the events of the Rising forced a reappraisal of their positions, with debates raging as to the appropriate manner by which to interpret canon law and the Rising.[87] There was, as ever, no single or unified position on the part of the Church, rather expressions on the part of various individuals who did or did not react to these events within the framework of the Church.[88]

This reappraisal took many different forms. In one case, Bishop O'Dwyer of Limerick had refused to discipline two priests who were sympathetic to the cause of radical nationalism on the grounds that pleas for mercy on behalf of the 'poor young fellows who surrendered to you in Dublin' had gone unheeded.[89] He went on to express his own personal opinion that Maxwell's 'abuse of power' had been 'as fatuous as arbitrary' and that it had served to 'outrage the conscience of the country'.[90] Bishop O'Dwyer was consistently outspoken in public condemnation against British reactions to the Rising, making a pronouncement in the spring of 1917 condemning the treatment of Irish prisoners still imprisoned in British jails. While noting the 'fruitlessness' of the Rising itself, he claimed that it served to 'galvanise the dead bones in Ireland, and breathed into them the new spirit with which England now has to reckon'.[91] Even for other prelates, less sympathetic than O'Dwyer to the radical nationalist cause, it was clear that it was not worth 'troubling' their congregations with a denunciation of the actions which had led to the 'awful tragedy' of Easter week, but that rather to denote the morality of the participants, such that the Volunteers had died 'bravely and unselfishly' even if 'foolishly'.[92] This heavily qualified version of condemnation was ultimately intended to provide comfort to the survivor's of the Volunteers, and not explicitly to denounce Pearse and his companions.[93]

At a popular level, religious nationalism now became a central form of expression of radicalism. Although martial law was being strongly implemented, popular sympathy with radical nationalism was evident the large number of masses said for the men who died during and after Easter Week.[94] The *Catholic Bulletin* proclaimed that 'the founts of our nationality have been stirred to their depths' with a searching of one's heart, and that the expression of this is piety, as evidenced through the recitation of requiem masses for the dead of the Easter Rising.[95] There were even stories, by June 1916, of a little girl praying to 'St Pearse' to intercede on her behalf for a new hat.[96] Curran, and therefore the Archbishop, were very much aware of the 'altered attitude of the public mind towards the Rising' illustrated in the popular support for, and significance assigned to, requiem masses in November 1916 for those who had died in the Rising.[97] General Maxwell had identified this trend, writing to Walsh to intervene in the holding of requiem masses because 'There is a section of the people who are taking advantage of the requiem masses said for the repose of the souls of those unfortunates who suffered death for the leading part they took in the late deplorable rebellion'.[98] Maxwell was especially concerned that the masses were being used as excuses 'to make political demonstrations outside of the churches and chapels in which these masses are said'.[99] These demonstrations included the waving of 'Sinn Féin flags [and] booing at officers and soldiers'.[100] Walsh responded to these requests by saying that while he had had an informal word with those involved to remedy this situation, the 'real difficulty is that there is a very widespread feeling of discontent, already sufficiently strong, ... and growing stronger everyday'.[101] To this end, Walsh informed Maxwell that actions 'taken from purely humane motives for the avoidance of bloodshed may be misinterpreted' within this context.[102] Maxwell's attempts to quell religious, cultural and political expressions of radical nationalism had failed in almost every conceivable way.

Sympathy for radical nationalism went beyond expressions of

public opinion. The Rising stopped recruiting almost entirely throughout Ireland.[103] There was a sense that in the aftermath of the Rising, Irish participation in the imperial war effort was no longer 'an issue of friendship' but rather a matter of power and necessity dictated by the British authorities.[104] There was another aspect to the transformation which was occurring. The debates over the introduction of conscription and its expansion to include Ireland, which occurred on 9 May, broadly indicated the potential for a new reckoning for Ireland's post-Rising role in the empire. Opposition to conscription was widespread throughout the empire, in so far as conscription had barely passed in a Canadian referendum, failed twice in Australian referenda, and was not even proposed in South Africa.[105] Asquith and Redmond agreed that the application of conscription to Ireland would serve to add 'petroleum on a fire', with Churchill commenting that it would not be worthwhile to court a 'serious Irish row'.[106] The Archbishop of Dublin was made aware of this evolving situation, and expressed concern about its possible outcome.[107] The issue of participation in the war effort triggered popular reactions, as farmers' sons would come to flood the ranks of the IRA in 1917–18, desperate to prevent the application of conscription to Ireland and equally antipathetic to British authority in Ireland which had, by now, for many lost a sense of political and moral legitimacy.[108]

War, Famine and Popular Radical Nationalism

By the end of 1916/beginning of 1917, the already existing antagonism to enlistment and the imperial war effort had become even more pronounced, with one priest stating to his parishioners that 'he did not see the use of providing corn, etc. if John Bull is going to seize it all which he will do and leave the people to starve, the same as happened in '47 when John Bull ... created Famine in Ireland'.[109] This was echoed in letters received by Archbishop Walsh from prominent public figures in October 1917, concerned that there would be a 'grave danger of food shortage in large cities ... during the coming winter and spring'.[110] The danger which they identified, was that Ireland was exporting more than the country could spare to aid the British war effort; and these public figures were trying to organise 'for the retention and distribution of such a quantity as will prevent a recurrence of the appalling disaster of '47 and '48' i.e. the Famine.[111] Other priests also said, on the topic of recruitment, that they did not want Irish Catholic soldiers 'in the realm when they were evicting their forefathers' whereas now the British establishment 'wanted [the sons of the forefathers] to fight for them'.[112] Here we see the operation of what I have termed the cultural trigger point – here is the repertoire of past events evoking interpretations of current actions as injustice, informing a sense of collective identity, and creating a sense of agency and urgency found in popular and radical nationalism. The myths, memories and symbols of the Famine were being used to communicate the broader sense of British injustice towards Ireland – reifying the collective identity of the Irish nation by assuming such imagery was familiar and accessible to its members.

The aftermath of the Rising transformed elements of cultural practice and political symbolism. Symbols of moderate and constitutional nationalism, the green flag and the song 'God Save Ireland', were replaced with the 'Soldier's Song' and the tricolour.[113] The 'Soldier's Song' went from a marching song of the Irish Volunteers to the '*de facto*' national anthem of Ireland after the events of 1916, and ultimately became the official anthem of the Irish Free State in 1926.[114] On the first anniversary of the Rising, a tricolour was raised over the GPO.[115] One observer reported an incident in Cork in 1917 when British soldiers tried to pull down a Republican flag hanging over the City Hall, but, finding the building shut, had to hail down a passing fire truck to use its ladders to pull it down.[116] In the view of this observer this story was indicative of the way in which Republican symbols could be found in more and more public locations over the course of 1916/1917 and of how the presence of such symbols 'did much to propagate the Sinn Féin policy'.[117] By the autumn of 1916, even before the release of internees from Frognoch, the authorities noted the 'revival' of 'Sinn Féin' activity, in the GAA, the formation of cycling clubs, holding of social events, advocating the wearing of a 'distinction ring by Irish speaking persons and members of the Gaelic League', the wearing of similar Sinn Féin badges, and the general 'movement of suspects throughout the country'.[118] These visible and tangible symbols, flags, badges, and so on, made palpable and demonstrable the transformation which had already occurred in the minds of individual members of the Irish nation. Even the terminology used to describe the events of Easter Week was undergoing a process of transformation; one schoolchild remembered being told by a nun not to refer to these events as a rebellion, which was 'against a lawful authority' but rather as an insurrection or rising, which denoted action 'against injustice'.[119]

The dissemination of these symbols of radical nationalism was no accident. From the outset, in the *immediate* wake of the Rising, Sinn Féin and radical nationalists also underwent a process of transformation. Frognoch became the site of a university 'both educational and revolutionary and from that camp came the hard core of the subsequent guerrilla war in Ireland'.[120] The reorganisation that began in the camps included not only the making of new links and contacts, but also elements of cultural and political training. Back in Ireland, the authorities had, by this point, also recognised that 'for every one potential rebel ... six months ago, there are now probably five'.[121] On the return of the internees, their specific intentions were to reorganise and to 'try and buck up the language, the Gaelic League and any other organisation that wasn't banned and we could get into'.[122]

After the release of the detainees, and on the anniversary of the Rising, the perceptions, myths, and memories of symbols of this event had been transformed so thoroughly that the 'Irish National Aid and Volunteers Dependents Fund'(INAVDF) could be found holding a two-day fundraising event in the Mansion House, Dublin.[123] The object of the INAVDF was 'to make provision for the families and dependents of the men who were executed, of those who fell in the events, and of those sentenced to penal servitude in connection with the insurrection of Easter 1916, and to provide for the necessities of those others who suffered by reason of participation or suspicion of participation in the Insurrection'.[124] Items for sale in the two-day 'gift sale' included the highly symbolic and the mundane, from Pearse's sword – an antique which had been used in the United Irishmen Rebellion in 1798 – to the block upon which Emmet was beheaded, to a basket with a sitting of Rhode Island Red hen eggs.[125] Other items included a first edition of Yeats' poems, an edition of Connolly's *Labour in Irish History*, a 'Frognoch Harmonium' and a full report from the foundation meeting of Sinn Féin in 1905.[126] There was an accompanying pamphlet produced by the INAVDF, stating that 'a year ago one might have said "here is a garland for the graves of those who died," now one must say "here are the flowers for the altars of those who live forever"'.[127] This transformation of opinion and broad sympathy translated into greatly expanded membership in Sinn Féin clubs throughout Ireland, so that there were 1,039 clubs with 66,270 members in 1917, 1,354 clubs with 112,080 members in 1918 and 1,454 clubs with 118,649 members by 1919.[128]

In this way, 'after the Rebellion, the Sinn Féin movement attracted many new adherents' and the actions of the British authorities was understood to effect 'a feeling of sympathy with those who had previously condemned the movement'.[129] By the end of 1916, the British authorities reported that while there had been little to no Sinn Féin activities, there was evidence of the popular institutional revival of radical nationalism in the guise of the GAA, cycling clubs, social evenings, the wearing of the *Fainne* and Sinn Féin badges, and the formation of a 'Repeal League'.[130] The newly popular radical nationalism in Ireland was evident in a pamphlet published by the Gaelic League which stated that 'the future of Ireland, spiritually and temporally is bound up with the Irish Ireland movement, a movement to free the Irish Nation from intellectual dependence on outsiders'.[131] Over this same period, crime rates in Ireland gradually began to change such that a previous downward trend in crime was beginning to reverse. This was despite the period of initial shock in the aftermath of the Rising concerning the action of the radical nationalists, and the complete disorganisation of radical nationalists after the Rising. By 1917, overall crime had risen by 6 per cent from 1915, and this trend became even greater in 1918 and 1919.[132] Compared to the figure of 1907, crime in 1917 was still some almost 7 per cent lower, demonstrating that it was a relatively quiet period while Sinn Féin and the IRA went through a process of reorganisation. By 1918, crime had risen more than 26 per cent compared to 1907, and by 1919, this figure had risen by more than 77 per cent what it had been some twelve years before.[133] This was true not only of the general overall crime statistics, but specifically of 'agrarian crime' as well.

By 1918, the equation of Irish political, cultural and religious nationalisms was complete. A quintessential example of this was the production of the *Sinn Féin Catechism*. Modelled on religious catechisms, it emphasised the ideology of nationalism and national identity to the Irish population asserting, amongst other things, what it means to be Irish, and how this is antithetical to being loyal to England, as only 'Frenchman can be loyal to France, a Chinaman to China and an Englishman to England'.[134] If an individual insisted that they were Irish and loyal to England, this would be nonsense as 'No one can serve to two masters, no one can be loyal to somebody else's nation'.[135] For the Irish nation, specifically this meant 'hating England's cruelty in Ireland since the beginning ... we must hate England's power that holds us in bondage against our will'.[136]

* * *

There is clear evidence to suggest that the effects of British policies on the Irish nation were understood though the prisms of religious and cultural nationalism. The first part of this chapter demonstrated the manner in which perceptions of the Rising changed in the Irish nation. Initially individual perceptions were typified by hostility, outrage, fear, and disbelief. In the aftermath of the Rising, British actions were considered to be overly belligerent, retributive and secretive. In this context, the reactions of individuals in the Irish nation became increasingly hostile to the British authorities. The executions and the imposition of martial law, both of which seemed as arbitrary as they did harsh, appeared to make the prophesies of the radical nationalists come true, and furthermore tapped into the deep vein of conceptions of Irish organic distinctiveness and latent sectarianism.

The second part of this chapter has shown the manner in which transformed perceptions of the events of the Rising led to participation in and sympathy for radical nationalism. At the institutional level, the Catholic Church, though broadly anti-radical, was forced into a process of re-conceptualising both Canon Law and their attitudes towards radical nationalism in Ireland. In part, this was a reaction to the grassroots groundswell of 'folk' Catholicism, evident in the popular requiem masses for the Easter Week dead, which led to public expressions of anger against the British regime, and support for radical nationalism. The popular beatification of Pearse and his companions, and the radicalisation in public opinion, would go on to undermine support for the moderate constitutional nationalism of the Irish Party, and, despite the efforts of Asquith and the British government, serve permanently to destroy previously held aspirations for a Home Rule settlement. The next chapter will demonstrate how these religious, cultural and political shifts in outlook would have direct political implications in the rise of Sinn Féin from February 1917 onwards.

NOTES

1   From herein these sixteen executions will be simply referred to as 'the executions'. The set of events which I will describe as 'the aftermath' of the Rising will include the executions and the imposition of martial law by the British authorities in reaction to the events of the Rising.
2   Kautt, 1999, p. 57.
3   Report in the situation in Co. Cork, East Riding, May 1916, CO904/100 PRO Kew.
4   Report on the situation in Kilkenny, 1916, CO903/19 PRO Kew.

5   Wells and Marlowe, 1916, p. 203.
6   Ibid.
7   Kautt, 1999, p. 47.
8   *Daily Freeman's Journal*, 9 May 1916.
9   See Kautt for discussion of Wylie and Campbell, Kautt, 1999, pp. 46–9, see also newspapers, including *Freeman's Journal*, 9 May 1916.
10 Letter from Mabel Fitzgerald to Archbishop Walsh, 24 May 1916, Walsh Papers Reference Number 385/1, 5–7.
11 Papers Relating to Alphonsus Sweeney, MS. 35454, 1-14 NLI, 'A Dubliner's Diary by Thomas King Moylan', MS. 9620 NLI.
12 Letter from Mabel Fitzgerald to Archbishop Walsh, 24 May 1916, Walsh Papers Reference Number 385/1, 5–7.
13 Kee, 1982, p. 7.
14 Statement of Monsignor Michael J. Curran to Bureau of Military History, MS 27728, NLI.
15 Dillon Papers in Hennessey, T., *Dividing Ireland: World War One and Partition* (London: Routledge, 1998, p. 139.
16 Dillon's Speech to Commons, in Kautt, 1999, p. 47.
17 Kautt, 1999, p. 48.
18 *Freeman's Journal* April, 26–May 5, 1916.
19 Kautt, 1999, p. 49.
20 Statement of Monsignor Michael J. Curran to Bureau of Military History, MS. 27728, NLI.
21 Dillon's speech in Kautt, 1999, p. 48.
22 Dillon in Kautt, 1999, p. 50.
23 Dillon in Kautt, 1999, p. 51.
24 Birrell in Hennessey, 1998, p. 140.
25 Wells and Marlowe, 1916, p. 208.
26 Resolution passed by Urban District of Fermoy, 25 May 1916 in O'Day and Stevenson, 1992, p. 162.
27 Report on Co. Meath, 1917, CO903/19 PRO Kew.
28 Papers Relating to Alphonsus Sweeney, MS. 35454, 1–14 NLI, 'A Dubliner's Diary by Thomas King Moylan', MS. 9620 NLI.
29 Letter quoted in Kautt, 1999, p. 52.
30 Letter from Patricia Lynch, quoted in Kautt, 1999, p. 50.
31 Wells and Marlowe, 1916, p. 208.
32 Redmond-Howard, 1916, p. 59.
33 See Report of the Royal Commission on the Arrest and Subsequent Treatment of Francis Sheehy-Skeffington, etc., in *The Irish Uprising 1914–21*, 2000.
34 Royal Commission on the Arrest and Subsequent Treatment of Francis Sheehy-Skeffington in *The Irish Uprising 1914–21*, 2000, pp. 144–5.
35 Report of the Royal Commission, p. 146.
36 Hennessey, 1998, p. 142.
37 Hennessey, 1998, pp. 141–2; Lee, 1989, pp. 35–7.
38 *Daily Freeman's Journal*, 9 May 1916.
39 Statement of Monsignor Michael J. Curran to Bureau of Military History, MS. 27728, NLI.
40 *Kilkenny People*, quoted in Hennessey, 1998, p. 140.
41 *The Nation* as quoted in *Daily Freeman's Journal*, 9 May 1916.
42 Dillon in Kautt, 1999, p. 50.
43 *Kilkenny People*, quoted in Hennessey, 1998, p. 140.
44 *Dungannon Democrat* in Hennessey, 1998, p. 141.
45 Stephens, 1992, pp. 89, 92.

46   Murphy in Hennessey, 1998, p. 142.
47   Letter cited in Edwards and Pyle, 1968, pp. 204–5.
48   Kee, 1982, p. 15; *Contemporary Review* as cited in Whyte, J. H., '1916 – Revolution and Religion' in Martin, 1967, p. 224.
49   See especially the work of Drumm, 1996.
50   *Freeman's Journal*, April 26–May 5, 1916.
51   Ellis, 2001, p. 28.
52   Ibid.
53   Ibid., p. 29.
54   Ibid., p. 28.
55   Ibid., p. 30.
56   Letter in Kautt, 1999, p. 52.
57   Hart, P., *The IRA and its Enemies: Violence and Community in Cork, 1916-1923* (Oxford: Oxford University Press, 1998), p. 207; Novick, B., 'Propaganda I: Advanced Nationalist Propaganda and Moralistic Revolution, 1914–1918' in Augusteijn, J. (ed.), *The Irish Revolution, 1913–1923* (New York: Palgrave, 2002), pp. 38–40.
58   McGee, 2001.
59   Ibid.
60   See Ellis, 2001, for a description of this process.
61   Brennan-Whitmore, 1996, p. 117.
62   Letter dated 29 May 1916, 385/7 Walsh Papers.
63   Two letters from P. O'Connor, Irish Prisoner, Knutsofrd, 20 June 1916, MS. 4615.
64   From account of internee, MS. 31326 NLI.
65   Birrel in Kee, 1982, p. 1.
66   O'Malley in Kautt, 1999, p. 50.
67   Report on Co. Tyrone, 1916, CO 903/19 PRO Kew.
68   Report on the situation in Co. Tyrone, 1916, CO 903/19 PRO Kew.
69   See Stephens, 1992, pp. 87–92.
70   Wells and Marlowe, 1916, p. 208.
71   Report in the situation in Co. Clare, May 1916, CO904/23 PRO Kew.
72   Minutes for Release of Interned Sinn Féiner Denis Doran, 23 August 1916, CSB Files, 3/716/24 NAI.
73   Wells and Marlowe, 1916, p. 205.
74   *The Daily Freeman's Journal*, 9 May 1916.
75   Dillon in Kautt, 1999, pp. 50–1.
76   Wells and Marlowe, 1916, p. 207.
77   Kautt, 1999, p. 49.
78   See especially Kee, 1982.
79   Draft Petition for Casement, 385/6, Walsh Papers.
80   Dillon in Kee, 1982, p. 10.
81   Kautt, 1999, p. 51.
82   Ibid.
83   Report on Co. Tyrone, 1916, CO 903/19 PRO Kew.
84   'Miscellaneous Mimeograph' possibly by Msgr Curran or alternatively S. T. O'Kelly, Special Papers/Political Papers, Archbishop Walsh.
85   Report on Co. Meath, 1916, CO903/19 PRO Kew.
86   Miller, 1987, p. 198.
87   Correspondence between Bishop Foley and Bishop O'Dwyer, in Kautt, 1999, p. 46.
88   McHugh, 1966, p. 198.
89   Letters of correspondence between Maxwell and Bishop in O'Dwyer, MS. 32,695; Miller, 1987, p. 198.
90   Hennessey, 1998, p. 142; letters of correspondence between Maxwell and Bishop in O'Dwyer, MS. 32,695; Miller, 1987, p. 198.

91   'Important Pronouncement by Rev. Dr O'Dwyer, Bishop of Limerick, printed material, in Special Papers/Political Papers, Walsh Papers.
92   Whyte, 1967, p. 221.
93   Ibid.
94   Kee, 1982, p. 15.
95   *Catholic Bulletin* as cited in Whyte, 1967, p. 224.
96   Kee, 1982, p. 15.
97   Statement of Monsignor Michael J. Curran to Bureau of Military History, MS. 27728, NLI.
98   Letter from Maxwell to Walsh, June 1916 Walsh Papers, Ref No. 385/7.
99   Ibid.
100   Ibid.
101   Letter from Walsh to Maxwell, 26 June, 1916 Walsh Papers, Ref No. 385/7.
102   Ibid.
103   See especially CSB Files, 3/716/24 NAI; Intelligence Reports in CO 904 100 PRO Kew.
104   Finnan, 2000, p. 187.
105   Ibid., p.185.
106   Statement of Monsignor Michael J. Curran to Bureau of Military History, MS. 27728, NLI.
107   Ibid.
108   Hart, 1999, 219; Kee, 1982, 8. For further in depth analysis of the role of conscription and its effect on the rural population of Ireland, see Boyce in Boyce and O'Day, 2004 and Chapter 9.
109   CSB Files, 1913–20 3/716/24 NAI.
110   Letter from De Markievicz, Ginnell, Lynn (from Sinn Féin Offices) to Walsh, 6 October 1917, Walsh Papers 389 I.
111   Ibid.
112   CSB Files, 1913-20 3/716/24 NAI.
113   Alter, 1987, p. 16.
114   Ibid., p. 17.
115   Account of Maire Comerford in Griffith and O'Grady, 1998, p. 107.
116   Cork in Easter Week, MS. 31330 NLI.
117   Cork in Easter Week MS. 31330 NLI; account of Maire Comerford in Griffith and O'Grady, 1998, 107.
118   CSB Files, 1913–20, dated 5 September, 1916 3/716/24 NAI.
119   Account of Patrick Clare, MS. 33571.
120   Sweeney's account in Griffith and O'Grady, 1998, p. 94.
121   CSB Files, 1916 3/716/24 NAI.
122   Walton's account in Griffith and O'Grady, 1998, p. 98.
123   Walsh Papers, Special Papers/Political Papers.
124   From INAVDF Hand Bill, 1917 Walsh Papers 385/1, 5–7.
125   NAVDF Gift Catalogue, April 21–22, 1917, Archbishop Walsh Papers, Special Papers/Political Papers.
126   Ibid.
127   From pamphlet entitled 'Aftermath of Easter Week' September, 1917 produced by INAVDF, in Walsh Papers, Special Papers/Political Papers.
128   County Inspector's Reports, 1916, CO 903/19 PRO Kew.
129   Reports on Dublin and Kildare, 1916, CO903/19 PRO Kew.
130   Memo, Irish Command, 5 September 1916, CSB Files, 3/716/24 NAI.
131   Appeal by the Gaelic League, March 1917, Walsh Papers, Special Papers/Political Papers.
132   The extent to which the represented the extent of a change on the Irish scene, versus the extent to which it demonstrates altered perceptions of what kinds of crimes should be

or must be reported is debatable. This is an issue which, had time and space permitted, I should have liked to explore more fully. I have, however, used these statistics in this instance to demonstrate that there was some sort of general shift in Irish society at this point in time.

133 See Inspector's Reports, CO 903/19 PRO Kew.
134 *Sinn Féin Catechism*, by Darrel Figgis, 1918, Archbishop Walsh Papers, Special Papers/Political Papers.
135 Ibid.
136 Ibid.

7

The End of Moderate Nationalism

This chapter will trace the fall of the Irish Party, and the manner in which the Irish Party, and its leader, John Redmond, became increasingly alienated from and unrepresentative of the Irish nation. It will therefore chart the fall of the Irish Party as a result of its failures to secure Home Rule between May 1916 and April 1918, ultimately leaving no viable 'Imperial solution' to the Irish question. This series of events, when combined with the unleashing of support for radical nationalism, and the resultant rise of Sinn Féin, served to permanently close the door on a moderate and constitutional solution to Irish nationalist demands as imagined prior to the Rising. This chapter and the next will contend that the willingness of the Irish Party to accept the exclusion of Ulster as part of a Home Rule settlement, when combined with the 'outrage' emanating from the Irish nation in the aftermath of the Rising, reinvigorated the previously moribund and stagnant radical nationalist institution of Sinn Féin. This had the effect of redefining a sense of Irish identity and agency. Although the release of the 1916 internees and the reorganisation of Sinn Féin had a major invigorating effect on radical nationalism in Ireland, the success of radical nationalism depended in large part on the apathy felt for the discredited moderate nationalists and their constitutional means. Their collapse reinforced the burgeoning sympathy with, and resonance of, the radical nationalist agenda in Ireland.

The End of the Irish Party

As has been discussed in earlier 'pre-Rising' chapters, the Home Rule question had dominated Irish politics since at least the formation of the Home Government Association in 1870. Whether this desire for some form of Home Rule grew out of an inherent fear of the return of the Famine, concerns over the subjugation of Irish Catholics in the Union, or an expression of the political desires of a rising Catholic middle class, it was a dominant issue in Irish politics. The Home Rule question had dominated Irish politics to such an extent that prior to the outbreak of the First World War, Ireland had witnessed the formation of armed paramilitary groups, and even saw a rebellion in the British army in response to these orders to disarm Ulster Unionists opposed to a Home Rule settlement. It had seemed as though these tensions had disappeared in the frenzy of patriotic and pro-imperial sentiment that accompanied the outbreak of the First World War. This impression was reinforced by the apparent decline and absence of radicalism amongst nationalists and unionists after August 1914. The reasons for this were the outbreak of the war and the passage of the Home Rule Act, despite its suspension for the duration of the War.

The Irish Party had benefited from this passage of events. It had dominated nationalist politics since the end of the nineteenth century, because of its extensive political network throughout Ireland. It held a grip on the politics of the Irish nation not least because it had been able to apparently deliver the ultimate prize after forty years of nationalist agitation. The Home Rule Act was more than had been previously gained by Irish nationalists, and promised as much freedom as Ireland had enjoyed in the mythical golden age before the Act of Union. For the Irish Party, its elites and supporters, this gain was thought to be the result of shrewd politicking on the part of Redmond.[1] One incident held up as an example of this was Redmond's taking control of the executive of the Volunteer movement, and its subsequent co-optation to the will of the Party. His ability to deliver the support of the Volunteers to the imperial war effort at the outbreak of the war, from a moderate nationalist's perspective, showed Irish loyalty, and evidence of how much Ireland deserved Home Rule. It was also an action that was intended to allay Unionist fears of Irish extremism, again by showing Irish loyalty to the Imperial project. In addition, the Irish Party's alliance with the Liberal Party, something on which the Liberal Party had depended to retain power throughout the end of the nineteenth century/ beginning of the twentieth centuries, while no longer politically necessary, provided evidence for the Irish Party supporters of how their political loyalty in Westminster ultimately paid dividends. In short, the achievement of Home Rule appeared to the party and its supporters to be the result of the political manoeuvring of Redmond, both at Westminster and at home.

The Easter Rising and British reactions to the Rising damaged the party's vision of moderate nationalist politics in Ireland. As was shown in the previous three chapters, the Rising re-stimulated the resonance of Irish national myths, memories and symbols, reignited nationalist passions, and unleashed sectarian extremes that lay behind Irish nationalist demands for self-rule. For example, the manner in which these events had brought recruitment to the British army to a standstill has already been established, and it is a good example of the imperial legitimacy crisis in Ireland. Irish apathy if not outright antipathy towards the British army, prior to the Rising, at mass and elite levels, had apparently been overcome by Redmond's political will. He ensured that British recruiting efforts were at least respected, if not supported. The aftermath of the Rising – its effects on British perceptions of Irish loyalty, and Irish perceptions of British rule – struck at the very core of the party's strategy and Redmond's reputation.

The Irish Party's demise began with its reaction to the transformation and radicalisation of the Irish nation after the Rising. The party initially hesitated to react strongly to the executions after the Rising, and then hesitated again when the transformation of the Irish nation became popularly apparent. The previous chapter established Dillon's and Redmond's reactions in the Commons to the executions of Pearse and his companions and to the British authorities' implementation of martial law; however, it rapidly became apparent that Redmond and the party lacked any power to effectively lobby Asquith to prevent these events from occurring. Dillon had observed that military rule in Ireland was 'doing everything in its power to turn people against you and us'.[2] Asquith, despite assuring Redmond that the executions had ended, either was 'out of the loop' in Maxwell's decision-making process as regards the carrying out of sentences in Ireland, or was misrepresenting the truth to Redmond. Redmond's political power and personal reputation was being made to look dependent on individuals and institutions who simply disregarded his requests.

In the immediate aftermath of the Rising, therefore, it seemed as though the actions of the Irish Party's politicians, and their ability to influence British government policy, were not in tune with the transformed Irish nation. Even the 'mouthpiece' of the party was forced to change its opinions on the Rising and its participants. The *Freeman's Journal* went from condemning the Rising and its leaders to an attitude of grudging respect, and it generally followed the grassroots process of transition regarding the depiction of Pearse and his companions – first as 'devils' then eventually as saints.[3] This change occurred after its 'dogmatic' reporting of the party line almost ruined its reputation, with its circulation dropping precipitously as compared to that of the *Irish Independent* in October 1916.[4] Redmond, amongst others in the Irish Party, now recognised that it was necessary to act if the party was to have any chance of political survival. The question then arose as to whether or not action meant changing in the party's strategy – Dillon wanted to break the party's traditional alliance with the Liberals and become a true party of opposition, in order to put forward the case for Irish nationalism.[5] Redmond hesitated – wanting to see what response would be put forward by Asquith and his cabinet.[6] Redmond had staked his political career and political ambitions for Ireland on supporting the British war effort – he could not simply withdraw from this course now.

Initially this appeared the right decision, as it seemed as though the Irish Party would be able to turn these events to their advantage by gaining the immediate implementation of their ultimate ambition, Home Rule. As the executions were taking place, Asquith announced that he would visit Ireland to gain a first-hand knowledge of the Irish situation. Prior to his departure, Asquith had stated that the system of government in Ireland had 'completely broken down' and that some form of Home Rule, as agreed to at the start of the War, would have to be implemented to solve Irish problems.[7] This heartened nationalists who thought that they would finally have Home Rule as it was passed by Westminster in 1914, i.e. Home Rule for all of Ireland.

In the immediate aftermath of the Rising, Asquith met with Nationalists and Unionists, moderate and radical in Ireland. Asquith's visit undermined support for the Irish Party and moderate constitutional nationalism in Ireland, by serving to reinforce the apparent effectiveness of the actions of the radical nationalists.[8] There was the popular perception that there had been no movement on Ireland and Home Rule prior to the Rising, because of the war. The actions of Pearse and his companions sparked the British to address this situation. Asquith's visit helped to transform and radicalise popular political opinion in favour of the radical nationalists, as the

Rising, as foolish as it initially had seemed, had apparently forced a change in policy on the part of the British government which had previously seemed impossible.[9] On his visit, Asquith visited men being held in Dublin jails who had participated in the Rising. For these men who had not yet been shipped off to prisons in England and Wales, Asquith's visit had the effect of transforming them from being 'despondent' to 'insulting their guards, throwing up their caps and shouting victory'.[10] The county inspectors made reference to the way in which Asquith's actions, through his speeches and visit, when 'coupled with the executions of the leaders completely changed the feeling of large numbers of the people'.[11] Another wrote that 'it was felt that the rebellion had done more than ten years of constitutional agitation to convince the Government of the urgent necessity of Home Rule'.[12] Even General Maxwell believed that 'there is a growing feeling that out of the Rebellion more has been got than by constitutional methods'.[13] Asquith's visit bolstered the legitimacy of radical nationalism in Ireland – even whilst his regime was in the middle of carrying out a policy of suppression.

On his return from Ireland, Asquith reported to the Commons that the Rising had created 'a unique opportunity for a new departure for a settlement of outstanding problems' and reasserted that Castle Rule in Ireland had irreparably collapsed.[14] Some British critics and observers believed that the reaction of the British authorities to the Rising was 'verification of all that [Sinn Féin] had feared and prophesised, and for which they had until that point been looked upon as fools and scaremongers'.[15] However, Asquith's actions on Ireland must be contextualised, in so far as they went beyond immediate governmental concerns over the fate of Ireland itself. The situation in Ireland was alienating US support for the Allied war effort, and it was causing much concern amongst the Imperial Dominions, which was having a detrimental effect on recruiting efforts.[16] The Government was receiving reports from the British Ambassador in Washington that there was now a 'wave of fury sweeping through Irish America originating with the executions'.[17] This concern was particularly keenly felt by the British Government, acutely aware of the upcoming American presidential election in the autumn of 1916.[18] The cabinet worried that Irish-American attitudes towards Westminster were being shaped by the reactions to the Rising, which had served to horrify and radicalise Irish-Americans. This had the potential effect up of forcing a change towards a pro-German stance in the US presidency.

Asquith now approached Lloyd George about brokering the negotiations over Home Rule in Ireland. Lloyd George was already serving as minister for munitions, and this position made him aware of the potential damage that a change in the outlook of the USA could have on the supplies of munitions.[19] By 24 May, Lloyd George agreed to take on this special role to negotiate the implementation of a set of proposals entitled 'Headings of a Settlement as to the Government of Ireland'.[20] These proposals were based on the Home Rule Act of 1914, but were altered to include the exclusion of six counties in Ulster, although whether or not there was a time limit on the exclusion of this six-county entity was left vague.[21] This meant that these negotiations began at a point before the passage of the Home Rule Act in 1914, which did not include a provision for the exclusion of Ulster, though whether exclusion would have always occurred is a matter for debate. These Lloyd George-led negotiations were therefore beginning where the failed Buckingham Palace negotiations of the summer of 1914 had left off. These 1914 negotiations had occurred when tensions were at their highest, and Ireland was on the brink of civil war.[22] This new set of negotiations, in the aftermath of the Rising, took place between Northern Unionists, led by Carson, and Nationalists, as represented by Redmond and the Irish Party. A third group would come to a play a significant role in these negotiations as they progressed, the Southern Unionists, led by Lords Lansdowne and Long.

The Cabinet had two preconditions for these negotiations. First they determined that the negotiations would pick up where the Buckingham Palace negotiations had left off. This meant a rehash of the same issues that had dominated the previous sets of negotiations – would Ulster be excluded from a Home Rule settlement, and if so, for how long? Indeed, the second and unstated, though implicit, precondition for these negotiations was that the period of exclusion of Ulster from Home Rule would be indefinite. From the outset the Cabinet believed in exclusion lasting for as long as desired by Ulster Unionists. This is not surprising because, though Asquith's Cabinet was a broadly Liberal wartime coalition, it had Conservative and Unionist members who were hostile to any Home Rule settlement in Ireland. Redmond and the Irish Party had been offered a position in Asquith's Cabinet, but had declined on the grounds that 'the principles and history' of the Irish Party made it impossible to accept a position in the cabinet.[23] Now Redmond and the party found the institutional reins of power beyond their grasp, initially leaving them unable to prevent the British policy of retribution after the Rising, and now unable to effect the setting of the parameters for the negotiations over Home Rule. They were caught in a political no-man's land – lacking a strategic advantage in power and position.

The importance of the proposal to exclude a part of north-eastern Ireland – whether it was the full nine counties of the historical province of Ulster, only six of them, or simply the four with a majority Unionist population – cannot be over-emphasised.[24] Even though it had almost led to civil war before the outbreak of the First World War, Redmond now believed that the Irish dilemma could ultimately be solved by compromise. He recognised that there was most likely no way to immediately convince Ulster Unionists, led by Carson, to accept an all-Ireland implementation of Home Rule. There was also a recognition that the party lacked the political strength to force the Cabinet to make Unionists accept Home Rule without exclusion. Therefore he concluded that it was up to the Irish nation themselves to convince the British government and their Unionist compatriots of their deserving of Home Rule. In this way, Redmond did not stray from his 1914 strategy of committing the National Volunteers to the war effort. From this perspective, Redmond calculated that the exclusion of a six-county entity in Ulster might be a *temporary* price worth paying while convincing the Unionists of the benefits of Home Rule. However, any form of exclusion of the north-east of Ireland for any period of time was very difficult, if not impossible to 'sell' to nationalists outside of the Irish Party elite.[25] By the time Redmond and the Irish Party realised this, they had been backed into a political corner – to oppose exclusion meant the collapse of the Home Rule negotiations, but to push on meant accepting the principle of exclusion. Despite the passage of the Home Rule Bill in 1914, which, apparently, applied to all of Ireland, they were now forced to accept some form of exclusion as a precondition for Home Rule.

Lloyd George had shown the Home Rule proposals which he had put forward to the Cabinet to Carson and Redmond by 29 May.[26] Negotiations were carried out individually, so that Lloyd George met with Carson and Redmond at separate times. This enabled Lloyd George to give differing impressions of the issue of exclusion to Carson and Redmond. Redmond gained assurances that the exclusion of the proposed six-county entity of Tyrone, Fermanagh, Armagh, Down, Londonderry and Antrim was temporary. Lloyd George had told Redmond that he 'placed his life upon the table and would stand or fall by the agreement come to'.[27] Simultaneously, Lloyd George had provided a *written* assurance to Carson that 'we must make it clear that at the end of the provisional period Ulster does not, whether she wills it or not, merge in the rest of Ireland'.[28]

In the meantime, there were heavy defeats for the British navy at Jutland on 31 May. Southern Unionists took this opportunity to declare that the time was not right for negotiations over Home Rule, because the war was a much more pressing issue than the Irish situation. They therefore declared that they could no longer negotiate over this issue. They wanted the entire project to be shelved, and they had the political clout, if they could ally themselves with sympathetic Conservatives, to wreck the Bill and bring down Asquith's Cabinet. Like the Northern Nationalists, who were concerned about being left behind in the area of exclusion in Ulster, Southern Unionists felt that exclusion would render them a vulnerable minority in a Home Rule entity dominated by Nationalists and Catholics. In the Cabinet, they threatened, both explicitly and implicitly, to wreck the Bill and bring down the government, and generally to do everything in their power to prevent the implementation of Home Rule.[29]

At the same time Northern Nationalists were aghast that Redmond and the Irish Party could conspire to leave them out of a settlement. Ulster Unionists were also broadly in opposition to this development Carson, encountering Ulster Unionist Council hostility, proclaimed that the Unionists should support this measure because of 'Imperial necessity'.[30] While there were various questions and concerns over issues such as parliamentary representation for the area of Home Rule after its implementation, most of the basic factors for an agreement appeared to be in place. Despite the opposition within the Unionist and Nationalist camps, Carson and Redmond were both supporting the efforts of Lloyd George, and participating in the negotiations. Therefore, despite the apparent shakiness of popular support for their efforts, both of these politicians were carrying their parties, however reluctantly, with them.

Redmond, in particular, found that the support for the plan was patchy. Beyond the Irish Party elites, and outside of Westminster, this proposed settlement was unpopular. There was a great deal of concern amongst rank-and-file nationalists that the exclusion of the six-county entity would be permanent, despite the assurances of Redmond and the Irish Party. One commentator observed that 'everywhere [in the North] the proposed terms were rejected with contempt'.[31] There was a sense that 'once we assent to the theory of partition ... we cease to believe in Ireland's national entity ... if once we admit this theory of exclusion ... there is no knowing how far or into what absurdities it will carry us'.[32] For the Irish Party the disagreement over the interpretation of whether or not exclusion was permanent or temporary was 'more apparent than real ... it actually represents two legitimate views of the same proposal, and may easily be cleared up afterwards'.[33] This explanation wasn't enough, however, to allay Northern Nationalist fears.

Nationalist critics pointed out that the population of the proposed area of exclusion in Ulster was being created in such a way as to ensure a Protestant majority; this was despite its returning seventeen Nationalist MPs to sixteen Unionist ones in the Imperial Parliaments.[34] In order to forge ahead, the Irish Party systematically attempted to convince Nationalists in the area of exclusion, particularly those in Tyrone and Fermanagh, that the arrangement was temporary, and that the final fate of their region would be sorted out at an Imperial conference at the end of the war.[35] Out of the six counties to be excluded, Tyrone and Fermanagh were the only two to have a Catholic majority, while some other areas, such as Derry City, also had large concentrated Catholic populations.[36] Yet other critics pointed out that there was no real choice being presented in the Lloyd George led negotiations – the options were either this form of incomplete Home Rule, or martial law. The effect of such a choice would be to 'traffick the grave of St Patrick and the See of our only Cardinal to the men whose oath of initiation is to "wade knee deep in Papish blood"'.[37] This would mean ceding the fate of those Catholics and Nationalists in the exclusion area to a 'people in whom ... religious jealousy and sectarian distrust are as rampant as in the days when we were struggling for emancipation' and it would mean that those left behind would be 'consigned to an Egyptian bondage that nobody alive is in a position to say will pass away in this generation or the next'.[38]

These sentiments were crystallised in the Catholic Church's opposition to exclusion. As an institution it rejected these proposals, citing the fears that a Protestant-dominated administration for the area of exclusion would have a very negative impact on Catholic education and religious practice.[39] One bishop claimed that the threat of partition was 'the grossest insult to the spirit of Irish nationality' and that it was 'utterly subversive of the National ideals'.[40] For Archbishop Walsh the 'segregation' of the six counties was a 'bastard policy' that would have a 'deplorable effect on Religion and Education' and was to be resisted by the Church.[41] Redmond had recognised this potential threat to the negotiations from the outset, and had met with the bishops to try to allay their fears on 16 June. Even more traditionally moderate bishops supportive of the Irish Party reacted strongly to these proposals. The Bishop of Derry had described the proposals as rot, and the Bishop of Raphoe said that the 'party could not support the scheme and survive'.[42] Redmond sought the support of the bishops knowing that without the institutional support of the Catholic Church, he would be accused of using the Irish Party machine to undemocratically foist partition on to Catholics and Nationalists in the areas of exclusion.[43] This meeting did not lead to an agreement, with the result that the Church in the North became alienated from Redmond and the Irish Party.[44] One week later, an Ulster Conference of nationalist supporters met, and a measure supporting the negotiations was passed. This occurred in large part because its representatives were heavily comprised of Ancient Order of Hibernian Members, who supported Redmond's Northern allies because they were subject to the patronage of Irish Party MPs. Indeed, of the 740 representatives who had been at the conference, 270 had been from Tyrone-Fermanagh-Derry, and 183 of them, some 68 per cent, had voted against the proposals.[45] An accusation had even been made in the *Irish Independent* that those who supported the proposals for partition had prolonged their speeches to ensure that those who wished to catch the last train home (i.e. those not from the party's stronghold of Belfast) were unlikely to stay to the end to vote.[46]

The interpretation of these events were coloured by the sentencing of Sir Roger Casement to execution. As was shown in previous chapters, this execution, though legal and perceived as necessary by the British authorities, further antagonised nationalists and did little to inspire their confidence in moderate and compassionate British rule. Coming as it did on the heels of this vote amongst Northern nationalists, one could deduce that it was perceived as an action that seemed only further to call into question Redmond and the Irish Party's supposition that demonstrations of Irish loyalty would be rewarded. Furthermore, Casement's prosecution had been carried out by a Unionist member of Asquith's cabinet, F. E. Smith, in his capacity as attorney-general. There was an irony in Smith's prosecution of Casement, in light of his participation in 'extra-parliamentary' activities on behalf of Ulster Unionists to block Home Rule some two years before, and this irony did not go unnoticed by nationalists. This further strengthened perceptions of alienation and isolation in the Irish nation from Westminster and Asquith's Cabinet, and further brought into question what power, if any, Redmond and the Irish Party still possessed.[47] An event of equal significance for Unionists was the beginning of the Battle of the Somme on 1 July, which saw the decimation of the Ulster Volunteers in the 36th Division with 2,000 killed and 3,000 wounded. This must have seriously brought into question what prize their loyalty unto death for the empire would now bring.[48]

By 11 July, the negotiating process had begun to seriously falter. Lord Lansdowne made a speech at Westminster in which he produced the written assurance which Lloyd George had given to Carson, praised General Maxwell, and proposed that the Defense of the Realm Act be further extended to maintain the rule of law in Ireland with or without a Home Rule settlement.[49] He furthermore put it to the Cabinet that Lloyd George had in fact exceeded his brief by promising Redmond the immediate implementation of Home Rule, and by promising that the exclusion of the six counties would be temporary.[50] These actions antagonised the Irish Party and nationalist support for Home Rule, and constituted an attempt to wreck the Bill. He succeeded, and the negotiations over Home Rule fell apart by the end of July 1916. The Cabinet endorsed the promise made by Lloyd George to Carson. Redmond, felt completely betrayed by this turn of events. He declared all negotiations at an end, stated that he found Lansdowne's speech to be a 'declaration of war on the Irish people' and made it known that he and the Irish Party now opposed the new Home Rule Bill in its entirety.[51]

Castle Rule Reinstated

In the wake of the failure of the negotiations over Home Rule, Asquith reinstated a form of government in Ireland which was the same as had been in place prior to the Rising – a system of government which he had previously claimed had broken down entirely. It had been proposed that a new Irish administration be appointed by an advisory council, comprised of representatives of the different Irish parties, but Asquith dismissed this on the grounds that it was 'attractive but impracticable'.[52] Instead, Asquith selected an administration that had a distinctly Unionist tone, to replace the military regime of

Maxwell. The combination of a return to this form of rule, along with the selection of Unionist politicians to fill the positions in the Irish administration, was hugely unpopular with the Irish nation. One member of Maxwell's staff, Brigadier General Sir Joseph Byrne had been chosen as the inspector-general of the RIC, in part because he had been singled out for praise by Maxwell for his 'handling of captured insurgents'.[53] For the Irish nation, now transformed and radicalised, this was damning praise. The Irish Attorney-General was also a controversial appointment, as he had been Carson's 'lieutenant' in the Ulster Unionist movement.[54] Even Dillon refused to initiate any kind of contact with the new administration.

Not only had there been no tangible evidence for headway or advancement on Home Rule despite all the political machinations on the part of the Party and Asquith, but the re-imposition of Castle Rule was now seen as evidence of a Unionist victory. Unionist success in thwarting Home Rule, along with its domination of the Irish administration, especially given its draconian form, with extended DORA powers and martial law still in place, all served to increase nationalist anger and fears. In fact this fear was not completely unjustified, as imprisonment without trial became increasingly common and provision for its implementation was continually extended.[55] The more these powers were implemented, the more the population shunned the police and turned against the British regime as a whole, and the more the nation became radicalised, which in turn led to the further justification, in the minds of the British officials, of the use of the courts-martial and extra-judiciary powers.[56] With the re-establishment of Castle rule, and this cycle of radicalisation in place, all Redmond and the rest of the Irish Party could do was to futilely demand that these powers be rescinded, propose fruitless debates at Westminster, and demand that the British authorities 'trust the Irish people once and for all by putting home rule into operation'.[57]

The Price of Failure

It is apparent, in retrospect, that as great an impact as the events of Easter Week had popularly on the Irish nation, its impact was almost negligible in terms of a shift in the political thinking of the elite. The exclusion of Ulster, as it had been proposed by the British government and accepted by the Irish Party, and the supposition that negotiations over Home Rule should simply take up where they had left off before the outbreak of the war and the events of the Rising, demonstrated their lack of comprehension regarding the transformation of the Irish nation.[58] Redmond had misjudged the change brought about by the cultural trigger point in the Irish nation – swelling up from the masses were expressions of a *Sinn Féin Amháin* mindset, and a project that was based in part on a broader sense of British patriotism would not now suffice, especially if it included exclusion.[59] Redmond's failure to adjust to the changed political circumstances of the Irish nation, left the political potential of Home Rule in Ireland 'discarded and discredited'.[60] Redmond's pledging of the National Volunteers to the war effort had been a calculated political gamble to get Home Rule, but now it seemed that this gesture had ultimately gone unrecognised by the British government. The sense that this gesture had not been successful was already prevalent, as Kitchener had previously failed to create an equal companion nationalist regiment for the 36th 'Ulster' Division. Now it seemed overly hazardous to risk Irish lives for little political gain.[61] In assessing the situation during the autumn of 1916, Redmond rued the fact that 'from the very first hour our efforts were thwarted, ignored and snubbed. Everything we asked for was refused, and everything that we protested against was done.'[62] In this mindset, Redmond's commitment of the Volunteers and support for the imperial war effort had gained no advantage for the advancement of Irish nationalism.[63]

Redmond's problem was now that 'constitutionalism in a country whose grievance is that it possesses no constitution is an historical humbug'.[64] It had now become apparent that the Party's 'leaders ... had ceased to be representative'.[65] Observers within the Irish Party felt that Redmond's personal influence had been 'irreparably broken'.[66] One local politician declared: 'It was John Redmond's fault, everything was his fault.'[67] The fact that he had tried to compel those Northern nationalists who were dissatisfied with the proposals only further brought his political judgement into question.[68] For one county inspector, it was blatantly obvious that nationalists in Tyrone 'did not view with favour the proposed settlement excluding Tyrone ... and viewed its failure with great satisfaction'.[69] It was contemporarily observed that only the abandonment of Lloyd George's proposals had 'prevented a split in the Nationalist Party as serious as the Parnellite split and the repudiation of Redmond by a large body of his nominal followers'.[70]

Redmond's brother, and political ally, Willie, an Irish Party MP representing East Clare, argued that the party had now become obsolete, suggesting that he and his brother should retire and 'hand over the task of representing Ireland at Westminster to younger men'.[71] In fact, there was some basis for his concern that the younger generation was alienated from the party and its leadership, or, perhaps more correctly stated, that the leadership had become alienated and isolated from the younger generation. O'Brien wrote that the British 'have driven all that is best and more unselfish among the young men of Ireland to despair of the constitutional movement by ... bungling [and] double-dealing in reference to Home Rule ... above all by the methods by which you governed Ireland during the last six months'.[72] That this younger generation had despaired of moderate constitutional nationalism would later become apparent – it was the young who would go on to agitate most strongly on behalf of the burgeoning Sinn Féin movement. Redmond now believed that it was the British government that had set upon a political course that was 'bound to do serious mischief to these high Imperial interests which we were told necessitated the proposal of the [Home Rule] settlement ... they have taken the surest means to accentuate every possible danger and difficulty in this Irish situation'.[73]

This crisis led to state in which contemporary observers found that 'Every fool and semi-illiterate ass is busy with his "I never trusted Asquith", "I always said the Party was not strong enough"'.[74] Even the party's subscriptions suffered, dropping from £1,127 in March 1916 to £674 in June.[75] In various papers, it was proclaimed that the Irish Party's leadership had now discovered what the average person knew all along that they were being 'tricked, deceived, and humbugged by the Liberal Government' and that it had been a mistake to call for the Irish people to 'help to strengthen the empire' and to leave behind the nation.[76] For Dillon 'enthusiasm and trust in Redmond and the Party [was] now dead so far as the mass of the people is concerned'.[77] The impression left by the failure of these negotiations was that the leadership of the Irish Party ultimately lacked competence, that in choosing the empire over Ireland they had made a terrible blunder, and ultimately the transformation and beatification of the Rising and its participants was further emphasised by these points of view.[78] One historian put it succinctly, stating that 'the reward of compromise [was] distrust, distaste, and political death'.[79] Laffan points out that by August, the Irish Party had been so thoroughly defeated in the House of Commons that

Redmond and his colleagues found that even the time in Ireland, which had been twenty-five minutes faster than GMT, had been changed to harmonise it with English time, despite the vociferous protestations of the party.[80] There was therefore a sense that somehow Redmond and the Irish Party had been defeated at every level over the issue of Home Rule, and as a result they lost power and legitimacy.[81]

The Final Failure of Home Rule

Throughout the summer of 1916, there were attempts on the part of the Irish Party and Asquith to 'keep the negotiating spirit alive' despite the setbacks and apparent decline in political fortunes.[82] In December, a Lloyd George-led coalition replaced Asquith's after he resigned. Lloyd George's Cabinet was promptly stocked with the same Unionists with whom he had negotiated that summer. Sinn Féin's by-election victories over the course of the spring of 1917 demonstrated the potential dangers of an Ireland without some sort of Home Rule settlement, and there was now some impetus on the part of Lloyd George's government to move on the Irish situation.[83] By March, in the wake of a by-election in Roscommon, there was some definite movement within Lloyd George's Cabinet towards this end. In debates on Ireland in the Commons on 7 and 22 March, Lloyd George made speeches which reiterated the British government's position that they were willing to grant Home Rule to those areas which wanted it, but would not impose it where it wasn't.[84] The first proposals on how to resurrect a Home Rule settlement included a provision for negotiations led by a commission comprised of statesman from the Dominions where 'the problem of local autonomy has presented itself in different forms and has been solved in different ways'.[85] This may have had an ulterior motive, to try to reinvigorate recruiting in the Dominions by making them part of the solution to the Irish problem. However, when the Colonial Secretary approached various individuals to serve on the commission, representatives of the dominions declined to take part 'since their own countries were divided over the Irish issue'.[86]

By April these matters had become more pressing, a bill to prolong the life of the existing Parliament was coming up for a second reading in the Commons, and the Irish Party was threatening to obstruct its passage. This left Lloyd George's Cabinet with one of two alternatives

– to force through the legislation despite the risk that Irish Party opposition would 'become a focus for opposition from other quarters of the House' or to call a general election.[87] The Cabinet chose the former while simultaneously pursuing a policy that would attempt to appease Irish demands for Home Rule.[88] As part of this effort, a modified proposal emerged which provided for the parties in Ireland to negotiate a solution to the Irish problem between themselves, rather than directed or moderated by British or Dominion representatives. While the Irish Party failed to block the Bill, the episode served to put Ireland back on the political agenda of Lloyd George's cabinet and restarted the negotiations over Home Rule.

By 16 May, Lloyd George had sent two Home Rule proposals to Redmond and Carson. The first was that Home Rule should be implemented immediately with the exclusion of the six counties. Exclusion would be reconsidered after five years, and a Council of Ireland would be formed that would be comprised of representatives from both the Home Rule and excluded areas to deal with problems that would affect all of Ireland, in this way creating an all-Ireland dimension. The second proposal, a last minute addendum, was put forward by Lloyd George as a 'last resort'. It proposed 'a convention of Irishmen of all parties for the purpose of producing a scheme of Irish self-government.'[89] By 21 May, because of its appeal to the Irish Party and Southern and Ulster Unionists, and despite Lloyd George's original intentions, this second proposal was adopted as the way to move forward, such that 'Ireland should try her hand at hammering out an instrument of government for her own people' and Lloyd George agreed that whatever 'substantial agreement' was reached by the Convention would be implemented by the government.[90]

The makeup of the members of the convention was a particularly contentious issue, especially when what constituted a substantial agreement had yet to be agreed. Eventually a compromise emerged that called for ninety-five representatives to make up the body of the Convention. It would therefore be made up of fifty-two Nationalists, twenty-six Ulster Unionists, nine Southern Unionists, six Labour Representatives, and two Liberals. Lloyd George's Cabinet was, in particular, concerned that all aspects of Irish society were represented at the Convention, including religious representatives, representatives of those who held 'advanced nationalist opinions' and representatives of organised labour. Of course it was the latter two groups that had come together to carry out the Easter Rising, so their participation was seen as being crucial, though in a strictly controlled and limited manner.[91] Sinn Féin refused to officially participate unless the Convention's representatives were democratically elected and possessed the power to declare Ireland independent, and unless the British government would pledge itself to the ratification of whatever the majority of the convention decided.[92] They recognised that they were being asked to participate in a limited capacity, and, flushed with their electoral successes, would not participate in a body that did not adequately recognise their new-found political status, as Sinn Féin had only been assigned five seats in the convention. Sinn Féin also did not participate because its entire political rationale was dependent on its holding an anti-status-quo stance towards constitutional politics in Ireland, and this strategy had already aided them to by-election victory.[93] Eventually the places for 'advanced nationalist opinions' were filled by members who met daily with Sinn Féin representatives, but who could not officially 'be regarded in any sense a representative of the party'.[94] Of the other representatives, four came from the hierarchy of the Catholic Church, and their main concern was to prevent any form of exclusion that would lead to Protestant control of Catholic education in the excluded area.[95] This was, of course, problematic, because it was one of the aspects of a potential settlement sought by the Ulster Unionists. The leadership of the Nationalist delegation was left to Redmond – once again he staked his political reputation, and potentially the fate of the party, on Lloyd George-inspired negotiations over Home Rule.

The Irish Convention convened in July 1917 and collapsed in March 1918. Although it was long and arduous, it did produce some real compromise between and fundamental changes among Unionists, Southern and Ulster, and Nationalists. The key issues of the Convention were Ulster and customs – and it was in fact these issues on which the negotiations ultimately foundered.[96] Fiscal control of Home Rule Ireland constituted the thin legal membrane between a glorified devolved local authority under the control of the Imperial Parliament, and the achievement of full Dominion status, to rival that of Canada, South Africa and Australia. It therefore comes as no shock that this issue was the main point of contention between Ulster Unionists, who wanted no form of fiscal devolution between Ireland and Britain, and Nationalists, who believed there could be no liberty for Ireland without substantial economic independence. Nationalists, in particular, were concerned that a dominant British parliament would always put the economic and industrial concerns of Britain first. Therefore to ensure the ultimate security of the Irish nation it would be necessary for the Irish Parliament to be able to enforce customs and excise duties as it saw fit, rather than at the behest of Westminster. This approach was informed in no small part by the memories of the Famine and Irish economic under-development and dependence. It would also be necessary, from this point of view, for an Irish Parliament to be empowered to negotiate foreign trade treaties to ensure that they would have independent access to resources for which they might find themselves in competition with Britain itself. This was anathema to Ulster Unionists, and the negotiations rapidly ground to a halt.

In late 1917, Southern Unionists proposed a compromise to overcome this stalemate. The position of the Southern Unionists had altered from the one which they had held in the first set of negotiations. Many in this group now recognised the apparent inevitability of some sort of Home Rule settlement, and were therefore seeking to shape this settlement to their advantage. In accepting an inevitability of an all-Ireland Home Rule solution, the Southern Unionists had diverged from their Ulster Unionist counterparts, and this change of position was a cause of conflict within Unionism. The compromise which was put forward by the Southern Unionists suggested that the right of internal taxation should indeed be held by an Irish Parliament, but that the right of raising customs duties and tariffs should remain with Westminster. This left the bulk of Irish economic policy in the hands of Westminster, a situation that was historically and symbolically 'problematic' for Irish Nationalists with memories of the nineteenth century.

In early January, 1918 Redmond forged ahead with this compromise despite the misgivings of nearly all nationalists in the Convention, including his own advisors and allies. This was a compromise too far. When the negotiations collapsed, Redmond was subjected to hostility from elites from his own party. In the aftermath of the collapse of this compromise, and in a cloud of political defeat and embarrassment, Redmond withdrew from the Convention, on the grounds that 'he could no longer be of service'.[97] His health was already in decline, and he would be dead within two months. The Convention had, in the meantime, become hopelessly deadlocked, and three months later delivered three different reports to Lloyd George, a sign of its inability to come to a substantial agreement as to the future of Ireland. The majority report, passed 44 to 29, represented a new compromise which suggested that the matter of customs be deferred for a period after the cessation after the war.[98] Nationalists, this was ultimately a 'dangerous' concession, in so far as it ultimately meant the implementation of a 'federal Home Rule' rather than 'colonial' Home Rule, i.e. limited self-government rather than full Dominion status.[99] This débâcle was reminiscent of the disgrace attached to the end of the first set of negotiations, and it was unclear to what extent the Irish Party had now gained anything in participating in these negotiations. This perception was only further reinforced by debates over Irish representation in Westminster, with Nationalists believing that it would justify and sanction further British interference in Irish affairs, and Unionists believing it to be evidence of attachment to the Empire.[100]

Military Service Bill

Ultimately, the proposals of the Convention failed not only because of the inability of the Irish Parties to come to terms over the Home Rule fate of Ireland, but also through the actions of the British government in April 1918. There were massive defeats for the Allied forces in late March, with a German advance capturing some 98 square miles, penetrating as deeply as four and a half miles into the British lines, and on one day killing 7,000 British soldiers with another 21,000 being taken prisoner.[101] Between 21 March and the end of April, Britain had lost 300,000 men – and throughout April the British army was engaged in a series of actions to save Amiens, which, if it were overrun, could have meant the failure of the entire British defence system on the Continent.[102] The Cabinet now decided to extend the application of the Compulsory Military Service Bill in England, to include 17-year-olds, vicars, etc. and to apply conscription to Ireland. The introduction of conscription was not a surprising proposal, given the negative effect all of these events had had on recruiting, and it had been foreseen by one county inspector as early as 1916, who thought that with recruiting having virtually ceased, 'it is not expected many more will join unless compelled to do so'.[103] A Military Service Bill for Ireland was introduced, along with a Home Rule Bill, ostensibly to sweeten the bitter pill for Nationalists. This was part of an effort to raise some 550,000 more men in Britain, and some 150,000 in Ireland. The bill served to alienate Nationalists and Unionists in equal measure, and drove yet more 'farmer's sons' into the ranks of Sinn Féin and the Volunteers.[104]

Sir Horace Plunkett, chair of the Irish Convention, viewed this situation as critical.[105] He felt that the decision to introduce the Bill in Ireland, coming just when the Convention reported, proved 'unhappy' and that it was pushed ahead by the government as 'unwise'.[106] Opposition to conscription created a basis for an alliance of disparate elements of the Irish nation, the clergy, moderate nationalists and radical nationalists could come together to oppose conscription, and as a result it would finalise the process of radicalisation in Ireland.[107] In fact it would provide Sinn Féin with the final mantles of national legitimacy. Plunkett believed, as a result, that any resistance to the implementation of conscription in Ireland would be 'very effective' and 'no levy could be effected in response without bloodshed'.[108] It was Sir Horace Plunkett's ultimate belief that 'to accompany the concession of Home Rule for Ireland with conscription by England was a tyrannical act'.[109]

The Bill more or less finished the Irish Party's nationalist political legitimacy, in so far as it destroyed any semblance of the Irish Party strategy of loyalty to and cooperation with a Westminster regime in order to gain political favour, Home Rule, and to protect Ireland from compulsion and coercion, and this turn of events created a context in which Nationalists of all political persuasions began to question the rights Westminster to enforce such laws. In fact, the Military Service Bill was being introduced without any consultation of the Irish Party whatsoever, an action that called into question what purpose was being served by its presence in the Commons. The party attempted to renounce its moderate position and associate itself with the radical and anti-conscriptionist nationalism of Sinn Féin to form 'one general movement,' but this ultimately failed for a variety of reasons – not least its loss of political legitimacy because of previous failures.[110] In fact Lloyd George delivered the final blow to the Irish Party in November 1918, when he declared that Home Rule would be withheld 'until the condition in Ireland made it possible to implement', completely undermining the Irish Party's *raison d'être* in the run-up to the general election in December.[111] After this collapse, Home Rule was dead, despite several half-hearted attempts to resuscitate it. The Irish Party was, as a result, now finished, and the reformed and reorganised institutional expression of radical nationalism in Ireland, in the guise of Sinn Féin, now possessed the sole political legitimacy of the nationalist cause and resonated strongly and popularly throughout the Irish nation.

* * *

The effect of this course of events was twofold. First it created a perception for members of the Irish nation of the potential dangers attached to negotiation with the British authorities. This had the further more fundamental effect of raising the question for the Irish nation of its role in the British imperial project. Second, Home Rule had failed twice after the Rising, and in so far as each time it had hinged on Redmond's personal reputation and that of the party, these failures ultimately doomed them both. Political miscalculation and isolation from the nation led to the party no longer being representative. Its position on exclusion had shown how out of touch the elites of the moderate constitutional nationalist movement had become. For Redmond this became especially apparent with his 'compromise too far'. Before the ultimate failure of Home Rule and the collapse of the party, while there was still some potential for a constitutional settlement to Irish nationalist demands, there may have been a great deal of sympathy for, even resonance of, radical nationalism, but its development as a popular political movement was greatly hindered by the viable constitutional alternative. With the door firmly shut on a constitutional remedy, there were no more barriers and distractions from the full of development of an unhindered radical nationalist movement in Ireland and its full force was unleashed. The failure of the Irish Party changed national political identity in Ireland in so far as it created a political vacuum. With this transformation, there was a fundamental question over what the new politics of nationalism should be – and the sense of agency and urgency that resulted from the cultural trigger point therefore changed as a direct result of the collapse of the party. This situation would prove particularly fertile soil for the growth of Sinn Féin.

NOTES

1   Martin, 1967, p. 243.
2   Dillon in Kautt, 1999, p. 58.
3   See Chapter 6.
4   Fitzpatrick, 1998, p. 99.
5   Rees, R., *Ireland 1905–1925, Volume 1: Text and Historiography* (Co. Down: Colourpoint Books, 1998), p. 217.
6   Ibid.

7   Kee, 1982, p. 8.
8   Ibid.
9   Ibid.
10   Ibid., p. 9.
11   Co. Kilkenny Inspector Report, 1916, CO 903/19 PRO Kew.
12   Co. Monaghan Inspector Report, 1916, CO 903/19 PRO Kew.
13   Maxwell, memo, 16 June 1916, cited in Laffan, M., *The Resurrection of Ireland: The Sinn Féin Party, 1916-1923* (Cambridge: Cambridge University Press, 1999), p. 61.
14   Asquith in Kee, 1982, p. 9; O'Day 1998; Wells and Marlowe, 1916.
15   'English Critic', quoted in Redmond-Howard, 1916, p. 57.
16   O'Day, 1998, p. 270.
17   British Ambassador in Washington cited in Kee, 1982, p. 9.
18   Rees, 1998, p. 217.
19   For a discussion of Lloyd George's motivations, see amongst others O'Day, 1998, Rees, 1998, McBride, 1991.
20   Rees, 1998, p. 215.
21   O'Day, 1998, p. 271; Rees, 1998, p. 215.
22   See Chapter 3.
23   McDowell, R. B., *The Irish Convention, 1917-1918* (London: Routledge and Kegan Paul, 1970), p. 45.
24   The potential plans, geographical and political, for the exclusion of Ulster in a Home Rule solution are dealt with in Chapters 2 and 3 of this book.
25   See especially Hennessey, 1998, for an in-depth discussion of these issues.
26   See Kee, 1982.
27   Lloyd George quoted in Kee, 1982, p. 11.
28   Quoted in O'Day, 1998, p. 271.
29   See Kee, 1982, p. 12; McDowell, 1970, pp. 57–61.
30   Wells and Marlowe, 1916, p. 213.
31   Devlin quoted in O'Day, 1998, p. 271.
32   *Irish Independent*, cited in Hennessey, 1998, p. 147.
33   Devlin quoted in O'Day, 1998, p. 272.
34   *Irish Independent*, cited in Hennessey, 1998, p. 149.
35   Hennessey, 1998, p. 145.
36   Kee, 1982, p. 10.
37   *Midland Reporter*, cited in Hennessey, 1998, p. 149.
38   *Fermanagh News* and *Fermanagh Herald* cited in Hennessey, 1998, p. 149.
39   McBride, 1991, p. 214; Miller, 1987, p. 199.
40   Bishop McKenna, cited in Hennessey, 1998, p. 148.
41   Dictated by Walsh, 22 June 1916, Walsh Papers 385/7.
42   McDowell, 1970, p. 53.
43   Rees, 1998, p. 219.
44   Miller, 1987, p. 199.
45   McDowell, 1970, p. 54.
46   Ibid.
47   Rees, 1998, p. 215.
48   Ibid., p. 222. As has been previously noted, this event, in particular, seemed to underpin the repertoire of Unionist myths, memories and symbols of their sacrifice for Britain, and therefore seemed, from the Unionist perspective, supreme justification of their vehement opposition to Home Rule.
49   Ibid., p. 221.
50   Ibid., p. 218.
51   Hennessey, 1998, p. 148.
52   McDowell, 1970, p. 64.

53   McBride, 1991, p. 215.
54   Phillips, 1923, p. 112.
55   Fitzpatrick, 1998, p. 14.
56   Ibid., p.15.
57   Redmond's speech to the Commons, 24 July 1916, cited in McDowell, 1970, p. 66.
58   Mansergh, N., *Nationalism and Independence: Selected Irish Papers* (Cork: Cork University Press, 1997), p. 13.
59   Boyce, 1995, p. 288.
60   Mansergh, 1997, p. 11.
61   Rees, 1998, p. 222.
62   Redmond, October 1916, cited in Mansergh, 1997, p. 29.
63   Kee, 1982, p. 18.
64   O'Brien in *Longford Independent* 28 April, 1917, as cited in Boyce, 1995, p. 289.
65   Wells and Marlowe, 1916, p. 214.
66   Gwynn cited in Hennessey, 1998, p. 152.
67   Member of Ennis 'Board of Guardians', 1916, cited in Fitzpatrick, 1998, p. 102.
68   Hennessey, 1998, p. 152.
69   Co. Tyrone Inspector's Report, 1916, CO 903/19 PRO Kew.
70   Wells and Marlowe, 1916, p. 214,
71   Fitzpatrick, 1998, p. 97.
72   O'Brien in Commons, 24 July, 1916 as cited in Foster, R. F., *Modern Ireland: 1600–1972* (New York: Penguin, 1989), p. 486.
73   Redmond in Commons, cited in Kee, 1982, p. 12.
74   Michael Conway, former Irish Party MP, quoted in Hennessey, 1998, p. 160.
75   Laffan, 1999, p. 61.
76   *Kilkenny People* and *Sligo Nationalist,* cited in Hennessey, 1998, p. 160.
77   Dillon cited in Kee, 1982, p. 15.
78   See especially Hennessey, 1998 and O'Day, 1998.
79   O'Hegarty cited in O'Duibhgall, 1966, p. 86.
80   Laffan, 1999, p. 62.
81   Intelligence Report 'Attitude of the People Towards the Empire', February, 1917, CSB Files, 3/716/24 NAI; see also Laffan, 1999.
82   Letter from Asquith to Redmond, 28 July, 1916 in O'Day, 1998, p. 275.
83   For more on these by-elections, see Chapter 8.
84   McDowell, 1970, p. 71.
85   Speech by Asquith in the Commons, cited in McDowell, 1970, p. 71.
86   McDowell, 1970, p. 72.
87   McDowell, 1970, p. 73.
88   Cabinet Minutes, 16 April 1917 cited in McDowell, 1970, p. 73.
89   Lloyd George quoted in *The Times*, 17 May 1917, cited in McDowell, 1970, p. 76.
90   McDowell, 1970, p. 77.
91   Ibid., p. 82.
92   Ibid.
93   See especially Coogan, 1993 amongst others.
94   Lysaght's Diary, cited in McDowell, 1970, p. 84; Jackson, 1999, p. 209.
95   Miller, 1987.
96   O'Day, 1998.
97   Hennessey, 1998, p. 233.
98   Ibid., p. 228.
99   Ibid., p. 211.
100 Ibid., pp. 207–215.
101 Ibid., p. 220.
102 McDowell, 1970, p. 185.

103   Co. Carlow Inspector's Report, 1916, CO903/19 Pt. II PRO Kew.
104   See Chapter 6.
105   Plunkett to Col. House, 20 April 1918 in O'Day and Stevenson, 1992, pp. 164–6.
106   Ibid.
107   See Chapter 8.
108   Plunkett to Col. House, 20 April 1918, in O'Day and Stevenson, 1992, pp. 164–166.
109   Ibid.
110   Fitzpatrick, 1998, p. 98.
111   Foster, 1986, p. 490.

8

The Rise of Sinn Féin

While the Irish Party had been busy negotiating with the British government and Unionists over the possibility of the implementation of Home Rule in Ireland, radical nationalism, initially shattered by the aftermath of the Rising, was starting to reorganise. In part this reorganisation was driven by its adherents – they had been motivated enough to act when there was no support for their cause before the Rising and its aftermath, and now a period where it seemed that there might be some cause for optimism was all that it took to hearten them and make them redouble their efforts. More importantly, however, reorganisation was being driven by the effects of the cultural trigger point – the collapse of the Irish Party released an unfettered popular expression of radical nationalism, and there was a new sense of urgency and agency after the failure of the constitutional option. In the wake of the Rising, especially once Home Rule had failed (twice over) there was a demand from the nation for a new and more representative set of political institutions to come into being to replace the now discredited Redmond and the Irish Party. The institutional re-emergence and resurrection of Sinn Féin in the aftermath of the Rising can be charted from the initial foundation of alternative political organisations after the Rising, and through a series of by-elections from November 1916 onwards. The process was not necessarily a smooth one, but by the end of the war the radical nationalist party of Sinn Féin was able to claim to be the dominant political force in all of Ireland, and the effects of the cultural trigger point became apparent.

Burgeoning Radicalism: the Irish Nations League

For Redmond and the Irish Party, the failure of the Home Rule negotiations represented a major setback. Redmond and the party had been willing to accept the temporary exclusion of the six counties of Ulster, when popular nationalism would not.[1] There was a strong reaction to this willingness to compromise the geographic unity of Ireland, and for radical nationalists it was summed up by Michael Collins' sentiment that he was delighted by 'the smashing of the Home Rule proposals', believing that there should be 'anything but a divided Ireland'.[2] At the same time, for one contemporary observer it was clear that radical nationalists, now larger and continuing to grow, accepted 'the fact of the proposed [Lloyd George] settlement as a reward for rebellion and used the form of the settlement, which was repugnant to the national instincts ... to recruit and strengthen further'.[3] A Sinn Féin-inspired 'advanced nationalist' movement was appealing to the undercurrent of unrest and disaffection, especially 'amongst the younger section of the people' to the detriment of the Irish Party.[4] Redmond and the party's failed political gambles provided new political space for radical nationalism to operate.

After the failure of the Lloyd George-led Home Rule negotiations, over the summer of 1916, the influence of the National Volunteers was on the wane, while the popularity of the Irish Volunteers was on the increase. The RIC believed that while the membership of the Irish Volunteers was small, it had 'much influence with the labouring classes and shop boys, and through the relations with the rebels'.[5] There was a sense that there was an 'undercurrent of unrest and disaffection, especially amongst the younger section of the people due to current political events', and this disaffection was leading to the reorganisation and increased drilling amongst the Irish Volunteers.[6] There was, however no single body to which those who were feeling disaffected could turn. Radical nationalism was limited in its capacity to agitate, with an observer stating that 'owing to the absence of leaders the movement is in abeyance, but it would not require a clever organiser to create a dangerous organisation'.[7] This untapped potential was recognised by radical nationalists who were lamenting that in the absence of these leaders, Redmond and the Party were making attempts to rehabilitate themselves, and those 'that had been fighting parliamentarianism for nearly a quarter of a century now find ourselves without a leader when there is a chance to win the country to our view'.[8]

In the wake of the failure of Home Rule, there were calls for a political organisation to replace the disgraced and denuded Irish Party. While some organisations already were in existence, such as O'Brien's All-For-Ireland League, various new political organisations now started up and vied to represent the transformed and radicalised Irish nation, including the 'Irish Ireland League', the 'Repeal League' and the 'Anti-Partition League'. At the start of August 1916, the Anti-Partition League became the Irish Nations League (INL). The Church, under the direction of several Northern bishops, came together with Northern nationalists to form the Anti-Partition League on 20 July, to oppose the Irish Party's planned Home Rule compromise to exclude the six north-eastern counties from Home Rule. Two weeks later this body had become the Irish Nations League. Although the content of these organisations was now more radical, their form, and even the style of their leadership, retained aspects of their moderate forerunners. This was due in part to the fact that many of their organisers, sympathisers and agitators had previously done the same for Home Rule and moderate nationalism, and they brought with them experience and assumptions as to what form a political organisation should take.[9] Although the Irish Nations League was ultimately to have little political impact, it is indicative of the popular calls for the representative reorganisation of nationalism in Ireland.

The expressed aims of the Irish Nations League were to avert partition, participate in independent opposition in the Commons, perform 'militant agitation' at home, and demand a form of rule in Ireland along Dominion lines.[10] It believed that 'the Irish leaders, having betrayed their trust, the people of Ireland can have no further confidence in them, they have acted in direct opposition to the National sentiment'.[11] Its aims, however, were expressed in 'dulcet tones', in that it sought to 'preserve and cherish the National ideals … to cultivate patriotism and good citizenship … to develop the natural resources of the country'.[12] The Irish Nations League saw itself not as a separatist party but rather as a 'revived, purified and reinvigorated Parliamentary Party'.[13] The Irish Nations League was therefore compared to various parliamentary-orientated forerunners, such as the United Irish League, and for one contemporary the comparison was obvious, in so far as 'both looked to London and Parliamentarianism to remedy Ireland's grievances'.[14] It was a transitional step from radicalised perceptions of the events of the Rising to full-blown participation in radical nationalist politics. As one priest put it, the Irish Nations League was a type of purgatory, 'a place or state of punishment where some Parliamentarians suffered for a time before they joined Sinn Féin'.[15]

While this group had some elements of radical nationalism, its power never extended beyond the areas affected in Ulster and its main base of power lay in Tyrone–Fermanagh–Derry. Of its forty-two branches that were established between August and October 1916, twenty were in Tyrone.[16] In fact it did not hold its first meeting outside of Ulster until 10 September.[17] It did, however represent the institutional growth of grassroots radical nationalism. It also made contact with other groups who were disaffected with the Irish Party, but very much within the constitutional tradition, such as William O'Brien's 'All for Ireland League', centred in Co. Cork.[18] The emergence of the Irish Nations League was an explicit demonstration that there was a constituency in Ireland that felt that the Irish Party was no longer representative, and that it was necessary to set up an alternative political institutional structure to achieve Irish nationalist aims. The cultural trigger point was definitely having an impact, but the extent of its impact on the political behaviour of the Irish nation had yet to be determined. The Irish Nations League was not a full-blown radical nationalist organisation, but it was representative of radicalisation.

These expressions of anti-party sentiment suffered inherent drawbacks, in so far as they lacked clear leadership, policies and structures by which to accomplish their goals. In the Irish Nations League policies were being decided and felt out as they were being made. As part of this process of shedding off the institutional and parliamentary mentality of the Irish Party, it was noted that 'people are beginning to think and act for themselves' beyond the stifling leadership and machine of the party.[19] This was marked by a demonstrable shift to what might be considered to be a more 'traditional' or 'orthodox' nationalist ideology, i.e. that the nation is best governed by itself, independent of non-national influences. In the Irish case, after the failures of Home Rule, and with the process of radicalisation having firmly taken root, the popular belief in an Irish-Ireland became increasingly important. This meant an understanding of Ireland as not only culturally distinct but also politically independent from its Anglo-Protestant counterpart. This resurgence in the popularity of a *Sinn Féin Amháin* outlook marked a radical departure from the moderate and constitutional politics of the preceding forty to fifty years.[20] The organic distinctiveness of the

Irish nation, as expressed in this *Sinn Féin Amháin* ideology, now even posed the ultimate question – why participate in Westminster or a 'Home Rule' scheme at all? This question, expressed in the issue of abstention, would now increasingly come to dominate radical nationalist politics. In fact the Irish Nations League's first stated aim was to secure self-government for the Irish nation, and its provisional constitution stated that Irish MPs should withdraw from Westminster 'whenever called upon to do so'.[21]

The West Cork By-Election

By November 1916 there was a by-election in West Cork which would provide a gauge by which political change in the aftermath of the Rising would become apparent. The election was chiefly between a pro-Redmond Irish Party candidate, Daniel O'Leary, who was running despite Redmond's instructions to the contrary, a 'self-styled Sinn Feiner', Frank Healy, who was running at the behest of O'Brien for his All-for-Ireland ticket, and a local independent All-for-Ireland candidate, Michael Shipsey. Healy had been selected by O'Brien, Redmond's bitter enemy in the Irish constitutional nationalist movement, to try to court a protest vote.[22] Healy was an O'Brienite, who had been deported by the British authorities after the Rising, a friend of Sinn Féin's founder, Arthur Griffith, and was known as a sympathiser with the 'Sinn Féin rebellion'.[23] He was not, however, officially involved in or representative of Sinn Féin itself. The potential for a split vote for Healy and Shipsey amongst West Cork's All-For-Ireland ranks did not bode well for Healy's candidacy, and says more about O'Brien's political manoeuvrings than for the content of Healy's electoral platform.[24]

Healy's electoral platform was based on the supposition that, while he gloried and took pride in the achievements and heroism of Irish soldiers in the British army, he wondered 'was it fair for a man who boasts himself the leader of the Irish people to tell these men on their way to Flanders "I have blown the bugle for you, and when you come back your country will have shrunk from 32 counties to 26".'[25] His brother, T. M. Healy, campaigned on his behalf, stating that 'if they elected O'Leary it meant conscription for Ireland; if they elected Frank Healy it meant no conscription but amnesty for prisoners'.[26] The commander of the Cork section of the Irish Volunteers, incarcerated in Reading Jail, was livid upon hearing that

Healy was running under a Sinn Féin banner, and took out a newspaper ad stating that 'neither Healy, nor any of the other candidates for Parliament in West Cork represented the views of either the interned prisoners or Sinn Féin' [27] One of the issues which had led to a radical nationalist rejection of Healy was his refusal to entertain running his campaign on a policy of abstention, to their mind implicitly meaning that his political orientation was towards a Westminster status quo.

The pro-Redmond Irish Party candidate, O'Leary, won this by-election by 116 votes, with the number of votes for the other two candidates combined equalling more than those polled for O'Leary. This result was not disturbing to radical nationalists as there was hardly any political institutional infrastructure to express radical Irish nationalism. O'Brien had tried to capitalise on the transformation in the Irish nation and the anti-Redmond and anti-Irish Party sentiment which had resulted from the failures of the Lloyd George negotiations. However, this is evidence that radical nationalists, though in a state of organisational chaos and disarray, were making it known that they would not be drawn into status quo Irish politics, nor were such politics particularly attractive to the electorate.

Release of the Frognoch Internees

Two events of major significance would occur in December 1916 which would greatly change the institutional ineffectiveness of radical nationalism in Ireland. First of all, Asquith was replaced as prime minister by Lloyd George. One of Lloyd George's first actions was to release the 560 internees who had been detained and held without trial in the aftermath of the Rising. Not only did Lloyd George publicly state that a solution to the Irish situation was one of his chief objectives, but, as was shown in the last chapter, there were many external pressures which made finding a solution attractive. If the situation in Ireland could be sorted out, it could unlock Irish manpower, adding as many as 150,000 new soldiers to the British army and releasing the division currently 'locked up' in Ireland. Moreover, releasing the internees would help to 'facilitate' recruiting in the Dominions and 'favourably influence' US opinion towards the allies.[28] Therefore the release of the internees held without trial was part of a strategy to allay American fears over Ireland, and to entice them further into supporting the allies in the War.[29] The second significant event, as was discussed in some detail in the last chapter, was the Irish convention, to allow Irishmen to solve Irish problems, and again to address American and Dominion concerns about the situation in Ireland. To facilitate these negotiations, Lloyd George ordered the release of all remaining Irish '1916 Prisoners' in June 1917.[30]

The release of the Frognoch internees had an immediate impact on the organisation of radical nationalism in Ireland. The British government had assumed that to restore Irish confidence and to return Ireland to its *status quo ante* required little more than appeasement – that is, the release of the remaining prisoners and the resumption of negotiations over Home Rule.[31] However, upon their release, the prisoners were received with open enthusiasm, and 'Everything began precisely where they had left off'.[32] Whether or not their release actually meant a direct return to the way things had been, it definitely had a reinvigorating effect on the radical nationalist movement, from top to bottom. Before the release of the prisoners, one contemporary lamented that 'the absence of all the leaders to whom the rank and file Sinn Féin party look for guidance was an insurmountable obstacle'.[33]

The released internees did not return as the same men as those that had departed in the immediate aftermath of the Rising. Frognoch had served as a kind of training ground for radical agitators from all over Ireland, and it had given these men the chance to discuss strategies for their return. By being interned, disparate individuals were brought together to 'receive one pattern of thought and to know one another and to learn of one another'.[34] MacNeill, interned with the leadership of the Rising at Lewes Jail, described his time in jail as 'a sort of school' in which prisoners were learning Irish language and history.[35] Upon their release, these new ideas, contacts and skills were put into action by men such as Michael Collins, who immediately threw themselves into institutions such as the Irish National Association and Volunteers Dependents' Fund (INAVDF). This organisation was busy providing relief to released internees who found themselves unemployed, and provided assistance to the widows and families of those who were killed during Easter Week. The money for their activities came from both home and abroad, particularly from the USA and Australia. The INAVDF was viewed with suspicion by the British authorities, and they gave strict orders that their activities were to be constantly monitored to ensure that they were not participating in Sinn Féin agitation.[36] In fact, it was not so much that the INAVDF was a hotbed of agitation – rather, it was a focal point for the popular expression of radical nationalism so that newly opened branches of Sinn Féin and other 'advanced nationalist' organisations sending contributions to the fund, raising it in their capacity as social clubs as much as through political agitation, through events such as sponsored dances, Irish poetry reading and so on.[37] In the immediate aftermath of the Rising, it had been apparent to some county inspectors that various nationalist organisations such as 'the GAA and Gaelic League though nominally non-political are in reality strongly Sinn Féin'.[38] What these organisations provided was a network for radical nationalists to organise and keep in contact, a cover for the burgeoning radical nationalist political organisation.

The Roscommon By-Election

The first indication that radical nationalism was undergoing a process of reorganisation was its victory in the North Roscommon by-election of February 1917. The by-election was contested by three candidates, although it was really only a two candidate race. The candidates included a pro-Redmond Irish Party candidate, Thomas J. Devine, an independent, Jasper Tully, who was the publisher of the *Roscommon Herald*, and the radical nationalist candidate, Count George Noble Plunkett. Plunkett was the father of one of the Easter Week 'martyrs', Joseph Plunkett, a signatory of the Proclamation. His two other sons were imprisoned for their actions over Easter Week. In fact, when selected by Collins, Griffith and others to run for the seat, Plunkett was in England, himself having been deported there by the British authorities after the Rising. He arrived back in the constituency only two days before the election. His candidature was not an obvious choice for the radical nationalists, as prior to the events of the Rising he had been an intellectual who had run the National Museum of Science and Art in Dublin, and he had been president of the Royal Irish Academy on two occasions.[39] Plunkett was even a member of the Royal Dublin Society, although he was expelled upon his selection for this seat, and because of the activities of his family during Easter Week. These were not typical radical nationalist credentials. Despite Plunkett being in England recovering from illness, Collins, Griffith and other radical nationalist agitators were undeterred from running a vigorous campaign on his behalf in his absence.

Plunkett won this by-election by twice as many votes as his Irish Party competition. Archbishop Walsh believed that 'there had been nothing like it since Butt's victory in Limerick'.[40] Plunkett benefited from the support of a discontented and disaffected electorate. These groups included Sinn Féin, the Volunteers and the Irish Nations League.[41] This broad umbrella of nationalist support would later play a crucial role in the organisational development of radical nationalism. While there had been a transformation and radicalisation in the outlook of individuals in the Irish nation, lagging institutional representation meant there were a variety of potential outlets for this transformed outlook, none of which dominated the Irish political scene. This new support and energy was going politically unharnessed. Before this by-election victory, disparate groups, such as pre-Rising Sinn Féin, the Gaelic League, the Volunteers, *Cumann na mBan* and the IRB were attempting to focus their efforts to regroup and reorganise the greater project of radical nationalism – but they lacked a coherent structure and strategy.[42]

Plunkett's campaign reflected this, as he asked that the people of Roscommon should vote for him because he was 'father of his dead boy and his two sons were suffering penal servitude'.[43] His entire platform was based on an appeal for sympathy, and on highlighting the incompetence and failure of the Irish Party.[44] Laurence Ginnell, a rebel MP who would eventually come to fully support Sinn Féin in the summer of 1917, campaigned on Plunkett's behalf, and claimed that 'If elected Count Plunkett would prevent the young men of Ireland being forced into the British army'.[45] For Ginnell, the fear of serving in the British army formed the basis of his campaigning on behalf of Plunkett again. At one meeting he stated that 'Redmond promised Home Rule to the Irish people and thereby got 150,000 men to fight for England but now these men were feeding the worms in Gallipoli' and reiterated this message at another meeting stating that 'As a result of Redmond's action thousands of Irishmen are buried to-day at the bottom of the Dardanelles, in Sulva Bay, and in the trenches of Flanders who ought to be at home breaking up the ranches of Roscommon.'[46]

This was highly indicative of the issues which the radical activists identified as potentially appealing to the voters. But at this point, there was no unified radical nationalist policy – and radical nationalists were in such disarray that Plunkett even refused to submit to

Griffith's request that he pledge to abstain from Westminster should he be elected. Officially Plunkett was running without any party affiliation, though it had been made clear from the start that he represented Sinn Féin.[47] One jibe accused all those who were canvassing on Plunkett's behalf, as really being Irish Volunteers rather than Sinn Féiners.[48] In fact, Sinn Féin was at this point nominally a defunct political organisation in Ireland, a condition due, in large part, to the incarceration and only recent release of its leaders, organisers and activists.

In Roscommon, however, it was the efforts of the newly freed radical nationalists combined with local agitation that actually helped to get Plunkett's campaign off the ground.[49] Local agitation in Roscommon was masterminded by a radical priest, Father Michael O'Flanagan. O'Flanagan had been elected to the Sinn Féin executive in 1910, had given a funeral oration for O'Donovan Rossa along with Pearse in 1915, and had often been chastised for his political involvement by his bishop, Dr Coyne of Elphin. He would go on to play a major role in the Republican movement, becoming vice-president of Sinn Féin in 1917.[50] O'Flanagan made a variety of speeches on Plunkett's behalf during the by-election, making statements such as 'the rotten policy of Redmond and his Party caused the rebellion in Dublin' or that 'only for the Dublin Rising the Irish Party would be inducing their unthinking followers to give their very lives for England ... in exchange for sweet words and false promises of British ministers'.[51] In fact the role of clergymen, especially young clergymen, in this and the following Sinn Féin by-election victories was to prove crucial, despite the fact that it often meant defying their ecclesiastical superiors.[52] The radicalisation of the younger clergymen which had been semi-apparent in their participation in organisations such as the GAA and Gaelic League before the Rising, became especially so from 1916 onwards.[53]

This combination of local agitation, and the budding institutional organisation of radical nationalism made images such as the carrying of elderly voters over snow drifts on the shoulders of young Irish Volunteers to reach the polling booths one of the 'most enduring images of the campaign'.[54] Images like this served to reinforce the 'saintly' and 'fastidious' portrayals of the radical nationalists which had begun in the aftermath of Easter Week. After North Roscommon, radical nationalism had a new group of leaders, and a new strategy – dependent on a mix of centralised organisation and local agitation – that worked, and as a movement it also began to develop an agreed programme for policy and action. This process of reorganisation would eventually come to form Sinn Féin. Sinn Féin grew like a shoot from the diverse roots of cultural nationalism, and that was part of the reason that on the ground at this time, in the by-elections, it appeared as a conglomeration of disparate organisations – the GAA, Gaelic League, and so on.[55] Radical nationalism, as a political movement, had been able to camouflage itself in the garb of cultural nationalism, and this allowed it to grow, culturally and institutionally, under the noses of those who had disapproved of this movement before 1916.[56] It also allowed for the popular dissemination and consolidation of the myths, memories and symbols of the Irish nation. The final step in the ascendancy of Sinn Féin would be its reconstitution as a unified electorally representative body, to replace the increasingly disgraced Redmond and the Irish Party, and fill the vacuum.

At the rally to celebrate his victory, Plunkett declared that he could not bring himself to represent the people of Roscommon in a foreign parliament, but that rather he would remain in Ireland where 'the battle for Irish liberty was to be fought'.[57] Of course, abstention was one the earliest of Sinn Féin policies, and it featured prominently in Dolan's 1908 campaign. He had asserted that abstention went against the Irish Party's 'politics as usual' and status quo relationship with the British authorities. In December 1916, Sinn Féin's policy was one of passive resistance to foreign aggression, the development of national natural resources, and the 'fostering of national characteristics'.[58] The only 'tangible' element of its policy was its commitment to abstention. This now became a particularly potent and resonant idea. This policy of abstention – the refusal to send elected representatives to Westminster – was predicated on the belief that for the 116 years that Ireland had been sending representatives to Westminster it had suffered two famines, four open insurrections, 'long periods of partly suppressed insurrections, wholesale evictions, abnormal emigration, scores of Coercion Acts, ever-increasing taxation, destruction of industries, decrease of tillage, and "mind-stupefying' methods of education'.[59] Abstention, as a policy, was in part justified on this basis that it could prevent another potentially imminent ethnocidal famine.[60] As a policy and symbol of the rejection of status quo politics, abstention helped to underpin the organisational evolution of Sinn Féin in Ireland.

In its institutional form, as it was being reconstituted Sinn Féin appeared very much like the Irish Party. However, it differed from what preceded it in so far as its attachment to the policy of abstention meant that it was attempting to turn the *de facto* difference of an Irish nation, as recognised by nationalist ideology and by British negotiations over Home Rule, into a *de iure* form of state.[61] They were, however, forced to do this through the traditional mechanisms of recognition and legitimacy throughout Irish society.[62] Prior to the reorganisation of radical nationalists, O'Brien had been able to exploit the lack of cohesion amongst radicals in West Cork the previous autumn. Plunkett's by-election victory now provided a blueprint for radical nationalist electoral success, and Plunkett's victory helped to unify the disparate forces of radical nationalism.

The Reorganisation of Sinn Féin

For Father O'Flanagan, newly enthusiastic following Plunkett's triumph in Roscommon, Sinn Féin was 'an old policy under a new name, the policy of '48, or Robert Emmet and Wolfe Tone, it was the 1500 Volunteers that saved you from conscription'.[63] While it was clear that a 'Sinn Féin' movement had been victorious in North Roscommon, it was unclear what it stood for, as it had brought together a variety of nationalist groups under one banner. While there was a sense that it brought together those disaffected with British rule, there was no agreement on how to solve this disaffection. When these differences became increasingly obvious, the shine quickly wore off Plunkett's victory. Plunkett's leadership was also terribly divisive; he had a 'dogmatic and unbending' character and poor political judgement, lacking basic diplomatic political ability.[64] He alienated Irish Nations League supporters, who had worked to get him elected, and he began feuding with its members and representatives.[65] Flushed with his own success, Plunkett now proposed to disband the entire Sinn Féin organisation in favour of his self-styled 'Liberty League', a proposal which upset Griffith, brought the two into conflict, and had the potential to divide and wreck the entire radical nationalist project.

Plunkett called for a conference to be held in the Mansion House in Dublin, on 19 April 1917, to which he wished to invite representatives of all aspects of advanced nationalist opinion in Ireland. Plunkett called this convention because he felt that the duty had been 'cast' on him as the deliverer of advanced nationalist politics by virtue of his victory in North Roscommon.[66] While only sixty-eight of 277 invited public bodies attended, the conference had over 1,200 attendees, including Sinn Féiners, priests and students. After a great deal of debate and action, Plunkett's proposal to disband Sinn Féin was rejected. A major split was ultimately avoided, by fitting a loose collar around all of the disparate radical nationalist groups in the guise of the Mansion House Committee.[67] The Mansion House Committee's main aim was 'to deny the right of any foreign parliament to make laws for Ireland'.[68]

A major split had been averted, and the path was now clear for the emergence of Sinn Féin as the dominant nationalist political organisation in Ireland. It has been suggested that the British government misnomer for the Rising – the Sinn Féin Rebellion – helped to ensure the prominence of the party in the institutional reorganisation of radical nationalism, and that this in part helped to ensure its survival.[69] At the Mansion House Convention, a Sinn Féin representative also commented that it 'would be a pity to lose a name which had so distasteful a flavour in the mouth of their Saxon friends'.[70] Eventually the Liberty League was subsumed into Sinn Féin, and the party would begin growing rapidly, from 11,000 members in July 1917 to 200,000 in 1,200 Sinn Féin clubs by October of the same year.[71] The county inspectors' reports put these figures closer to 66,000 members in 1917 and 112,000 in 1918, but nevertheless the movement was clearly growing.[72] In Kilkenny, for example, the effect of Sinn Féin's momentum was quite apparent, in so far as there were six more Sinn Féin clubs at the end of December 1917, than there had been in June of that hear, rising from 15 to 21, and an increase of 600 members, from 1,290 to 1,869 over the same period.[73] While only a handful showed up for the Manchester Martyr Celebrations in Ennis, Co. Clare, in November 1916, the growth of Sinn Féin clubs in the same county a year later was 'killing the Ancient Order of the Hibernians'.[74] Indeed after April 1917, Sinn Féin's rise was meteoric, and by July there were some 336 affiliated Sinn Féin clubs, compared to the forty-one that had attended the Manor House Convention.[75] The expansion was, in some cases, the result of Sinn Féin organisers travelling from Dublin throughout the countryside, something which was duly noted by British observers.[76] In other cases, however, there are examples of groups of individuals spontaneously founding local Sinn Féin clubs, and as a result of their foundation meeting writing to the central executive to affiliate themselves, and to receive literature and membership cards.[77] It was as though Sinn Féin served as a mechanism to facilitate the popular expressions of a radicalised Irish nation.

The South Longford By-Election

In May 1917, there was another Sinn Féin by-election victory. This time the victorious candidate was Joe McGuinness, a republican and a prisoner in Lewes Jail. McGuiness and his companions in Lewes Jail believed that his candidature was inappropriate, in part fearing the potential cost of defeat. South Longford had not appeared to be a particularly fertile location for advanced nationalist opinion before the Rising, so if Sinn Féin were to win, it was recognised that it would take a great deal of effort.[78] Furthermore, McGuinness' electoral platform could not use the 'sympathy' card in the same way as Plunkett's campaign, and, given the infighting in the Mansion House Committee, coming up with an agreed, unified and appealing platform would not be easy. If the radical nationalists lost this by-election, it would not only be a political setback but could have signalled a rejection of the participants in the Rising themselves, sullying the power of the myths, memories and symbols attached to them. Despite these concerns, choosing McGuiness as the candidate indicated a new-found confidence in the radical nationalist movement.[79]

The formula which had proved successful in North Roscommon was used in South Longford, with the harnessing of local agitation and a loose coalition of radical nationalist institutional organisations, although in this case it was nearly defeated. McGuinness defeated the pro-Redmond Irish Party candidate by around only thirty votes, and needed a recount to do so. Despite this close call, Sinn Féin's institutional organisation was now much healthier than it had been in Roscommon, although it was still far from perfect. It weathered the internal divisiveness that could have torn it apart the month before, and now possessed the organisational know-how to bombard South Longford with motor cars, petrol to run the cars, organisers, pamphlets, posters, and so on. The rhetoric of the campaign centred on cries to 'put him in to get him out'. More significantly, however, the stump speeches indicated a shift in rhetoric to reminding people of the tragedies of the Irish past and the revolutionary tradition. In one speech, it was stated that it was 'men like Joe McGuinness that prevented the men of Ireland from being torn away from their lands to fight for England' and that 'we will see that the crops which you planted to feed yourselves and your children will not be taken away from the county as they were in '46 and '47'.[80] In another speech it was asserted that 'Ireland stands for complete freedom; it is a separate nation'.[81]

The most significant aspect of the South Longford by-election was, however, Archbishop Walsh's support for McGuinness. While the Church had supported the foundation of the Irish Nations League, it had remained silent over the emergence of a radical nationalist alternative. In fact it was doctrine for the Church and its priests not to get involved in politics. An 'instruction' had been sent out to remind priests that it was forbidden by the National Synod 'to speak of politics of any kind in Church'.[82] The 'instruction' also happened to be sent by Cardinal Logue, who was vehemently opposed to Sinn Féin, and by the Bishops of Cloyne and Ross who were staunch Irish Party supporters. Walsh, however, went ahead and wrote a letter to the *Evening Herald* the night before the by-election in which he attacked the Irish Party, and their acceptance of the policy of exclusion. Walsh finished his statement by saying 'I am fairly satisfied that the mischief has already been done, and that the country is practically sold.'[83] On its publication, this statement was telegraphed to Sinn Féin activists who immediately had it printed on a pamphlet which was distributed on the day of the election, with the additional statement that: 'This is a clear call from the great and venerated Archbishop of Dublin to vote against the Irish Party traitors and vote for Joe McGuinness.'[84] With the narrow margin of McGuinness victory, a great deal of importance has been ascribed to Walsh's intervention. Walsh's actions damned him among Irish Party supporters, but young radicals had found a new hero from the old guard.[85]

The East Clare By-Election

In June the leaders of the Rising were released from Lewes Jail, as a gesture of goodwill on the part of Lloyd George, a contribution to the auspicious beginning of the Irish convention, and an action intended for an American audience.[86] Bonar Law, in announcing their release in the Commons, stated that it was done so that 'the convention may meet in an atmosphere of harmony and good will'.[87] For Sinn Féin, however, their release seemed more like an expression of fear rather than goodwill on the part of the British government.[88] If the released Frognoch internees had been greeted with enthusiasm on their return, these men were fêted like heroes and treated like living saints. The arrival of one hundred released prisoners in Dublin was celebrated by a procession in which Sinn Féin flags were displayed, and in Cork their release brought on a riot against the British forces.[89] Eamon de Valera was chosen to stand for a seat in East Clare, as he had emerged as one of the leaders of the prisoners in Lewes Jail. Redmond's brother, Major Willie Redmond, had volunteered to serve in the British army, and his death at the front led to the by-election in East Clare in July, 1917. While there had been concern about South Longford as fertile ground for Sinn Féin's attention, there were no such concerns about East Clare.[90] Since 1909, Clare had had the third highest number of fully paid -up members of Sinn Féin.[91] The pattern of this by-election was similar to that of the others, in that it was a combination of the efforts of increasingly seasoned Sinn Féin campaigners and local agitators. In this case, the role of the Church, in the guise of the bishop and especially the younger clergy, was apparent. They were observed as 'moving heaven and hell' to secure a Sinn Féin victory.[92] The imagery used in this campaign also changed, in so far as there were increasing references to 'the enemy,' to fighting, to arming and to revolutionary methods.[93] In his victory speech, de Valera proclaimed 'You are worthy descendants of the Claremen who fought under Brian Boru, with the spirit in your hearts and body that your fathers had a thousand years ago'.[94] There were also references to the British exploitation of Ireland through the burden of over-taxation.[95] The by-election was won by de Valera, by almost 3,000 votes. From Curran's perspective in the archbishop's residence it seemed that 'a huge landslide is carrying away the Irish Party supporters into the Sinn Féin camp'.[96] In the aftermath of his victory, a banner hung from Birr Castle, proclaiming 'Irish Party wounded at North Roscommon, Killed in South Longford, Buried in East Clare. R.I.P'.[97] If East Clare was the burial, than Kilkenny in August 1917 represented the raising of the headstone. W. T. Cosgrave, the Sinn Féin candidate, defeated the Irish Party candidate by over 300 votes in the Kilkenny City by-election. This by-election fell into the same pattern as East Clare, given the constituency's pre-existing Sinn Féin orientation, and the ease for Sinn Féin supporters to canvass in the constituency.

The Content of Sinn Féin

As the moral stock of radical nationalism rose, that of British rule and the Irish Party's brand of constitutional nationalism fell. One sign of this was that wives of Irish soldiers serving in the British army, called 'separation women' because of their dependence on the separation allowance paid by the British authorities, became increasingly portrayed as 'drinking blood money' and as facing an 'awful reckoning' on judgement day.[98] This was linked explicitly in Sinn Féin political posters to alcoholism and sexual depravity so that there were 'dishevelled hoydens shown swilling porter and bearing Union Jacks and banners for the Irish Party candidates'.[99] In the same vein, British culture, especially in the form of dance hall music, was a particular target for nationalist propaganda, as something which promoted drunkenness and sexual immorality.[100] Count Plunkett's wife was particularly concerned about public advertisements asking for 'Irish girls' to offer themselves for employment in England because of the 'appalling state of immorality amongst the men in England' where 'seduction is not a punishable offence if the culprit is in the Army'.[101] She was making a protest on behalf of these 'poor Irish girls without the faintest idea of what they have to face once they leave Ireland ... it is as well as one might look on a flock of innocent sheep driven into the wolves' stronghold'.[102] The pervasive themes of cultural and religious nationalisms – the organic distinctiveness of the Irish nation, and the inherent distrust of and hatred for the Anglo-Protestant other – were also further promoted by this turn of events. In the nationalist imagination the Irish Party, associated as it was with British politics, constituted an internal threat to the organic, innocent, and pure moral character of the Irish nation.[103]

Other speeches over the course of 1917 emphasised the role of the 'saintly Rising martyrs' with the words 'I accept your cheers ... for the men who fell in Easter Week and who lie in Glasnevin, but also for my comrades who were executed in Kilmainham Gaol, and who lie in Barrack Yard at Arbour Hill and the only prayers that reaches their sacred bones are the blasphemous oaths of the British soldiery'.[104] These themes had been echoed in de Valera's victory speech and stump speeches by Ginnell and O'Flanagan. The Bishop of Limerick proclaimed that the events of the Rising had served to 'galvanise the dead bones in Ireland and created the spirit with which England now has to reckon'.[105] This was in marked contrast to the initial reactions to the Rising, and demonstrated the extent to which attitudes towards the Rising had become changed. A great deal of importance was continually attached to the memories of the Easter Week dead. It had, after all, been their executions that sparked the first actions of public defiance, such as the saying of requiem masses in their honour. A year on and their deaths were still being commemorated. Before the anniversary of their deaths, the families of the executed approached Archbishop Walsh about masses of commemoration, and according to Curran 'Numerous Requiem Masses were held ... Republican flags were hoisted'. and 'Cumann na mBan placed wreathes on the graves of the Rebellions victims'.[106] In the countryside, in places like East Down, Sinn Féin flags were flown on the anniversary of Connolly's execution.[107] On 5 August, on the anniversary of Casement's execution, there was, for example, a large march in Co. Kerry to 'Casement's Fort' during which 'Sinn Féin tricolours were worn and waved, and it was noted that large numbers of Volunteers appeared in uniform'.[108] New heroes were added to these ranks as well. Thomas Ashe, a popular and powerful figure in the burgeoning Sinn Féin movement had been rearrested after his release in June and interned under the DORA (Defence of the Realm Act) in Mountjoy Jail. Ashe was a heroic figure, his leadership of an action against British forces at Ashbourne was one of the only military successes during Easter Week. He died when being force fed during a hunger strike to protest his treatment. His death 'made a vast public impression'.[109] He was immediately 'canonised' in the nationalist propaganda, and his funeral was a massive occasion at which tens of thousands of mourners filed past his coffin.[110] In fact, over 150 priests attended and in its size, power and overall status it was compared to O'Donovan Rossa's funeral in 1915.[111]

Other imagery included that of Sinn Féin as protector of the Irish nation against conscription. In all of the various by-elections, Sinn Féin had attempted to get across the message that a vote for Sinn Féin had meant a vote against conscription. O'Flanagan and Ginnell had used this line in Roscommon, Longford and Clare. Other examples of this tactic include a priest who was campaigning on behalf of de Valera, stating that if it weren't for Sinn Féin, 'the bones of the young men of Ireland would be bleaching today in the blood sodden soil of France'.[112] In October, de Valera, now an MP, made a speech referring to the Famine, stating 'Your fathers could tell you of the Famine of black '46 and '47 when a million and one half of our people died by the roadside. If those who died of starvation had only turned with pitchforks a quarter as many would not have died ... if I had a million and a half soldiers of the Irish Volunteers I would drive every one of the English out of Ireland.'[113] The imagery of the Famine was used constantly during this period. In part this was a result of agitation against the system of food control being imposed by the British authorities in reaction to the U-boat blockade of Britain. Regardless of its root cause, the use of the call 'The clutching hand is out to capture your food' was clearly popular beyond any current sense of injustice.[114] In February 1918, Sinn Féiners seized pigs as they were driven through the streets of Dublin to Kingstown to be shipped to England, and butchered them, distributing their meat amongst the population of Dublin.[115] The effect was to force the British authorities into banning the export of pigs thereafter. There are a variety of similar reports of speeches and protests in the Dublin Metropolitan Police Special Branch files, with regular references being made to '47 and the Famine.[116] In May 1917, a proclamation from the King was read to the Protestant Churches in Dublin enjoining their parishioners to be economical with bread and flour. It was ignored in all the Catholic Churches, bar one in Coolock, where the priest publicly remarked that 'the people of Dublin should keep their own supplies in Ireland'.[117] Sinn Féin even approached Archbishop Walsh to gain the Church's support in establishing local committees to ensure the 'security' of Irish food.[118] This concern had even led to a policy of cattle driving and forcible land reclamation, especially in the west of Ireland, to ensure that there was more arable land, and to settle old scores, much to the disapproval of the Sinn Féin executive who thought that these actions were too radical.[119] All of these were actions which the nation thought it should have taken in retrospect of the events of the nineteenth century. On the one hand, the Famine afforded a useful and resonant political banner which could be used by Sinn Féin to mobilise the nation. On the other hand, the fears of Famine, as a result of the myths, memories and symbols of the Irish nation, still rang true for individuals in the nation.

De Valera's Rise to Prominence

By late October 1917, the reorganisation of Sinn Féin as the representative political movement in Ireland was complete, when a Sinn Féin *Ard-Fheis* elected de Valera as president and Arthur Griffith as vice-president. On the next day, de Valera was elected president of the Irish Volunteers. Over the course of the spring of 1917 the National Volunteers had severed their ties to Redmond and the Irish Party, and had sought and gained a reunion with the Irish

Volunteers.[120] The institutional rubric of radical nationalism in Ireland had now been completely formed and united. From Curran's perspective, it seemed that 'The old order has yielded, giving place to the new'.[121] As part of this exercise, 'departments' which were responsible to 'ministers' were now set up within Sinn Féin, and were responsible for matters such as military organisation, political organisation, education and propaganda, foreign relations and finance.[122] County inspector reports all make reference to the outward appearance of calm, but refer equally to a 'spirit of unrest' prevailing, and that this was combined with 'a spirit of disaffection ... ready to breakout if a suitable opportunity occurred'.[123] Part of this was due to 'the Sinn Féin movement making considerable strides' along with increased activities on the part of the Irish Volunteers.[124] While there was outward calm in some locations, in others such as Clare there was what was described by the British authorities as 'utter anarchy' – a state of affairs that entailed illegal cattle drives, land seizures, illegal drilling, and the general obstruction of policing.[125] Similarly in Cork, the RIC reported that 'since the police are regarded as the great obstacle to the realisation of their political aims, they are confronted in the discharge of their duties by an organised conspiracy'.[126] This resulted in the county being put under martial law, the first place to which it had been applied since the Rising.

The Conscription Crisis

Though the expression of radical nationalist agitation was beginning to get more heated in various spots in Ireland, Sinn Féin faced three by-election setbacks between February and April 1918. The first by-election defeat to the Irish Party occurred in February in South Armagh, which had been controlled by Devlin and the Ancient Order of the Hibernians, and it proved a difficult constituency to crack. A Sinn Féin victory was highly unlikely, because this was an Irish Party stronghold, and because while there was a great deal of support by the young for Sinn Féin, it was almost exclusively 'the older generation' that were listed on the electoral roles.[127] The next defeat occurred in March in Waterford City. It was the by-election for John Redmond's vacated seat. The seat had become vacant on Redmond's death in March, and his son now ran for this seat. In fact Redmond's death itself indicated how transformed the Irish political scene had become: the local bishop refused permission for a requiem mass to be said in his honour.[128] There was no hope of a Sinn Féin victory in this constituency. William Redmond campaigned dressed in his Irish Guards uniform, a particularly useful prop in what was historically, and continued to be a British army garrison town. This, along with the sympathy for his father, and the patronage attached to the Redmond family name meant that he handily won this seat. William Redmond won by 478 votes, but given the conditions it was not considered a decisive defeat.[129] Redmond had been the MP for East Tyrone, and so this third seat now became vacant. Sinn Féin initially had not even considered contesting this seat, but there was a grassroots movement in East Tyrone for a Sinn Féin candidate, and despite their initial hesitation and the Irish Party's head start, the Sinn Féin candidate nearly defeated the Irish Party candidate in April 1918.[130]

The negative impact of these events on the fortunes of Sinn Féin, and the positive impact on the fortunes of the Irish Party, were partially mitigated by the conscription crisis. The introduction of the Military Service Bill and conscription crisis in Ireland delivered the final blow to constitutional nationalism in Ireland, and secured Sinn Féin's place in the upcoming years. Its introduction created a massive public outcry. From Curran's perspective, it 'Set Ireland ablaze' and 'exhibited the blind hatred of the English people for Ireland'.[131] Conscription 'came as a thunderbolt to the leaderless masses of the Irish people for while the majority had lost their faith ... in the Parliamentary Party, many of the older generation were slow to commit themselves to the revolutionary policies of Sinn Féin'.[132] Therefore the crisis, from Curran's point of view, was 'the brutal shock that woke them to the political realities and unreliability of the Party'.[133] The immediate reaction of all Irish nationalists was to ratify a Sinn Féin-sponsored pledge at the 'Mansion House Conference' on 18 April. This pledge, modelled on the Solemn League and Covenant of the Ulster Unionists in reaction to Home Rule, declared that there was no right of the foreign parliament of Westminster to impose conscription on Ireland, and that the participants in the conference would 'solemnly ... resist conscription by the most effective means at our disposal'.[134] The day before, the Irish Party had withdrawn from Westminster, in what appeared to be the ultimate vindication of Sinn Féin's policy of abstention. The Catholic bishops also supported this effort, releasing a statement that directed 'the clergy of Ireland to celebrate a public mass of intercession ... in every church in Ireland to avert the scourge of conscription' and furthermore backing the pledge to resist conscription as agreed upon at the Mansion House Conference. As early as 9 April, the Standing Committee of the Catholic Bishops had released a statement which said 'we feel bound to warn the Government against entering upon a policy so disastrous to the public interest, and dangerous to all order, public or private'.[135] The anti-conscription movement brought together all elements of the Irish nation, secular and religious, in the guise of organised Labour and the Catholic Church, radical and moderate, in Sinn Féin and the Irish Party. Sinn Féin had already manoeuvred itself into being the anti-conscription party, and it had the track record of consistently not trusting or negotiating with the British government. Curran claims that he and de Valera had hatched the alliance of Sinn Féin and the Church at the surreptitious request of the Archbishop. They concocted a plan by which Sinn Féin would propose a bold and popular way forward on this issue, and that the sympathetic bishops would move right away to support them. In this way they could outmanoeuvre some of the more conservative and worried bishops, such as Cardinal Logue. That the Irish Party had been involved in the Irish Convention immediately prior to this crisis rendered them even more vulnerable to attacks that they had misjudged and miscalculated the politics of the Union.

The conscription crisis was a moment that also benefited Sinn Féin by bestowing upon it the vestiges of institutional legitimacy that it had not yet acquired. By working so closely with the Church in the anti-conscription movement, and by gaining the approval of many bishops and other clerics who had previously been so hostile to its rise, Sinn Féin had now gained recognition as the most powerful and the legitimate political force in the Irish nation. The bishops had decreed that masses of intercession should be said everyday so that conscription would not be implemented, stating that: 'The Irish people have a right to resist by every means that are consonant with the laws of God.'[136] Hundred of thousands of Irishmen signed the anti-conscription pledge, drafted by Sinn Féin and organised by the Church, and it was these actions which ultimately forced the British government to abandon their immediate intentions to implement conscription over the summer of 1918, thought the British authorities did not revoke their right to do so anytime in the future – thereby assuring conscription was a constantly looming which Sinn Féin could turn into an important politically mobilising issue.[137]

Indeed, regardless of how the alliance between Sinn Féin and Church came about over the issue of conscription, its effect was to mobilise the entirety of the Irish nation. Curran reported that as a result 'scenes were witnessed the length and breadth of Ireland that were never seen before ... a million hitherto divided, unorganised, demoralised rallied ... and signed the pledge' and that the 'press reported that the Dublin churches were thronged to overflowing, revealing in a remarkable way the spiritual unity and exultation of the nation'.[138] In several of the county inspector's reports, the central role of Sinn Féin in the organisation of the anti-conscription movement was apparent, especially in contrast to the little or no mention of the Irish Party's role in this movement.[139] It was also thought that 'the fear of conscription increased [Sinn Féin's] power and members more than anything else and now Sinn Féin is regarded as the power which saved the country from compulsory service'.[140] The threat of conscription had loomed so large in Sinn Féin's electoral imagery before this crisis that this turn of events only seemed to vindicate their warnings and helped to inspire their ever increasing popularity. New members where joining it as 'a means of resisting conscription' and even if they had been previously unsure of the movement, now joined so 'in the belief that it would be the means of staving off conscription'.[141]

Epilogue

In the wake of the conscription crisis there was a recognition on the part of the British authorities in Westminster and in Dublin that the republican movement was now growing so strong as to pose a real threat to their power. A new administration was put in place in Dublin, with 'stronger' men than those that had made up the previous regime. Within six days of their arrival, in early May, the 'German Plot' was 'uncovered' by the Castle authorities. This was the apparent discovery of a plot, organised by de Valera and Sinn Féin, to ally with the Germans to overthrow British rule in Ireland. Its veracity is strongly doubted. Regardless, by 20 May, de Valera, Griffith, Plunkett and others had been arrested. It was an eventuality that the Sinn Féin executive had already considered, and they had already made plans to ensure that they were able to turn this situation to their advantage – for example, that all the relevant leaders were arrested en masse to gain the maximum impact and exposure for the 'injustices' of these arrests. At this time, the Irish administration in Dublin Castle approached Archbishop Walsh about the possibility of having a memorial mass said for the war dead. Walsh rejected this request on the grounds that in light of 'recent events it would probably be regarded as a directly provocative challenge' thereby making its occurrence 'injudicious'.[142] In fact, Walsh thought the whole situation to be an 'outrage, in sending off a number of Dublin Catholics, prisoners, not only untried, but not even charged with any crime, to prisons in England where they have no possibility of even hearing Mass on Sundays'.[143] The arrests were meant to strike a surprising and crippling blow to Sinn Féin, but their effect was only to consolidate its position as the dominant political force in Ireland. As the prisoners were being driven through the streets to the Kingstown docks, thousands lined the streets to support and cheer them.

The effects of the Rising as a cultural trigger point are blatantly apparent when one considers the institutional growth of Sinn Féin and radical nationalism after Easter Week, 1916. The rise of radical nationalism was without precedent from the Irish point of view before the Rising. In the general election of December 1918, after the end of the war, Sinn Féin would win seventy-three of the 105 Westminster seats in Ireland. This was sixty-seven more than those gained by the Irish Party. For the County Dublin Inspector, while the general election was carried out in a peaceable manner, it revealed that 'Sinn Féin is a highly organised and efficient organisation'.[144] The Irish Party had even been forced to abandon twenty-five seats which had been 'safe seats' in the previous election of 1910. The organisational structure of the Irish Party could not organise or muster enough support to put forward candidates for these seats. This defeat though was also particularly galling as it had been the first where the franchise had been extended to all men over 21, and all women over the age of 30 through the Representation of the People Act of 1918.[145] This had the effect of tripling the electorate, and empowering Sinn Féin's younger supporters.[146] The next step would be violent agitation on behalf of the Irish nation, a phenomenon that would become increasingly apparent in the records of crimes kept by the British authorities between 1917 and 1919.

* * *

There are ultimately two points in this chapter which help to explain the rise of institutional radical nationalism in Ireland. These are 1) the change engendered by the release of the internees after the

Rising, and their ability to agitate for a particular type of radical nationalism amongst a transformed Irish nation who now found their message highly attractive, a changed indicated in the gain of political momentum made by Sinn Féin with the victories in the Roscommon, Longford and East Clare by-elections, and 2) the consolidation of this new found momentum and support after the conscription crisis in the spring of 1918, and the eventual landslide victory of Sinn Féin in the general elections of December 1918. These developments were made possible because of the end of the hope of repairing and/or restructuring an Imperial relationship with the failure of the Irish convention of 1917–18, especially over the question of the implementation of conscription to Ireland. While previous chapters described the 'grassroots' groundswell of support for and participation in radical nationalism amongst the masses of the Irish nation, this chapter charted the effects that this process had at an elite and institutional level. This final chapter reveals that the elite and institutional levels of Irish nationalism were initially dragged along by this transformation, despite the best efforts of Redmond and Westminster to put a positive spin on the changing Irish scene, but that in the wake of their failure to adjust, a new representative political organisational structure emerged in Ireland. Radical nationalism had now become the popular form of nationalism in Ireland – a turn of events virtually unimaginable some four years previously.

NOTES

1   Kee, 1982.
2   Coogan, 1993, p. 52; see also accounts in CSB Files from August, 1916, 3/716 NAI.
3   Wells and Marlowe, 1916, p. 215.
4   Co. Kilkenny Inspector's Report, 1917, CO 903/19 PRO Kew.
5   Intelligence Reports, 1916, CO903/19 PRO Kew.
6   Reports on Dublin and Kilkenny, 1917, CO903/19 PRO Kew.
7   Co. Meath Inspector's Report, 1916, CO 903/19 PRO Kew.
8   Letter to 'Dixon', 10 October 1916, MS. 35262 NLI Dublin.
9   See Chapter 4, Fitzpatrick, 1998.
10 Hennessey, 1998, p. 148.
11 Handbill from Irish Nations League, 3 August 1916, in Walsh Papers 385/7.
12 Pamphlet, 4 August 1916, cited in Laffan, 1999, p. 63.
13 Laffan, 1999, p. 63.
14 Letter to 'Dixon' 10 October, 1916, MS. 35262 NLI Dublin.
15 Sermon, 15 October 1917, cited in Laffan, 1999, p. 64.
16 Hennessey, 1998, p. 148.
17 Laffan, 1999, p. 63.

18   Ibid.
19   *Galway Observer* in Kee, 1982, p. 19.
20   Kee, 1982.
21   Ibid., p. 20.
22   Rees, 1998, p. 223; Laffan, 1999, p. 73
23   Laffan, 1999, p. 73.
24   For a full description of this situation see Laffan, 1999.
25   *Irish Independent*, 11 November 1916, cited in Kee, 1982.
26   *Cork Examiner*, 15 November 1916, cited in Laffan, 1999, p. 74.
27   Rees, 1998, p. 223.
28   McDowell, 1970, p. 68.
29   Kee, 1982.
30   Rees, 1998, p. 158.
31   O'Duibhgall, 1966, p. 303.
32   O'Duibhgall, 1966, p. 323.
33   Letter to 'Dixon', 10 October 1916, MS. 35262 NLI Dublin.
34   Darrell Figgis in Laffan, 1999, p. 65
35   Letter from MacNeill to Margaret MacNeill, 26 March 1917 cited in Laffan, 1999, p. 65.
36   Laffan, 1999, p. 68.
37   Fitzpatrick, 1998, p. 126.
38   Belfast Inspector's Report, 1916, CO 903/19 PRO Kew.
39   Laffan, 1999, p. 79.
40   Walsh quoted in Statement of Monsignor Michael J. Curran to Bureau of Military History, MS. 27728, NLI.
41   Rees, 1998, p. 224.
42   Ibid.
43   Kee, 1982, p. 22.
44   Laffan, 1999, p. 83.
45   Report on meeting for Count Plunkett, 19 January, 1917, CO 904/23 PRO Kew.
46   Report on meeting for Count Plunkett, 20 and 28 January, 1917, CO 904/23 PRO Kew.
47   Rees, 1998, p. 224.
48   *Roscommon Herald*, 3 February, 1917, cited in Laffan, 1999, p. 81.
49   Rees, 1998, p. 224.
50   See beginning of Chapter 3 for a quote Pearse's famous oration at this same funeral.
51   Report on Meeting for Count Plunkett, Elphin, 29 January, 1917, CO 903/23 PRO Kew.
52   Miller, 1987, p. 200; Phillips, 1923, pp. 122–3.
53   Co. Dublin Inspector's Report, 1916, CO 903/19 PRO Kew.
54   Rees, 1998, p. 224.
55   See Larkin, 1976.
56   Larkin, 1976; Hutchinson, 1987.
57   Kee, 1982, p. 23.
58   Phillips, 1923, p. 114; Coogan, 1993; Kee, 1982.
59   Hennessey, 1998, p. 164.
60   See Chapter 6 for further references to the Famine at this time.
61   Larkin, E., 'Church, State and Nation in Modern Ireland' in *The Historical Dimensions of Irish Catholicism* (New York: Arno Press, 1976), p. 1268.
62   Ibid.
63   Report on Speech in Elphin, 13 February, 1917 CO 903/23 PRO Kew.
64   Rees, 1998, p. 225.
65   Laffan, 1999, p. 88.
66   Ibid. p. 90.
67   Rees, 1998, p. 225.
68   Hennessey, 1998, p. 159.

69 Rees, 1998, p. 222.
70 Speech by Pim at Mansion House Convention cited in Laffan, 1999, p. 92.
71 Rees, 1998, p. 225.
72 Intelligence Reports, 1918, CO 903/19 PRO Kew.
73 Co. Kilkenny Inspector's Report, 1917, CO 903/19 PRO Kew.
74 Fitzpatrick, 1998, p. 98 The AOH had been an organisation associated with support for Redmond and the Irish Party.
75 Laffan, 1999, p. 94.
76 IO's report cited in Laffan, 1999, p. 95.
77 Laffan, 1999, p. 95.
78 Coleman, M. 'Mobilisation: the South Longford By-Election and its Impact on Political Mobilisation' in Augusteijn, J. (ed.), *The Irish Revolution 1913–1923* (New York: Palgrave, 2002), p. 53.
79 Laffan, 1999, p. 98.
80 Report on Speech of Mr. O'Mullane, Meeting at Ballymahon, 29 April, 1917, CO 903/23 PRO Kew.
81 Report on Speech of Mr. F. O'Connor, Meeting at Ballymahon, 6 May, 1917, CO 903/23 PRO Kew.
82 Phillips, 1923, p. 125.
83 Walsh cited in Laffan, 1999, p. 102.
84 Leaflet cited in Laffan, 1999, p. 102.
85 Letter from Students of the Nation to Walsh, May 1917, Walsh Papers 379/4.
86 Laffan, 1999, p. 106.
87 Phillips, 1923, p. 124.
88 Ibid.
89 Ibid. p. 125.
90 See especially Laffan, 1999 and Fitzpatrick, 1998.
91 Laffan, 1999, p. 108.
92 Letter from Moroney to Redmond, 4 July 1917, cited in Laffan, 1999, p. 109.
93 Laffan, 1999, p. 110.
94 *Cork Examiner* cited in Kee, 1982, p. 28.
95 Laffan, 1999, p. 110.
96 Statement of Monsignor Michael J. Curran to Bureau of Military History, MS. 27728, NLI.
97 Coleman, 2002, pp. 66–7.
98 Novick, 2002, p. 41.
99 Ibid.
100 Ibid.
101 Letter from Josephine Mary Plunkett to Walsh, 19 September 1917, Walsh Papers 379/5.
102 Ibid.
103 Novick, 2002, p. 48.
104 Report on Speech of Mr. Paul Culligan, August 1917, CO 903/23 PRO Kew.
105 Proclamation of Bishop of Limerick, Dr O'Dwyer, 30 April 1917, Walsh Papers Special Papers/Political Papers.
106 Walsh Papers 379/5 and Statement of Monsignor Michael J. Curran to Bureau of Military History, MS. 27728, NLI.
107 Gallagher, A. 'Nationalism in East Down' in Fitzpatrick, D. (ed) *Ireland and the First World War* (Dublin: Trinity History Workshop, 1986), p. 100.
108 Phillips, 1923, p. 133.
109 Statement of Monsignor Michael J. Curran to Bureau of Military History, MS. 27728, NLI.
110 Laffan, 1999, p. 269; Phillips, 1923, p. 134.

111   Statement of Monsignor Michael J. Curran to Bureau of Military History, MS. 27728, NLI.
112   *Clare Champion* 30 June, 1917 cited in Laffan, 1999, p. 130.
113   Report on Speech of E. de Valera, MP Meeting at Kilmaly, Co. Clare, 8 October 1917, CO 903/23 PRO Kew.
114   Phillips, 1923, p. 116.
115   Statement of Monsignor Michael J. Curran to Bureau of Military History, MS. 27728, NLI.
116   See CSB Files 3/716/24 NAI.
117   Statement of Monsignor Michael J. Curran to Bureau of Military History, MS. 27728, NLI.
118   Letter from De Markiviecz, Ginnell, and Lynn to Walsh, 6 October 1917, Walsh Papers 379/5.
119   See Kee 1976, Laffan 1999 and Fitzpatrick 1998.
120   Phillips, 1923, p. 126.
121   Statement of Monsignor Michael J. Curran to Bureau of Military History, MS. 27728, NLI.
122   Phillips, 1923, p. 135.
123   Counties Dublin and Kilkenny Inspector's Reports, 1917, CO 903/19 PRO Kew.
124   Co. Dublin Inspector's Report, 1917, CO 903/19 PRO Kew.
125   Phillips, 1923, p. 138.
126   Intelligence Reports, CO 904/09 PRO Kew.
127   McConnell, 2004.
128   Statement of Monsignor Michael J. Curran to Bureau of Military History, MS. 27728, NLI.
129   Kee, 1982, p. 43; Laffan, 1999.
130   Kee, 1982, pp. 42-3; Laffan, 1999; Coogan, 1993.
131   Statement of Monsignor Michael J. Curran to Bureau of Military History, MS. 27728, NLI.
132   Ibid.
133   Ibid.
134   Hennessey, 1998, p. 221.
135   Statement of Standing Bishops found in Statement of Monsignor Michael J. Curran to Bureau of Military History, MS. 27728, NLI.
136   Phillips, 1923, p. 142.
137   Kee, 1982, pp. 48–9.
138   Statement of Monsignor Michael J. Curran to Bureau of Military History, MS. 27728, NLI.
139   Intelligence Reports, 1918, CO 903/19 PRO Kew.
140   Co. Meath Inspector's Report CO 903/19 PRO Kew.
141   Counties Wexford and Meath Inspector's Reports CO 903/19 PRO Kew.
142   Letter from Walsh to Byrne copied into Statement of Monsignor Michael J. Curran to Bureau of Military History, MS. 27728, NLI.
143   Letter from Walsh to Byrne copied into Statement of Monsignor Michael J. Curran to Bureau of Military History, MS. 27728, NLI.
144   Co. Dublin Inspector's Report, 1918, CO 903/19 PRO Kew.
145   McConnell, 2004, p. 356.
146   Ibid.

9

Conclusions

Irish historians have done an excellent job of charting the broad social and structural changes in the Irish nation, demonstrating the various effects of the long nineteenth century on Irish nationalism, and the pressures it brought to bear on the political institutions created by the Act of Union in 1801. Such works go hand in hand with several of the more important contributions to theories of nations and nationalisms, such as notions of periphery versus centre conflicts, theories of relative deprivation, the processes of modernisation (as industrialisation was more or less absent from Ireland save several notable examples such as Belfast), and the sweep of the ideology of the nation and nationalism in the nineteenth century. These theoretical approaches, given their various strengths, directly relate to aspects of the growth of the Irish nation and its expression in nationalist movements.

The argument in this book has not concentrated on these broad factors, important though they are. Instead the book has explained why a population, so content with a moderate form of nationalism during one period of time, should subsequently support a previously unpopular and radical position. For too long, historians of the Rising have taken this moment of transformation for granted. In response, this book has proposed a mechanism to explain this moment of transformation, and to map out the process by which the Irish nation became radicalised in response to a specific and time-limited series of events. From the moment that the Proclamation of an Irish Republic was read in front of the Dublin GPO, through to the application of martial law, the courts-martial and the executions of the leaders of the Rising, perspectives on nationalism amongst individual members of the Irish nation were transformed and radicalised. This change of perspective within the Irish nation ultimately served to 'translate' these broader social, structural, ideological and institutional factors into a radicalised form of Irish nationalism.

In order to explain how this process works, the book began with an examination of the cultural trigger point. This trigger point, as a series of events that triggered a radicalisation in identity, sense of injustice and perception of agency which accounted for the shift in popularity from moderate to radical nationalism, was the Easter Rising. It was informed by the myths, memories and symbols of the Irish nation. From the outset, it has been established that two major themes lay at the core of these national myths, memories and symbols:

1) The sense of the **organic distinctiveness of the Irish nation,** especially from the 'Anglo-Protestant other.' The sense of distinction also had other implications, such as the inherent morality and spiritual purity of the Catholic, as opposed to Protestant, Irish nation.
2) The memories of **historical injustices** perpetrated against the moral Irish Catholic nation, at the hands of the Anglo-Protestant other, in the guises of Protestant proselytisers and the British authorities, and through their institutions such as the Irish administration, Westminster, soldiers and police force.

These factors were present in the Irish nation before the Rising, before the cultural trigger point took place, and before the trans-formation and radicalisation of Irish nationalism was even contemplated. In fact, these factors were clearly present during the Home Rule crisis in 1914. Irish nationalists, strongly and popularly committed to the constitutional methods of the Irish Party, only armed themselves after the Ulster Volunteers. These factors were also present when Redmond committed the National Volunteers to the war effort, and when this call was responded to by Irishmen who enlisted in their tens of thousands. These factors were present when the response to the outbreak of the war was not an upsurge in the popularity of Sinn Féin, but rather steady support in the Irish Party. So how do these factors explain the impact of the Rising?

The Rising itself was demonstrated to be an unpopular event. Its leaders were demonised, the participants labelled as fools, and the destruction which they had caused highlighted. However, in moments of high anxiety and drama, while there was a vacuum of information and rumours ran wild, it was in fact this sense of organic Irish distinctiveness and injustice which began to creep in and colour the reporting of events. This alone would not have been enough to radicalise the nation. When combined, however, with events such as Sheehy-Skeffington's murder and the subsequent persecution of his wife, the execution not so much of Patrick Pearse, but of his brother 'Willy', the draconian implementation of martial law and the courts-martial in general, all the national myths, memories and symbols of the persecution of the Irish nation at the hands of the Anglo-Protestant other were unleashed. Yeats' 'sixteen dead men' were stirring the boiling pot of cultural imagery, and through a combination of cultural and religious myths and symbols, these men were rehabilitated, indeed resurrected, as saints and martyrs for the Irish nation. The process of their 'beatification' in the pantheon of Irish heroes was a grassroots one – there were no radical institutions or organisations to propel this process as they had been destroyed or broken up after the Rising. Therefore this process came as a result of individuals in the Irish nation trying to make sense of these events using the already present and popular building blocks of national myths, memories and symbols. This grassroots process fuelled the radicalisation of the Irish nation *ex post facto* and forced institutions and elites to change their behaviours and attitudes in its wake.

The Anglo-Protestant other, in the guise of the Unionists and the British authorities, seemed to reinforce Irish national myths, memories and symbols. For the Irish nation, the sense of organic distinction and injustice was clearly apparent. For the Irish nation, it seemed as though the system had been constantly stacked in favour of the Unionists. The Ulster Volunteers had been allowed to land arms, with the authorities turning a blind eye, whereas the landing of arms by the Irish National Volunteers had culminated in deaths resulting from the Bachelor's Walk incident. The British army had mutinied when it was rumoured they were about to be ordered to disarm the Ulster Volunteers, but there was never a lack of calls for the disbandment of the National Volunteers, let alone the Irish Volunteers. Kitchener and the British army failed to establish a National Volunteer division to mirror that of the Ulster Volunteer 36th Division. Unionists had key seats in the Cabinet. Unionists wrecked the Irish Convention by limiting the proposed power of the Irish Parliament. Constant political manipulation of the British political establishment by the Unionists only seemed to prove that the organic distinction of the Irish nation needed political expression in independence to ensure the ultimate security of the Irish nation. At the same time, the British authorities failed to adequately address any of the changes brought about by the Rising in the Irish nation, and their attempts at appeasement only served to strengthen the radical nationalist position. The pursuit of retribution on the part of the military regime in the immediate aftermath of the Rising, and the continuing draconian implementation of martial law and the DORA further served to reinforce this viewpoint.

Those institutions of the Irish nation that did not adequately alter their perspectives and actions in light of this popular transformation, and that found themselves 'unrepresentative' of the Irish nation, either quickly changed or were replaced. Examples of this were the Irish Party, and elements of the Catholic Church. The fall of the Irish Party was accelerated by the double failure of the Home Rule negotiations after the Rising. While it was clear that the cultural trigger point of the Rising had effected a change in the masses of the Irish nation, it was equally clear that it had failed to make any deep impact on the political thinking of the Party, as evidenced by their readiness to accept partition. This was a compromise that a radicalised Irish nation was simply not willing to swallow, and as the negotiations were dashed against these same rocks twice, with Redmond willing the Party on to this compromise each time, its power, efficacy and legitimacy were lost. The Church, though always divided, was able to manoeuvre its way through this period successfully because

1) it was at the cultural centre of the Irish nation, and was a natural outlet for expression of the Irish nation, as evidenced through the requiem masses said for the 'Easter Week martyrs' and the praying for 'St Pearse' and
2) because its institutional splits allowed it to pursue more than one policy at the same time, thereby always allowing it to appear to be on the 'winning' side.

The conscription crisis cemented the institutional transformation reflecting the radicalised Irish nation. The crisis created the conditions under which the Church was able to bestow upon the newly reorganised and representative institution of Sinn Féin the sense of legitimacy and power. This shift in the political fortunes of the Irish Party and Sinn Féin served to further the process of the radicalising of the nation, providing efficient and popular institutions by which to express this popular brand of radical nationalism. By the general elections of December 1918, this process was complete.

What came after this process, in terms of the Irish War for Independence, the Black and Tan War, the signing of the Anglo-Irish Treaty and the subsequent Civil War have been successfully covered elsewhere and these events are outside of the scope of the cultural trigger point, and of this book. However, there can be no doubt that the myths, memories and symbols which radicalised the Irish nation in the wake of the Easter Rising also had an impact on these events, and that the Rising itself became an Irish national myth and symbol, which would influence the interpretation of these subsequent events. It is important, however, to remember that the Rising was unique in comparison to these subsequent events, as it was a moment of popular transformation. As the dust was settling and the smoke was clearing from the shelling of central Dublin, there was no set of radical institutions such as Sinn Féin to organise a popular response, and those leaders who could have rallied such a response were either dead or imprisoned. In the moment of crisis, and in the vacuum of political leadership, widely resonant Irish national myths, memories and symbols, resonant were released, providing a framework for the interpretations of and reactions to these events.

The effects of the transformation engendered by the Rising as a cultural trigger point, both in terms of the myths, memories and symbols of the Irish nation, and its effects on political events, institutions and structures is apparent throughout the island of Ireland even today. Given the relatively recent peace process in Northern Ireland, it seems gratuitous, but nonetheless relevant to highlight the role that these myths, memories and symbols play in every deeply held ethnic and/or national identity. Just as when the military regime assumed it was putting down a treacherous German plot which was a threat to the British state, serving to stimulate a strong reaction in the Irish nation, the unintentional or clumsy manipulation of myths, memories and symbols can have dramatic results, often antithetical to those intended. It therefore seems clear that the more that theorists of ethnicity and nationalism and practitioners of subjects such as ethno-national conflict regulation are able to understand about the power and importance of the role played by national myths, memories and symbols, the more likely it is, perhaps, that a more lasting peace can be achieved.

Bibliography

Primary Sources

Newspapers and Periodicals (1914–1918)

An Gaedal
Clare Champion
Connaught Telegraph
Contemporary Review
Cork Examiner
Daily Freeman's Journal
Dungannon Democrat
Evening Herald
Galway Observer
Guardian
Hibernian Journal
Irish Catholic
Irish Freedom
Irish Independent
Irish Times
Longford Independent
Kilkenny People
Midland Reporter
Nation
Roscommon Herald
Sligo Nationalist
The Spark
The Times
Weekly Irish Times

Diaries and Manuscripts

Available in National Library of Ireland

MS. 4615: Letter from Patrick O'Connor to F. W. Poulter

MS. 7880: An Account by George Berkeley of his experience in Belfast 1914

MS. 7981: Diary of Mrs. Augustine Henry 1914 – September, 1915

MS. 7984: Diary of Mrs. Augustine Henry, Vol. IV, Oct. 1915–June 1916

MS. 9620: Diary of Current Events – 'A Dubliner's Diary' 1914 –1918 by T. K. Moylan

MS. 15415 Letter of Ismena (i.e. Mrs. S. Ismena Rhode) 21 May, 1916 describing events in Easter Week

MS. 27697: Accounts of Easter Week and After, by Sean T. O'Kelly, 1916

MS. 27728 Statement of Monsignor Michael J. Curran to Bureau of Military History, 1913–1921

MS. 31326 An Account of Internee in Knutsford, 1916

MS. 31337 Irish Volunteer Handbill 'The Present Crisis', July 1915

MS. 32695 Letters of Correspondence between Maxwell and Bishop O'Dwyer, 1916

MS. 31330 Cork in Easter Week, 1916

MS. 33571 Account of Patrick Clare, 1916

MS. 35262 Letter to 'Dixon', 10 October, 1916

MS. 35454 Papers Relating to Alphonsus Sweeney, 1916

Archbishop Walsh Papers (1914–1918)

379/5
384/4
384/5
385/1
385/3
385/6
385/7
389 I
Special Papers/Political Papers

Public Records Office, Kew (PRO Kew)

CO 903: (1912–1919) Colonial Office, Confidential Print –Comprises reports of criminal and political activities in Ireland during the period 1885–1919.

CO 904: (1912–1919) Dublin Castle Records – This series contains records of the British administration in Ireland prior to 1922.

National Archives of Ireland (NAI Dublin)

3/716/24 Dublin Metropolitan Police Crime Special Branch Files (1911–1919)

Contemporary Books and Reprinted Sources

The Irish Uprising, 1914–21: Papers from the British Parliamentary Archive (London: the Stationery Office, 2000).

1916 Rebellion Handbook (Dublin: Mourne River Press, 1998).

Brennan-Whitmore, W. J., *Dublin Burning: The Easter Rising From Behind the Barricades* [1916] (London: Gill and MacMillan, 1996).

Green, A. S., *Loyalty and Disloyalty: What It Means in Ireland* (Dublin: Maunsel, 1918).

Green, A. S., *The Making of Ireland and Its Undoing 1200–1600* (London, 1908).

Mitchel, J., *Jail Journal: with an Introductory Narrative of Transactions in Ireland* [1854] (London: Sphere, 1983).

Norway, M. L. and A. H., *The Sinn Féin Rebellion as They Saw It* [1916] (Dublin: Irish Academic Press, 1999).

Paul Duboio, L., *Contemporary Ireland* (Dublin: Maunsel and Co., 1911).

Phillips, W. A., *The Revolution in Ireland 1906–1923* (London: Longmans, Green and Co., 1923).

Redmond, J., *Some Arguments for Home Rule: Series of Speeches by John Redmond* (Dublin, 1908).

Redmond-Howard, L. G., *Six Days of the Irish Republic: A Narrative and Critical Account of the Latest Phase of Irish Politics* (London: Maunsel, 1916).

Stephens, James, *The Insurrection in Dublin* [1916] (Buckinghamshire: Colin Smythe, 1992).

Warwich-Haller, A. and S. (eds), *Letters from Dublin, Easter 1916: Alfred Fanning's Diary of the Rising* (Dublin: Irish Academic Press, 1995).

Wells, Warre B. and Marlowe, N., *A History of the Irish Rebellion of 1916* (Dublin: Maunsel and Co., 1916).

Secondary Sources

Alter, P., 'Symbols of Irish Nationalism' in O'Day, Alan (ed.), *Reactions to Irish Nationalism, 1865–1914* (London: Hambledon Press, 1987).

Armstrong, J., *Nations Before Nationalism* (Chapel Hill: University of North Carolina, 1982).

Augusteijn, J., 'Political Violence and Democracy: An Analysis of the Tensions Within Irish Republican Strategy, 1914–2002', *Irish Political Studies*, Vol. 18, No. 1, 2003, 1–26.

Augusteijn, J., *From Public Defiance to Guerrilla Warfare* (Dublin: Irish Academic Press, 1996).

Augusteijn, J. (ed.), *The Irish Revolution, 1913–23* (New York: Palgrave, 2002).

Augusteijn, J., 'Motivation: Why did they Fight for Ireland? The Motivation of Volunteers in the Revolution', in *The Irish Revolution, 1913–23* (New York: Palgrave, 2002).

Baily, M., 'The Parish Mission Apostolate of the Redemptorists in Ireland, 1851–1898', in Gallagher, R. and McConvery, B. (eds), *History and Conscience: Studies in Honour of Sean Ó Riordan* (Dublin: Gill and MacMillan, 1989).

Barth, F. (ed.), *Ethnic Groups and Boundaries: The Social Organisation of Cultural Difference* (London: Allen and Unwin, 1969).

Berg, D. and Purcell, L. E. (eds), *Almanac of World War I* (Lexington, KY: University Press of Kentucky, 1998).

Billig, M., 'Rhetorical Psychology, Ideological Thinking and Imagining Nationhood' in Johnston, H. and Klandermans, B. (eds), *Social Movements and Culture* (London: UCL Press, 1995).

Bowman, T., 'Composing Divisions: The Recruitment of Ulster and National Volunteers into the British Army in 1914', *Causeway Cultural Traditions Journal*, Spring 1995.

Bowman, T., 'The Ulster Volunteer Force and the Formation of the 36th Ulster Division' *Irish Historical Studies*, Vol. XXXII, No. 128, November 2001, 82–103.

Boyce, D. G., 'A First World War Transition: State and Citizen in Ireland, 1914–1919' in Boyce, D. G. and O'Day, A. (eds), *Ireland in Transition, 1867–1921* (London: Routledge, 2004).

Boyce, D. G. and O'Day, A. (eds), *Ireland in Transition, 1867–1921* (London: Routledge, 2004).

Boyce, D. G., *Nationalism in Ireland* (London: Routledge, 1995).

Breuilly, J., *Nationalism and the State* (Manchester: Manchester University Press, 1993).

Butler, J., 'Extracts from Lord Oranmore's Journal', *Irish Historical Studies*, Vol. XXIX, No. 119, November 1995.

Campbell, F., *Land and Revolution: Nationalist Politics in the West of Ireland, 1891–1921* (Oxford: Oxford University Press, 2005).

Caulfield, M., *The Easter Rebellion* (Dublin: Gill and MacMillan, 1995).

Coakley, J., 'Religion, National Identity and Political Change in Modern Ireland', Irish Political Studies, Vol. 17, No. 1, 2002, 4–28.

Codd, P., 'Recruiting and Responses to the War in Wexford', in Fitzpatrick, David, *Ireland and the First World War* (Dublin: Trinity History Workshop, 1986).

Coleman, M., 'Mobilisation: The South Longford By-election and its Impact on Political Mobilisation', in Augusteijn, Joost (ed.), *The Irish Revolution, 1913–23* (New York: Palgrave, 2002).

Connerton, P., *How Societies Remember*, (Cambridge: Cambridge University Press, 1999).

Connolly, S. J., (ed.) *The Oxford Companion to Irish History* (Oxford: Oxford University Press, 1998).

Coogan, T. P., *de Valera: Long Fellow, Long Shadow* (London: Random House, 1993)

Corish, P. J., 'Cardinal Cullen and the National Association of Ireland', in O'Day, Alan (ed.), *Reactions to Irish Nationalism, 1865–1914* (London: Hambledon Press, 1987).

de Weil, J. A., *The Catholic Church in Ireland, 1914–1918* (Dublin: Irish Academic Press, 2003).

Denman, T., 'The Red Livery of Shame: The Campaign Against Army Recruitment in Ireland, 1899–1914', *Irish Historical Studies*, Vol. XXIX, No. 114, November 1994, 208–33.

Denman, T., 'From Soldiers Three to The Irish Guards in the Great War: Rudyard Kipling and the Irish Soldier, 1887–1922', *The Irish Sword*, Vol. XXII, No. 88, Winter 2000, 159–173.

Drumm, Fr. M., 'Irish Catholics: A People Formed by Ritual', in Cassidy, E. (ed.), *Faith and Culture in the Irish Context* (Dublin: Veritas, 1996).

Edwards, O. D. and Pyle, F. (eds), *The Easter Rising* (London: MacGibbon and Kee, 1968).

Edwards, R. D., *Patrick Pearse: The Triumph of Failure* (London: Gollancz, 1977).

Edwards, R. D. and Williams, T. D., *The Great Famine: Studies in Irish History, 1845–52* (New York: Russell and Russell, 1957).

Ellis, J. S., 'The Degenerate and the Martyr: Nationalist Propaganda and the Contestation of Irishness, 1914–1918', *Eire-Ireland*, Fall/Winter 2001, 7–33.

Falls, C. B., 'Maxwell, 1916, and Britain at War', in Martin, F. X. (ed.), *Leaders and Men of the Easter Rising: Dublin, 1916* (London: Methuen and Co., 1967).

Finnan, J., *John Redmond and Irish Unity, 1912–1918* (Syracuse, NY: Syracuse University Press, 2004).

Finnan, J., 'Let Irishmen Come Together in the Trenches: John Redmond and Irish Party Policy in the Great War, 1914–1918', *The Irish Sword*, Vol. XXII, No. 88, Winter 2000, 174–192.

Fitzpatrick, D. (ed.), *Ireland and the First World War* (Dublin: Trinity History Workshop, 1986).

Fitzpatrick, D., *Politics and Irish Life, 1913–1921* (Cork: Cork University Press, 1998).

Fitzpatrick, D. (ed,) *Revolution? Ireland 1917–23* (Dublin: Trinity History Workshop, 1990).

Fitzpatrick, D., '"That Beloved Country, that No Place Else Resembles": Connotations of Irishness in Irish–Australasian Letters, 1841–1915', *Irish Historical Studies*, Vol. XXVII, No. 108, November 1991, 324–350.

Fleischmann, R., *Catholic Nationalism in Irish Revival* (London: Macmillan, 1997).

Foster, Roy F., *Modern Ireland: 1600–1972* (New York: Penguin, 1990).

Foster, R. F., *W. B. Yeats: A Life, II: The Arch-Poet, 1915–1939* (Oxford: Oxford University Press, 2003).

Foy, M. and Barton, B. (eds), *The Easter Rising* (Gloucestershire: Sutton, 1999).

Frijda, N., 'Commemorating' in Pennebaker, J., Paez, D. and Rimé, B. (eds), *The Collective Memory of Political Events* (New Jersey: Erlbaum Associates, 1997).

Gallagher, A., 'Nationalism in East Down', in Fitzpatrick, D. (ed.), *Ireland and the First World War* (Trinity History Workshop, Dublin 1986).

Gamson, W., 'Constructing Social Protest', in Johnston, H. and Klandermans, B. (eds), *Social Movements and Culture* (London: UCL Press, 1995).

Gamson, W., 'The Social Psychology of Collective Action', in

Morris, A. and Mueller, C. (eds), *Frontiers in Social Movement Theory*, (New Haven, CT: Yale University Press, 1992).

Garvin, T., *Nationalist Revolutionaries in Ireland, 1858–1928* (Oxford: Clarendon Press, 1987).

Garvin, T., 'Priests and patriots: Irish separatism and fear of the modern, 1890–1914', *Irish Historical Studies*, Vol. xxv, No. 97, May 1986, 67–81

Geary, L. M., *Rebellion and Remembrance in Modern Ireland* (Dublin: Four Courts Press, 2001).

Geertz, C., *Old Societies and New States* (New York: Free Press, 1963).

Gellner, E., *Nations and Nationalism* (Oxford: Blackwell, 1983).

Griffith, K. and O'Grady, T., *Curious Journey: An Oral History of Ireland's Unfinished Revolution* (Dublin: Mercier, 1998).

Grosby, S., 'Religion and Nationality in Antiquity', *European Journal of Sociology*, Vol. xxxii, 229–65.

Grote, G., *Anglo-Irish Theatre and the Formation of a Nationalist Political Culture Between 1890 and 1930* (Lampeter: The Edwin Mellen Press, 2003).

Grote, G., *Torn Between Politics and Culture: The Gaelic League, 1893–1993* (Munster: Waxmann, 1994).

Gwynn, D., *The Life of John Redmond* (New York: Books for Libraries, 1971).

Halbwachs, M. (translated by Coser, L.), *On Collective Memory*, (Chicago: University of Chicago Press, 1992).

Halbwachs, M. (translated by Ditter, F. and Ditter, V.), *The Collective Memory* (New York: Harper and Row, 1980).

Hart, P., 'Definition: Defining the Irish Revolution', in Augusteijn, Joost (ed.), *The Irish Revolution, 1913–23* (New York: Palgrave, 2002).

Hart, P., *The I.R.A. and Its Enemies: Violence and Community in Cork, 1916–1923* (Oxford: Oxford University Press, 1998).

Hennessey, T., *Dividing Ireland: World War I and Partition* (London: Routledge, 1998).

Henry, Robert M., *The Evolution of Sinn Féin* (New York: Books For Libraries, 1970).

Hepburn, A. C., *The Conflict of Nationality in Modern Ireland*, (London: Edward Arnold, 1980).

Hobsbawm, E. J., *Nations and Nationalism Since 1780: Programme, Myth, Reality* (Cambridge: Cambridge University Press, 1992).

Hutchinson, J., *The Dynamics of Cultural Nationalism: The Gaelic Revival and the Creation of the Irish Nation State* (London: Allen and Unwin, 1987).

Hutchinson, J., 'Archaeology and the Irish Rediscovery of the Celtic Past', *Nations and Nationalism*, Vol. 7, No. 4, October 2001, 505–519.

Igartua, J. and Paez, D. 'Art and Remembering Traumatic Events: The Case of the Spanish Civil War', in Pennebaker, J., Paez, D. and Rimé, B. (eds), *The Collective Memory of Political Events* (New Jersey: Erlbaum Associates, 1997).

Irwin-Zarecka, I., *Frames of Remembrance: Social and Cultural Dynamics of Collective Memory* (New Brunswick, NJ: Transaction, 1993).

Jackson, A., *Ireland: 1798–1998* (London: Blackwell, 1999).

Jeffrey, K., *The Sinn Féin Rebellion 'As They Saw It'* (Dublin: Irish Academic Press, 1999).

Johnston, H. and Klandermans, B. (eds), *Social Movements and Culture* (London: UCL Press, 1995).

Kautt, W. H., *The Anglo-Irish War, 1916–1921: A People's War* (London: Praeger, 1999).

Kee, R., *The Green Flag, Volume 2: The Bold Feinian Men* (London: Quartet, 1983).

Kee, R., *The Green Flag, Volume 3: Ourselves Alone* (London: Quartet Books, 1982).

Kelleher, M., 'Hunger and history: monuments to the Great Irish Famine', *Textual Practice*, July 2002, Vol. 16, No. 2, 249–76.

Kelly, M., 'Parnell's Old Brigade: The Redmondite–Feinian Nexus in the 1890's', *Irish Historical Studies*, Vol. XXXIII, No. 130, November 2002, 209–234.

Kennedy, Thomas C., 'The Gravest Situation of Our Lives: Conservatives, Ulster and the Home Rule Crisis, 1911–1914', *Eire/Ireland*, Fall/Winter 2001, 67–82.

Kerr, D. A., *The Catholic Church and the Famine* (Dublin: Columba Press, 1996).

Kissane, B., *Explaining Irish Democracy* (Dublin: UCD Press, 2002).

Klandermans, B., *The Social Psychology of Protest* (Oxford: Blackwell, 1997).

Laffan, M., *The Resurrection of Ireland: The Sinn Féin Party, 1916–23* (Cambridge: Cambridge University Press, 1999).

Larkin, E., *Church, State and Nation in Modern Ireland* in *The*

Historical Dimensions of Irish Catholicism (New York: Arno Press, 1976).

Larkin, E., 'The Devotional Revolution in Ireland', *American Historical Review*, 1972, Vol. 87, 625–652.

Lee, Joseph, *Ireland 1912–1985* (Cambridge: Cambridge University Press, 1998).

Lee, Joseph, *The Modernisation of Irish Society, 1848–1918* (Dublin: Gill and MacMillan, 1989).

Leonard, J., 'The Catholic Chaplaincy', in Fitzpatrick, D. (ed.) *Ireland and the First World War* (Dublin: Trinity History Workshop, 1986).

Lyons, F. S. L., *Ireland Since the Famine* (London: Fontana, 1985).

Mandle, W. F., 'The I.R.B. and the Beginnings of the Gaelic Athletic Association', in O'Day, A. (ed.), *Reactions to Irish Nationalism, 1865–1914* (London: Hambledon Press, 1987).

Mann, M., 'A Political Theory of Nationalism and its Excesses', in Periwal, S. (ed.), *Notions of Nationalism* (Budapest: Central European University Press, 1995).

Mansergh, N., *Nationalism and Independence: Selected Irish Papers* (Cork: Cork University Press, 1997).

Martin, F. X., (ed.), *Leaders and Men of the Easter Rising: Dublin, 1916* (London: Methuen and Co., 1967).

Martin, F. X., "1916 – Revolution or Evolution" in *Leaders and Men of the Easter Rising: Dublin, 1916* (London: Methuen and Co., 1967).

Maume, P., 'Young Ireland, Arthur Griffith and Republican Ideology: The Question of Continuity', *Eire-Ireland*, Summer 1999, 135–54.

McAdam, D. Tarrow, S. and Tilly, C. (eds), *Dynamics of Contention* (Cambridge: Cambridge University Press, 2001).

McBride, I. (ed.), *History and Memory in Modern Ireland* (Cambridge: Cambridge University Press, 2001).

McBride, L., *The Greening of Dublin Castle: The Transformation of Bureaucratic and Judicial Personnel in Ireland, 1892–1922* (Washington: Catholic University Press, 1991).

McBride, L. (ed.), *Images and Icons and the Irish Nationalist Imagination* (Dublin: Four Courts Press, 1999)

McCartney, D., 'Hyde, D. P. Moran and Irish Ireland', in Martin, F. X. (ed.), *Leaders and Men of the Easter Rising: Dublin, 1916* (London: Methuen and Co., 1967).

McDowell, R. B., *The Irish Convention, 1917–1918* (London:

Routledge & Kegan Paul, 1970).

McGee, O., 'God Save Ireland: Manchester Martyr Demonstrations in Dublin 1867–1916', *Eire-Ireland*, Fall/Winter 2001, 39–66.

McGrath, T. G., 'The Tridentine Evolution of Modern Irish Catholicism, 1563–1962: A Re-examination of the "Devotional Revolution Thesis"', in Ó Muirí, R. (ed.), *Irish Church History Today* (Dublin: Cumann Seanchais Ard Mhacha, 1992).

McHugh, R. (ed.), *Dublin, 1916* (London: Arlington Books, 1966).

Miller, D. W., *Church, State and Nation in Ireland, 1898–1921* (Dublin: Gill and MacMillan, 1973).

Miller, D. W., 'The Roman Catholic Church in Ireland, 1865–1914', in O'Day, Alan (ed.), *Reactions to Irish Nationalism, 1865–1914* (London: Hambledon Press, 1987).

Mitchell, A. and Ó Snodaigh, P. (eds), *Irish Political Documents* (Dublin: Irish Academic Press, 1989).

Mokyr, J., *Why Ireland Starved: A Quantitative and Analytical History of the Irish Economy, 1800–1850* (London: Allen and Unwin, 1983).

Moran, S. F., 'Images, Icons and the Practice of Irish History', in McBride, L. (ed.) *Images and Icons and the Irish Nationalist Imagination* (Dublin: Four Courts Press, 1999).

Moran, S. F., *Patrick Pearse and the Politics of Redemption: The Mind of the Easter Rising, 1916* (Washington, DC: The Catholic University Press, 1997).

Morash, C. and Hayes, R. (eds), *Fearful Realities: New Perspectives on the Famine* (Dublin: Irish Academic Press, 1996).

Murray, A. C., 'Nationality and Local Politics in Late Nineteenth-Century Ireland: The Case of County Westmeath', *Irish Historical Studies*, Vol. xxv, No. 98, November 1986, 144–58.

Nairn, T., *The Break-up of Britain: Crisis and Neo-Nationalism* (London: New Left Books, 1977).

Novick, B., 'Postal Censorship in Ireland, 1914–16', *Irish Historical Studies*, Vol. xxxi, No. 123, May 1999, 343–56.

Novick, Ben, 'Propaganda I: Advanced Nationalist Propaganda and Moralistic Revolution, 1914–1918', Augusteijn, Joost (ed.), *The Irish Revolution, 1913–23* (New York: Palgrave, 2002).

O'Broin, L., *Dublin Castle and the 1916 Easter Rising* (Dublin: Helicon, 1966).

O'Clery, C., *Phrases Make History Here: A Century of Irish Political Quotations, 1886–1986* (Dublin: O'Brien Press, 1986).

O'Day, A., *Irish Home Rule: 1867–1921* (Manchester: University of

Manchester Press, 1998).

O'Day, A. and Stevenson, J. (eds), *Irish Historical Documents since 1800* (Dublin: Gill and Macmillan, 1992).

O'Duibhghaill, M., *Insurrection Fires at Eastertide* (Cork: Mercier Press, 1966).

Ó'Duibhir, C., *Sinn Féin: The First Election 1908* (Nure, Co. Leitrim: Drumlin Publications, 1993).

O'Mahony, P. and Delanty, G. (eds), *Rethinking Irish History: Nationalism, Identity, and Ideology* (Hampshire: Palgrave, 2001).

Owens, G., 'Constructing the Martyrs: The Manchester Executions and the Nationalist Imagination' in McBride, L. (ed.), *Images and Icons and the Irish Nationalist Imagination* (Dublin: Four Courts Press, 1999).

Paez, D., Basabe, N. and Gonzalez, J-L., 'Social Processes and Collective Memory: A Cross-Cultural Approach to Remembering Political Events', in Pennebaker, J., Paez, D. and Rimé, B. (eds), *The Collective Memory of Political Events* (New Jersey: Erlbaum Associates, 1997).

Paseta, S., *Before the Revolution: Nationalism, Social Change and Ireland's Catholic Elite, 1879–1922* (Cork: Cork University Press, 1999).

Pennebaker, J. and Banasik, B., 'On the Creation and Maintenance of Collective Memories: History as Social Psychology', in Pennebaker, J., Paez, D. and Rimé, B. (eds), *The Collective Memory of Political Events* (New Jersey: Erlbaum Associates, 1997).

Rees, R., *Ireland 1905–1925, Volume I: Text and Historiography* (Co. Down: Colourpoint Books, 1998).

Reilly, E., 'Beyond Gilt Shamrock: Symbolism and Realism in the Cover Art of Irish Historical and Political Fiction, 1880–1914', in McBride, L., *Images and Icons and the Irish Nationalist Imagination* (Dublin: Four Courts Press, 1999).

Schöpflin, G., 'The Functions of Myth and Taxonomy of Myths', in Hosking, G. and Schöpflin, G. (eds), *Myths and Nationhood* (London: Hurst, 1997).

Shils, E., 'Nation, Nationality, Nationalism and Civil Society', *Nations and Nationalism* Vol. I, No. 1, 1995, 93–118.

Smith, A. D., *Chosen Peoples: Sacred Sources of National Identity* (Oxford: Oxford University Press, 2003).

Smith, A. D., *The Ethnic Origins of Nations* (London: Blackwell, 1986).

Smith, A. D., 'The Golden Age and National Renewal', in Hosking, G. and Schöpflin, G. (eds), *Myths and Nationhood* (London: Hurst, 1997).

Smith, A. D., *The Nation in History* (Hanover: University Press of New England, 2000).

Smith, A. D., *Nations and Nationalism in a Global Era* (Cambridge: Polity, 1995).

Smith, A. D., *Nationalism and Modernism* (London: Routledge, 1998).

Swidler, A., 'Cultural Power and Social Movements', in Johnston, H. and Klandermans, B. (eds), *Social Movements and Culture*, (London: UCL Press, 1995).

Taylor, A. J. P., *Politics in Wartime* (London: Hamish Hamilton, 1964).

Thompson, William I., *The Imagination of an Insurrection* (New York: Oxford University Press, 1967).

Tilly, C., *From Mobilization to Revolution* (New York: Random House, 1978).

Tilly, C., *Social Movements, 1768–2004* (Boulder, CO.: Paradigm Publishers, 2004).

Tumbleson, R., *Catholicism in the English Protestant Imagination* (Cambridge: Cambridge University Press, 1998).

Van den Berghe, P., 'Does Race Matter', *Nations and Nationalism* Vol. I, No. 3, 1995, 401–11.

Vermeulen, H. and Govers, C. (eds), *The Anthropology of Ethnicity: Beyond Ethnic Groups and Boundaries* (Amsterdam: Spinhuis, 1994).

Wheatley, J., *Nationalism and the Irish Party: Provincial Ireland, 1910–1916* (Oxford: Oxford University Press, 2005).

White, R., 'From Peaceful Process to Guerrilla War: Micromobilization of the Provisional Irish Republican Army', *American Journal of Sociology*, Vol. 64, No. 6, May 1989, 1277–302.

Whyte, J. H., '1916 – Revolution and Religion', in Martin, F. X. (ed.), *Leaders and Men of the Easter Rising: Dublin, 1916* (London: Methuen and Co., 1967).

Index